Denver Landmarks & Historic Districts:
A Pictorial Guide

For Jean,
Fellow author, fellow westerner and
stor of Colorado Indian History.
Cheers,
Tom Noel

For Jean, fellow Westward
author, Story of
Colorado Indian History.
Cheers,
Jon Noel

Denver Landmarks & Historic Districts: A Pictorial Guide

THOMAS J. NOEL

With a Foreword by Denver Mayor Wellington Webb

UNIVERSITY PRESS OF COLORADO

© 1996 by the University Press of Colorado

Published by the University Press of Colorado
P.O. Box 849
Niwot, Colorado 80544

The University Press of Colorado is a cooperative publishing enterprise supported, in part, by Adams
State College, Colorado State University, Fort Lewis College, Mesa State College, Metropolitan State
College of Denver, University of Colorado, University of Northern Colorado, University of
Southern Colorado, and Western State College of Colorado.

The paper used in this publication meets the minimum requirements of the American National
Standard for Information Sciences — Permanence of Paper for Printed Library Materials.
ANSI Z39.48-1984

Library of Congress Cataloging-in-Publication Data

Noel, Thomas J. (Thomas Jacob)
    Denver landmarks & historic districts: a pictorial guide / Thomas J. Noel
        p.   cm.
    Includes bibliographical references and index.
    ISBN 0-87081-427-3
        1. Historic districts — Colorado — Denver — Guidebooks.   2. Historic districts — Colorado
— Denver — Pictorial works.   3. Historic buildings — Colorado — Denver — Guidebooks.
4. Historic buildings — Colorado — Denver — Pictorial works.   5. Denver (Colo.) —
Guidebooks.   6. Denver (Colo.) — Pictorial works.   I. Title.
F784.D46A2 1996
917.88'830433 — dc20   96-24062
                                                                            CIP

10   9   8   7   6   5   4   3   2   1

For my students
who have educated me
and
for my fellow preservationists
who have shared cheers, beers, and tears

Contents

CONTENTS

Maps

Foreword

by Denver Mayor Wellington Webb

Since walking the city during my first mayoral campaign in 1990, I have often revisited Denver's seventy-three neighborhoods on foot to meet the people and enjoy the special ambience of each block.

Denver now has more than 250 locally designated landmarks and twenty-eight historic districts. I have supported designations because they stabilize and enhance Denver's older neighborhoods. Landmarking is a great way to establish deeper roots and a sense of place for this growing city, which is now welcoming a wave of newcomers.

In the 1990s, we can all be proud of our new Denver Public Library and restored branch libraries, Denver International Airport, Coors Field, revitalized parks and parkways, and many other achievements of our generation. But these new amenities are not as important as maintaining and respecting the residences, schools, businesses, libraries, fire stations, and churches that preceding generations of Denverites built. I have made understanding and respect for Denver's traditions a foundation of my leadership in Denver.

After taking some of Tom Noel's tours and enjoying his other books, I can recommend this guide. Tom is a longtime Denver Landmark Preservation commissioner, teacher of Denver history, author, and conductor of bar, cemetery, church, and neighborhood tours. Professor

Denver's squandered architectural heritage led to the creation in 1967 of the Denver Landmark Preservation Commission. During its first three decades, the DLPC oversaw designation of more than 250 individual landmarks and twenty-eight historic districts. The wrinkled hands on this plaque are those of pioneer commissioner and Colorado poet laureate Thomas Hornsby Ferril. (Photo by Glenn Cuerden)

Noel will steer you to Denver's special places with knowledge, zest, and humor.

I hope that you will visit our beautifully restored City and County Building and our handsome Civic Center Park on your tour of Denver's special places.

Acknowledgments

Tom and Laurie Simmons of Front Range Research Associates helped administer this project and provided data, editing, photographs, and preliminary maps. Ellen Ittelson of the Denver Planning Office captured and handled the Colorado Historical Society certified local government grant that made possible original research, photographs, and maps to tell the story of more than 250 designated Denver landmarks and twenty-eight historic districts.

Denver Landmark Preservation commissioners Philip E. Flores, Barbara S. Norgren, Stephen J. Leonard, and Edward D. White, Jr., reviewed the manuscript, making corrections and many helpful suggestions. William Bessesen, Charles Brantigan, Dennis Gallagher, Frank Hegner, Marjorie Hornbein, John Litvak, Earl McCoy, Vi Noel, Ann Student, and Bill West were also very helpful. Jack A. Murphy, curator of geology at the Denver Museum of Natural History, generously shared his pathbreaking research on the stones used in Denver buildings. Bob Damereau and the Denver Planning Office staff allowed my students and me access to the fat, overflowing DLPC files.

Sue Sethney of the University of Colorado at Denver History Department contributed to this project in many ways. CU–Denver students Sandy Beeson, Rosemary Fetter, Jennifer Fullmer, Marcia Goldstein, Eric Hammersmark, David Karlo, Nancy Kelly, Marcie Morin, Kevin Rucker, Rachel Smith, Chris Whitacre, and Nancy Widmann assisted with research and editing. Funding matches for the student research assistants — including an Undergraduate Research Opportunities Program grant for mapmaker Eric Hammersmark — were generously donated by the university.

Kathleen Brooker and the staff of Historic Denver, Inc., let me review their files and copy some of their photographs. Ace Denver photographers Glenn Cuerden, José Dole, Tom Simmons, and Roger Whitacre supplied contemporary photos to complement the historic ones from the magnificent collections of the Colorado Historical Society and the Denver Public Library. A special thanks to Krebs Uptown Photography for their first-rate reproductions. Robert Spude, National Park Service historian, and his staff, especially Chris Whitacre and Lisa Wegman-French, graciously shared their extensive records, including the Historic American Building Survey/Historic American Engineering Record (HABS/HAER) files and drawings.

Architects Mark Applebaum, Temple H. Buell, Rodney S. Davis, Peter H. Dominick, Jr., Paul Foster, Ken Fuller, Michael Graves, James Hartmann, Dan Havekost, Kathy Hoeft, Victor Hornbein, Dennis Humphreys, Brain Klipp, Gary Long, Stanley Pouw, John M. Prosser, Candy Roberts, Bob Root, David Owen Tryba, Ed White, and Alan Zeigel humored my inquiries and helped me to understand their work.

Despite outstanding efforts from so many people, mistakes and incomplete data haunt works such as this. If you find errors or information omitted here, please notify me in care of the University Press of Colorado. This book is financed, in part, with federal funds from the National Historic Preservation Act, administered by the National Park Service, U.S. Department of the Interior, through the Colorado Historical Society. However, the contents and opinions do not necessarily reflect the views or policies of either the Department of the Interior or the Colorado Historical Society.

Introduction

Si monumentum requiris, circumspice.

In the crypt beneath St. Paul's Cathedral in London, Christopher Wren's unpretentious tomb is marked with the preceding inscription. It translates as, "If you require a monument, look around."

Just as Wren's best building is his best tribute, Denver's buildings are the best monuments to the Mile High City's builders. Looking around at surviving architecture is a fine way to commemorate a city's architects and residents, to measure the community's booms and busts, to approach its history.

Denver's nineteenth-century masonry buildings reflect its gold rush origins. The discovery of a few specks of gold in the South Platte River near its junction with Cherry Creek led to the creation of Denver City on November 22, 1858. Founder William H. Larimer, Jr., named the town for Kansas territorial governor James Denver to help ensure its selection as the seat of what was then Arapahoe County, Kansas Territory. Larimer platted Denver City with streets parallel to Cherry Creek. Only after Denver began to blossom in the 1870s were outlying areas platted to conform to federal land grids based on cardinal compass points.

Aggressive town promoters, led by *Rocky Mountain News* founding editor William N. Byers and territorial governor John Evans, enticed railroads to this isolated town seven hundred miles from the Missouri River frontier communities. After railroads steamed into Denver in 1870, this crossroads in the middle of nowhere grew into the second largest city in the Far West. By 1890 Denver had a population of 106,713, making it smaller than San Francisco but larger than Los Angeles, Seattle, Phoenix, or any town in Texas.

Like other inland cities without navigable rivers, Denver's hub was the railroad station. Railroads hauled gold and silver ores from mountain mining towns into Denver's smelters, producing fortunes that built a grand opera house, elegant churches, majestic hotels, imposing office blocks, and masonry mansions.

Flush times ended with the silver crash of 1893. After federal repeal of the Sherman Silver Purchase Act that year, the price of silver dropped from more than a dollar to less than sixty cents per ounce, devastating Colorado's most lucrative industry. Responding to the economic slump and population loss in the mid-1890s, Denver's power elite set about diversifying the city's economy. While still serving a vast, if faltering, mountain mining hinterland, the city also focused on becoming the supply and food processing center for farmers and ranchers on the high plains.

Not content to be the regional metropolis only for Colorado, Denverites used railroads to extend their economic orbit to the neighboring states of Kansas, Oklahoma, New Mexico, Utah, and Wyoming. Agriculture and food processing, stockyards and meat packing, brewing and banking, and manufacturing and service industries became mainstays of Denver's economic base. More recently, federal jobs — civilian and military — have stabilized the boom-and-bust city, especially since the 1930s. Tourism has also emerged as one of the city's most reliable industries.

THE CITY BEAUTIFUL

Tourism and steady, more orderly growth were encouraged by Denver's City Beautiful movement. Robert W. Speer introduced this urban vision of the Progressive Era after his election as mayor in 1904. Speer had toured the 1893 World's Columbian Exposition in Chicago and, along with thirty million others, had marveled at the transformation of a swamp on Lake Michigan into an urbane, Neoclassical paradise. He brought the dream home and, as Denver's mayor, set out to turn a dusty, drab, unplanned city into "Paris on the Platte."

Speer served two-and-a-half terms as mayor before dying in office in 1918. He first engaged Charles Mulford Robinson, the New York City planner and author of *Modern Civic Art, or The City Made Beautiful* (1903), to prepare a master plan. The 1906 Robinson Plan, augmented by George Kessler's 1907 park and parkway plan and later revised and extended by Frederick Law Olmsted, Jr., Frederick MacMonnies, Edward H. Bennett, and others, was implemented by "Boss" Speer, who operated both over and under the table. Denver became one of the better examples of City Beautiful planning. These schemes were later expanded with the help of New Deal programs and, more recently, were revived by Denver's first Hispanic mayor, Federico Peña (1983–1991) and first African American mayor, Wellington Webb (1991–present).

Denver's City Beautiful landscape comprises Civic Center Park, surrounded by city, state, and federal office buildings. A network of parkways stretches out from Civic Center via Speer Boulevard to the neighborhoods. Neighborhood parks serve as mini civic centers surrounded by schools, libraries, churches, and other public buildings. The Denver Mountain Parks network consists of Winter Park Ski Area, Red Rocks Park with its Greek-style outdoor amphitheater, Mt. Evans, and forty-five other parks covering about 13,500 acres in Arapahoe, Clear Creek, Douglas, Grand, and Jefferson Counties.

George E. Kessler, who created the park and parkway plan, was a German-born, European-trained professional landscape architect who became this country's foremost parkway planner. Kessler worked on New York's Central Park, helped lay out the 1904 Louisiana Purchase Exposition grounds in St. Louis, Missouri, and gave Kansas City, Missouri, its park and parkway system. In Denver, Kessler abandoned the spoke-and-wheel model of diagonal avenues and connecting outer rings of boulevards. Too many buildings already obstructed that ideal scheme, so Kessler superimposed parkways upon the existing street grid. He placed parks at the highest points to permit mountain views, as exemplified

by Cheesman, Cranmer, Inspiration Point, and Ruby Hill Parks. These spacious parks set high architectural and landscaping standards for adjacent private homes and buildings. Driving, bicycling, or walking the park and parkway system is a good way to explore Denver.

The public-minded Progressive Era reformers of the early twentieth century created grand parks, parkways, and public buildings. These amenities still distinguish the city, giving it traditional classical moorings and generous landscaping. To preserve this legacy — an amenity unmatched by even the richest suburbs — the Denver Landmark Preservation Commission is in the process of landmarking much of Denver's park and parkway network.

THE ARCHITECTS

Robert S. Roeschlaub, Colorado's first licensed architect, came from Illinois to Denver in 1873. After the Denver School District appointed Roeschlaub its architect, his fine schools taught lessons in improved architectural standards in the hastily built boomtown. A half dozen Roeschlaub schools survive as designated landmarks.

Frank E. Edbrooke, Denver's most prominent nineteenth-century architect, was brought to Denver from Chicago in 1879 by silver-mining tycoon Horace Tabor. Tabor, a former stonecutter, explained, "Denver was not building as good buildings as it ought, and I thought I would do something towards setting them a good example." He did with the Tabor Grand Opera House, the city's finest structure, designed by Frank Edbrooke and his older brother, Willoughby. Although Willoughby moved on, Edbrooke remained in Denver. He introduced mainstream design influenced by Henry H. Richardson, the East Coast pacesetter whose use of Romanesque (round) arches of rough-cut stone in massive blocks characterized the popular Richardsonian Romanesque style. Edbrooke also introduced Denverites to technical achievements such as the steel skeleton of his best-known landmark, the Brown Palace Hotel.

Following Tabor's example, other capitalists commissioned out-of-state architects instead of local builders. The flush times of the 1870s and 1880s attracted such notable Illinois architects as William Lang, who designed wonderful stone and shingle homes in his own version of the Richardsonian Romanesque style. The Illinois influence may be seen in Denver's early skyscrapers, which tended toward the flat-topped Chicago school rather than New York City's stepped towers and dramatic spires.

A notable attempt to professionalize building design and raise architectural consciousness was Jesse B. Dorman's *Western Architect and Building News*. This illustrated monthly magazine extolled architecture as the most democratic and important art form. Dorman's magazine, as architectural historian Richard Brettell put it, was "a rudder guiding the course of the building boom." Although this Denver journal lasted only three years, from 1889 to 1891, it successfully promoted the Colorado Association of Architects, which in 1892 became the Colorado chapter of the American Institute of Architects (AIA). In 1909 the AIA persuaded the Colorado Legislature to begin licensing architects.

Nineteenth-century Denver architects such as the Baerresen Brothers, David W. Dryden, Frederick C. Eberley, Aaron M. Gove, John J. Huddart, Willis A. Marean, Albert J. Norton, and Frederick J. Sterner used local brick and stone to build in the Second Empire, Italianate, Queen Anne, and Richardsonian styles as each mode became successively popular in the eastern United States.

Neoclassical architecture, which became stylish after 1900, came to include Beaux-Arts revivals of Greek, Roman, and Italian styles. Jacques Jules Benoit Benedict, the first Denver architect to train at the École des Beaux-Arts in Paris, left many outstanding landmarks in that style. Sadly, his only known commercial building, Central Bank, was demolished in 1990 despite its landmark designation. The neoclassical tendencies of the early 1900s resulted in two very common Denver residential types: the foursquare and the modest, one-story classical cottage with its central attic dormer and Tuscan porch columns.

Brothers William E. and Arthur A. Fisher dominated both residential and commercial building in Denver between 1910 and 1930. They favored the red tile roofs and thick masonry walls of Mediterranean design that provided the durable weatherproofing required by Colorado's erratic climate. The Fishers and their most prominent employee, Burnham Hoyt, produced many notable interpretations of Southwestern styles.

The Fishers also used other revival styles trendy during the 1920s through 1940s — Italian, French, and, most notably, English, including Colonial, Georgian, and Tudor. The Fishers and other leading twentieth-century architects such as Maurice Biscoe, Theodore Boal and Frederick L. Harnois, Aaron M. Gove and Thomas F. Walsh, Harry James Manning, and Ernest P. Varian and Lester E. Varian gave Denver notable landmarked examples of various revival types.

Denver's most creative twentieth-century architect, Burnham Hoyt, designed the municipal outdoor amphitheater at Red Rocks Park, Colorado's finest piece of modern architecture. Here Hoyt sensitively integrates minimalist construction with the natural environment. Unfortunately, few other architects have achieved such sensitive use of natural terrain and vegetation in their work.

Twentieth-century styles such as Prairie, Art Deco, Streamline Moderne, and postmodern caught on slowly in Denver. As early as the 1930s, modern concepts, shapes, and materials were introduced by such architects as Robert K. Fuller, Eugene G. Groves, Victor Hornbein, Burnham Hoyt, Merrill Hoyt, Glen W. Huntington, G. Charles Jaka, and Eugene Sternberg. Before the 1950s, few architects could make a living by specializing in modern architecture. Temple Hoyne Buell, the state's most successful developer-architect, told this author in 1986 with a wink, "We don't fight over architectural styles. The client is always right."

Denver architects, like their tradition-minded clients, usually opted for the imitative rather than the original, giving Denver handsome, solid, but generally conventional buildings.

DENVER'S DISTINCTIVE ARCHITECTURAL CHARACTERISTICS

Denver buildings, although generally imitative of those in other cities, are often distinctive in three ways: spacious settings, masonry construction, and mountain views. Generous settings characterize a metropolis largely unconstrained by natural impediments. Denver developed with a western emphasis on elbow room, producing single-family detached homes. Such homes, with side yards as well as front yards and backyards, predominate even in the inner-city districts.

Unconstrained by any large bodies of water or by the mountains fifteen miles away, Denverites were free to build in every direction, and they did. Streetcars, and later automobile roads, shaped a metropolis that now sprawls through five suburban counties and over some 2,500 square miles, from the Front Range of the Rockies on the west to the most spacious airport in the United States on the east.

Denver is a brick city. Because the nearest forest lies some fifty miles away and clay beds underlie many areas of the city, brick was often easier and cheaper to use than timber. Bricks were also more fire resistant than frame and were encouraged by city ordinances after the Great Fire of 1863, Denver's only major blaze. Brick, reddish local sandstone, and, in recent years, tinted concrete, give Denver its ruddy complexion.

Denver's setting is special because of its backdrop — the snow-capped Rocky Mountains. Mayor Speer realized that this mountain view was the city's greatest asset and limited building heights to twelve stories. Not until the 1950s did a growth-hungry city abandon the height ordinance in order to court high-rise developers. With few exceptions, developers have had their way to this day — witness the demolition of the Central Bank Building and the 1996 demolition of I. M. Pei's Hyperbolic Paraboloid for a St. Louis hotel chain's aggressive expansion plans. To make matters worse, none of the forty- and fifty-story towers erected since 1980 have roof-level viewing areas open to the public. Recent mountain view ordinances have been only partially successful in preserving Denver's mountain views, a sight that can cheer up even the poorest and most depressed citizen or visitor.

ETHNIC ANGLES

Greek, Roman, Spanish, English, French, and Italian influences are prominent in early twentieth-century revival-style architecture used for both residential and commercial structures in Denver. Denver's early "brick" ordinances, which mandated the use of fire-retardant materials in building construction, excluded adobe bricks, discouraging a functional, handsome Hispanic building tradition. Denver lacked the solid German, Irish, Slavic, and Scandinavian neighborhoods of many

eastern cities, although heavily Jewish, Italian, black, and Hispanic areas did emerge.

Little Israel, the old Jewish neighborhood along West Colfax Avenue, is largely gone. Landmarked remnants are Golda Meir's relocated girlhood home and the Emmanuel Sherith Israel Chapel on the Auraria campus. On the east side lies Temple Emanuel Synagogue, now a public events center, whose Middle Eastern influences provide a contrast to Gothic and Romanesque elements of Christian churches.

Little Italy is represented by that area's heartbeat, Our Lady of Mount Carmel Catholic Church. Several other nearby North Denver landmarks — the Damascio House, Cerrone's Grocery, and the Hannigan-Canino Terrace — are reminders of this now dispersed Italian enclave.

Germans, Denver's largest foreign-born immigrant population in the nineteenth century, have left notable landmarks, such as St. Elizabeth's Catholic Church, the Tivoli Brewery, and the Buckhorn Exchange Restaurant. The oldest ethnic club in Colorado is commemorated by the landmarked Denver Turnverein in Capitol Hill and the Turnhalle Opera Hall within the Tivoli Brewery complex. Such institutions not only provided the food and drink but perpetuated the song, dance, music, and language of the homeland.

Anglo-Americans gave the city some of its finest landmark churches (Asbury Methodist and Trinity United Methodist), hotels (the Oxford and Brown Palace), and office blocks (the Boston, Equitable, Kittredge, and Masonic buildings). Episcopal churches with notable English Gothic architecture include several landmarks — St. John's Cathedral, St. Luke's, St. Mark's, and the Chapel of Our Merciful Savior. St. Patrick's Catholic Church, the first Irish parish, was a source of Irish pride and the inspiration for one of Denver's most popular civic festivals — the St. Patrick's Day Parade.

The French Gothic style is celebrated in Immaculate Conception Cathedral and the Ivy Chapel of Fairmount Cemetery, both designated landmarks. The Château style is best seen in the Croke-Patterson-Campbell Mansion, while later French Revival influences are showcased in the Frank Smith and Crawford Hill mansions.

Of the black community's institutions, Zion Baptist and Scott Methodist Churches are landmarked, as is the

Douglass Undertaking Parlor. The restaurant of Barney Ford, the pioneer black leader, and the residence of Dr. Clarence Holmes, a major twentieth-century spokesperson, are designated landmarks, although Dr. Justina Ford's House, now the Black American West Museum, is not.

Hispanos, the first European group to settle Colorado, have landmarks in Our Lady of Guadalupe and St. Cajetan's Churches and the Byers Branch Library, with its Spanish architecture and Spanish language programs. Denver has a Mexican-oriented commercial district on Santa Fe Drive between 7th and 12th Avenues. Unfortunately, the proposed designation of upper Larimer Street, with its many small and colorful Hispanic businesses, has been frustrated by the tremendous development pressures generated by the 1995 opening of Coors Field, the baseball park of the Colorado Rockies.

DENVER STYLES

No distinctive Denver style has emerged, although brick foursquares became so common as to be locally known as "Denver squares." Coloradans generally borrowed traditional styles from the eastern United States and Europe, whose cities they hoped to emulate. As Richard Brettell explained in his 1973 book *Historic Denver: The Architects and the Architecture, 1858–1893,* "Denverites gave their commercial buildings gravity by the use of the Renaissance rounded arch; they gave their churches a 'churchy' quality by the use of the Gothic arch; and they gave their homes a 'homey' quality by the addition of a balustraded front porch."

Denver's earliest landmarks, especially in Ninth Street Park and Curtis Park, reflect the Italianate style popular in the 1880s. Denver has only a few examples of the earlier Second Empire style, notably the Crawford Building in Larimer Square and the Knight House in Ninth Street Park.

More common in Denver are Queen Anne and Romanesque styles. Neoclassical types such as the foursquare and classic cottage also abound. Denverites, who used their buildings to convey a sense of tradition and permanence in a raw young city, favored historicist revivals like the colonial, Georgian, and Tudor. Most Denver buildings, it should be added, are not stylistically pure; rather, they are vernacular versions, often an eclectic mix of elements from two or more styles.

A few architects experimented with the Spanish Colonial and Mission Revival modes. Arthur A. Fisher and William E. Fisher, the principals of Denver's most prolific early twentieth-century architectural firm, argued that Spanish styles were ideal for a southwestern state with a Hispanic heritage. Furthermore, Colorado has a bright, sunny, dry climate, like the American Southwest and Spain itself, with temperature extremes that make stout masonry walls sensible because they keep buildings cooler in summer and warmer in winter.

A derivative of the Spanish hacienda is the ubiquitous post–World War II ranch house, of which there is not yet an individually landmarked specimen. Another common style, the bungalow popular from 1900 to the 1920s, is well represented in the city's largest historic district — East Seventh Avenue. Art Deco shaped only a few Denver residences, apartment houses, and commercial buildings. The Paramount Theater and the Cruise Room of the Oxford Hotel are landmarked examples. Denver has demolished or altered many of its few examples of Streamline Moderne commercial buildings, but residential examples may be found in Park Hill, Country Club, and, most notably, in the Bonnie Brae area. Twentieth-century styles remain underrepresented among designated landmarks.

THE DENVER LANDMARK PRESERVATION COMMISSION

Urban renewal projects, speculation, and rapid and reckless growth spurts have eliminated many notable structures, especially in the Central Business District and Capitol Hill. Wholesale demolitions led the mayor and city council to establish the Denver Landmark Preservation Commission (DLPC) in 1967. Since then, more than 250 individual landmarks and twenty-eight historic districts containing more than six thousand structures have been designated for preservation by the city council on the recommendation of concerned citizens and the DLPC. Designations are made on the basis of architectural, geographical, and historical significance. After a structure is landmarked, the DLPC

Helen Millett Arndt (1913–1985) persuaded Denver to establish a landmark commission in 1967. "Where an older generation will see nothing but obsolete and worn-out buildings awaiting demolition," Arndt argued, "a younger generation may see opportunities for restoring and recycling old structures for a new kind of space." (Alice Bakemeier photo)

reviews any exterior alterations requiring a building permit. The commission has ordinance authority to deny demolition in historic districts and to delay for one year destruction of individual landmarks that lie outside of historic districts.

The majority of landmarks in this book were constructed during Denver's greatest boom era, 1880-1893. These monuments in brick and stone commemorate an optimism that has characterized the city ever since its gold rush origins. The native stones of the Rocky Mountains — rhyolite (volcanic lava rock), Colorado Yule marble, sandstone, travertine, and granite — were used to trim and face brick structures.

Over the years Denverites have built many special places. This guide, whose entries are arranged to suggest a logical touring order, takes you to places the city has designated as having outstanding architectural, geographical, or historical importance. Although these are the officially designated buildings and neighborhoods of

note, the great fun in rubbernecking around Denver is discovering other special places on your own.

HOW TO USE THIS GUIDE

This is a guide to the buildings and districts identified by the Denver Landmark Preservation Commission and designated as landmarks by the city council and mayor as of 1995. It is arranged by neighborhoods and districts in tour order.

Structures are listed by their original names, with prominent later names also provided. Notable buildings that are not individually designated landmarks but fall within historic districts are discussed in the text but are not numbered or mapped. If a building is also on the National Register of Historic Places, it has been identified as NR (or, in the case of a district, NRD for National Register District). The National Register program established in the 1960s is like the DLPC program in that it identifies, designates, and attempts to preserve significant buildings and districts. Since 1990, Colorado has also identified locally significant landmarks by listing them on the State Register (SR).

Many buildings and districts are both National Register and Denver landmarks. The National Register program is administered for the federal government by the State Historic Preservation Office of the Colorado Historical Society. National Register administrators, unlike the DLPC, have no control over alterations and demolitions.

As with all architectural guidebooks, readers should be aware of some problems. Dates of building permits, building design, ground breaking, cornerstone laying, completion, and occupation usually stretch over several years. Here I have listed the date of completion.

Readers should also be wary of another pitfall in architectural history. Generally, buildings are attributed to the architect of record or to the head of a firm, rather than to the employee or employees who actually produced the design. When the actual designer could be determined, that person as well as the firm are listed. Unless identified as the builder, the name after the date of construction is that of the architect.

Like the barbarians who sacked ancient Rome, developers have leveled much of Denver's Neoclassical architecture. (Photo by Roger Whitacre)

Denver Landmarks & Historic Districts:
A Pictorial Guide

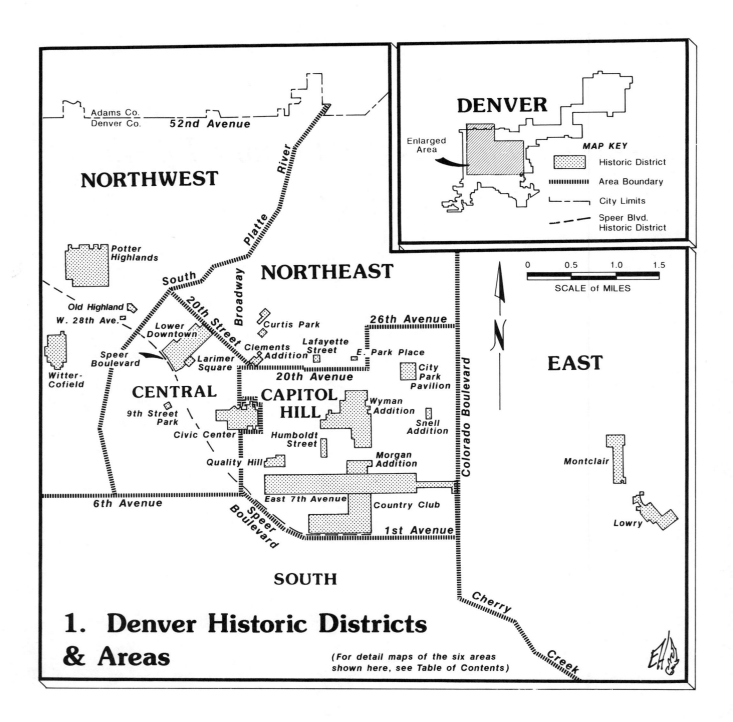

Adams Co.
Denver Co.
52nd Avenue

NORTHWEST

Platte River

South Broadway

NORTHEAST

DENVER

Enlarged Area

MAP KEY

▦ Historic District

▬▬▬ Area Boundary

▬ ▬ City Limits

▬ · ▬ Speer Blvd. Historic District

Potter Highlands

Old Highland

W. 28th Ave.

20th Street

Lower Downtown

Speer Boulevard

Witter-Cofield

Larimer Square

CENTRAL

9th Street Park

Civic Center

Quality Hill

6th Avenue

Curtis Park

Clements Addition

Lafayette Street

E. Park Place

26th Avenue

20th Avenue

CAPITOL HILL

Wyman Addition

Snell Addition

Humboldt Street

Morgan Addition

East 7th Avenue

Country Club

1st Avenue

Speer Boulevard

City Park Pavilion

Colorado Boulevard

EAST

Montclair

Lowry

Cherry Creek

N

0   0.5   1.0   1.5
SCALE of MILES

SOUTH

1. Denver Historic Districts & Areas

(For detail maps of the six areas shown here, see Table of Contents)

EH

CHAPTER 1
Central Denver Area

AURARIA
NINTH STREET PARK
SPEER BOULEVARD
LARIMER SQUARE
LOWER DOWNTOWN
CENTRAL BUSINESS DISTRICT
CIVIC CENTER

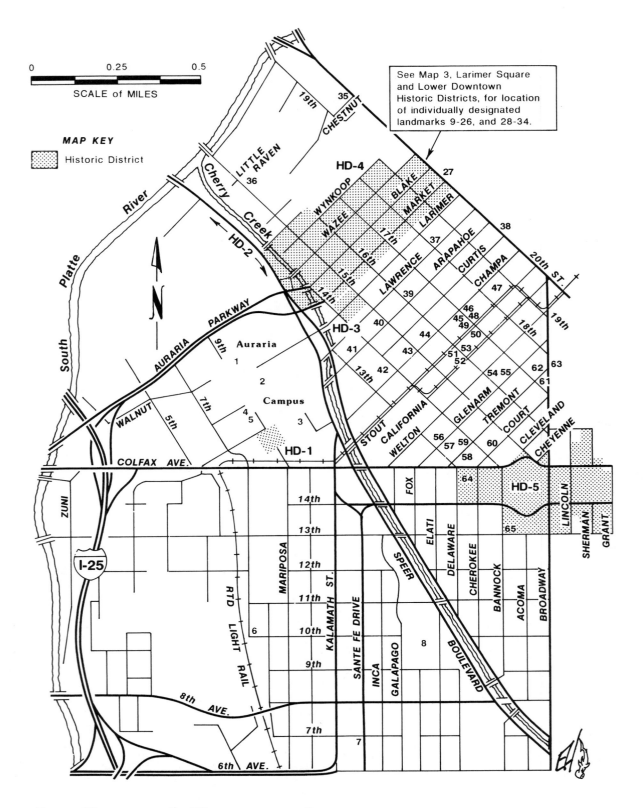

0   0.25   0.5

SCALE of MILES

MAP KEY

Historic District

See Map 3, Larimer Square and Lower Downtown Historic Districts, for location of individually designated landmarks 9-26, and 28-34.

2. Central Denver Area

2

AURARIA

William Greeneberry Russell, his brothers Joseph Oliver and Levi, and a few other prospectors from Auraria, Georgia, founded Auraria City on November 1, 1858. They gave their "city" a Latin word for gold, the heavy metal that they found that summer in Cherry Creek and the South Platte River.

Their discovery launched the Colorado gold rush. The rival camp of Denver City, founded November 22, 1858, on the northeast bank of Cherry Creek, merged with Auraria in 1860. After the railroads arrived in the 1870s, Denver's oldest neighborhood evolved into a mixed residential, retail, and industrial area. During the 1970s, it became a target of the Denver Urban Renewal Authority. Much of the Auraria neighborhood north of West Colfax Avenue was demolished to clear land for the 171-acre Auraria Higher Education Center, which houses the Community College of Denver, Metropolitan State College of Denver, and the University of Colorado at Denver.

The Denver Landmark Preservation Commission, in one of its first major campaigns, used designation to save from urban renewal bulldozers three Auraria churches, the Tivoli Brewery, and homes on Ninth Street Park. Historic Denver, Inc., a private preservation group founded in 1970, restored a full block of nineteenth-century homes on 9th Street in its most ambitious project. Historic Denver, Inc., donated the reconstructed block to what has become the most populous campus in Colorado, with more than thirty-two thousand students.

1. Tivoli Brewery/Auraria Student Union and Shopping Mall

(1881. 1890, many additions. 1980s, renovation by Hellmuth, Obata & Kassabaum), 900 block of Larimer St., NR

In this one-block complex, the seven-story mansard tower building (1890, Frederick C. Eberley) opened as the Milwaukee Brewery. The attached West Denver Turnhalle Opera Hall (1882, Harold W. Baerresen) retains its horseshoe-shaped balcony and proscenium arch stage. The brewery expanded over the years to incorporate surrounding structures, the oldest of which

1. Tivoli Brewery. (Courtesy Denver Public Library)

is the 1881 building at 10th and Larimer Streets. The bottling and storage building at the corner of 9th and Walnut Streets was a later addition. The complex operated as the Tivoli-Union Brewery from 1900 until it closed in 1969. The Auraria Higher Education Center leased the brewery to private developers who renovated the facility during the 1980s, creating a retail mall with a central skylighted atrium. Students voted in 1991 to use the Tivoli as their student center, a plan that had been rejected by less preservation-conscious students of the 1970s.

2. Emmanuel Sherith Israel Chapel/Student Art Gallery)

(1877. 1970s, renovation by Gale Abels & Associates), 1201 10th St., NR

Denver's oldest ecclesiastical edifice is a Gothic Revival vernacular chapel built for an Episcopal congregation. In 1903 the rhyolite chapel was purchased by some of the many East European Jews moving into the West Colfax neighborhood of Little Israel. The chapel's fifty-five years as a synagogue are commemorated by a Star of David on the roof and a Hebrew inscription over the door. The Gothic windows recall the Episcopalian origins of what is now a student art gallery for the Auraria campus.

2. Emmanuel Sherith Israel Chapel/Student Art Gallery. (Photo by Tom Noel)

3. St. Elizabeth's Catholic Church. (Photo by Tom Noel)

3. St. Elizabeth's Catholic Church

(1898, Frederick W. Paroth), 1062 11th St., NR

Brother Adrian, one of the German Franciscans assigned to Denver, helped the architect design this replacement for a smaller brick predecessor on the same site. This Romanesque Revival church of rough-cut Castle Rock rhyolite has a dominant single corner spire soaring 162 feet. Behind a curving arcade and fountain are cloisters (1936, J.J.B. Benedict) for the clergy, with an old private chapel and library retaining samples of the German stained glass and ornate woodwork now gone from the modernized church interior. Officially established as a German national parish, St. Elizabeth's used the German language in many parish activities for Denver's largest foreign-born nineteenth-century immigrant group. The Gothic prayer garden and monastery (1936, J.J.B. Benedict) joined the church to the extant monastery and to the old parish school (1890), which was replaced by the modern St. Francis Conference Center (1980, Marvin Hatami), with its contrasting expanses of glass and stark brick walls. The church remains active as part of both the Auraria campus and the community and stands as a monument to Colorado's German pioneers.

4. St. Cajetan's Catholic Church

(1926, Robert Willison), 9th and Lawrence Sts.

The first church for Spanish-speaking Catholics in northern Colorado is this stucco and red tile edifice in the Spanish colonial revival style. Millionaire flour miller John K. Mullen, whose house once stood here, donated both the site and $50,000 toward construction of the church. Curvilinear parapets, twin bell towers, and round arches make this a larger, refined version of small country churches in the San Luis Valley — or a smaller version of the great churches in Mexico. Although the church has been rearranged inside for use as a lecture and concert hall for the Auraria campus, it has been faithfully restored outside. With its parish credit union and Ave Maria Health Clinic, St. Cajetan's tended to the economic and physical — as well as spiritual — health of the community until moving to a new church in Southwest Denver in 1975. As the first major public building erected by and for Denver Hispanos, it is a tribute to what has become the city's largest ethnic minority.

4. St. Cajetan's Catholic Church (Photo by Michael Gamer)

5. Golda Meir House

(1911), 1146 9th St.

This single-story, flat-roofed duplex of pressed red brick with a corbeled and stepped parapet is a type so humble and common that it is generally overlooked. The restored dwelling, made significant by the residency of Golda Meir, a Jewish American who became the first female prime minister of Israel, was moved to 9th Street to avoid demolition. The house was built at 1606–1608 Julian Street in the working-class neighborhood of Little Israel along West Colfax Avenue between Santa Fe Drive and Sheridan Boulevard.

NINTH STREET PARK

HD-1 NINTH STREET PARK HISTORIC DISTRICT (see Map 2, page 2)

(1870s–1905. 1976, restoration by Edward D. White, Jr.), 9th St. between Champa and Curtis Sts., NRD

One of Denver's oldest surviving residential face blocks consists of a corner store and thirteen middle-class dwellings with restored exteriors and renovated interiors now used for campus offices. The pavement of 9th Street has been replaced with grass, but the original granite curbs and red sandstone sidewalks remain. Two of the dwellings are 1870s frame houses that predate early Denver fire ordinances mandating masonry construction.

The **Knight House** (1885), 1015 9th Street, in the Second Empire style, was the home of Stephen Knight, a pioneer miller. His descendants, who became prominent in Denver banking, business, educational, and political circles, helped restore what Don Etter, in *Auraria: Where Denver Began* (1972), calls "perhaps the most perfectly proportioned and tastefully embellished Victorian house in Denver."

Another Second Empire model, the **Witte House** (1883), 1027 9th Street, retains its crested entry tower. The **Madden-Schultz Duplex** (1890, Jason J. Backus, builder), 1045–1047 9th Street, is the simple, two-story brick house of Eugene Madden, a Larimer Street saloonkeeper who served as the area's councilman from 1918 until his death in 1941. The **Groussman Grocery** (1906, Frederick C. Eberley), 1067 9th Street, now the Mercantile Restaurant, is a two-story corner store with distinctive brickwork detail and globe finials. This grocery, a typical cornerstone of nineteenth-century neighborhoods, was operated by Albert B. Groussman's Jewish family, who lived upstairs. Descendants helped fund restoration.

The **Smedley House** (c. 1872), 1020 9th Street, a very early frame residence, retains its original bracketed eaves, but it is much altered and has a reconstructed porch. William Smedley, a Quaker dentist from Pennsylvania, built what later became the Casa Mayan restaurant, a social center for the Hispanic community. Ramon and Caroline Gonzales lived upstairs with their seven children, who helped run the street-level dining rooms. Casa Mayan was one of the first restaurants to introduce Mexican food — as well as music and art — to non-Hispanics.

Restraint heightens the impact of detail on the **Davis House** (c. 1873), 1068 9th Street, an Italianate dwelling with Carpenter Gothic porch woodwork. Houses at 1061, 1041, and 1024 9th Street are also Italianate. This handsome block from the past, with structures restored at $20 per square foot, outshines the campus's bland newer brick buildings erected for $30 per square foot during the 1980s.

HD-1 Ninth Street Park. (Photo by Tom Noel)

6. Buckhorn Exchange Restaurant

(1886), 1000 Osage St., NR

In 1893, Henry H. Zietz moved his saloon from Market Street into this typical two-story brick commercial building. The Zietzes supposedly brought the white oak front bar with hand-carved oak leaves and acorns from their family tavern in Essen, Germany. Three generations of Zietzes ran this legendary resort, where Buffalo Bill and U.S. presidents from Theodore Roosevelt to Ronald Reagan feasted on western delicacies ranging from rattlesnake steaks to Rocky Mountain oysters.

Wildlife murals by Noel Adams decorate the exterior. The interior is jammed with several hundred stuffed animals ranging from jackalopes to a golden eagle, from prairie dogs to a giant bison head. Besides doubling as a natural history museum, the Buckhorn is also packed with antique guns, trappers' tools, photographs, and antique furniture.

7. Byers Branch Library

(1918, Ernest P. Varian and Lester E. Varian. 1992, restoration by Stanley Pouw Associates), 675 Santa Fe Dr.

This exquisite branch library was named for William N. Byers, founder of the *Rocky Mountain News* and Denver's greatest booster. The father-and-son architectural team used concrete-covered brick with stone trim in a Spanish eclectic style. The single-room library is a large, finely crafted space with a fireplace under a vaulted ceiling and with basement meeting, storage, and office space. Denver artist Carlota Espinosa painted the large mural *Pasado, Presente, Futuro* (1975), capturing the sweep of Hispanic history. As a center for English-as-a-second-language programs, this library has become a cornerstone for the Spanish-accented business district on Santa Fe Drive.

6. Buckhorn Exchange Restaurant. (Photo by Tom Noel)

8. West High School

(1924–1926, William Harry Edwards), 951 Elati St. between W. 9th and W. 11th Aves.

Facing Speer Boulevard across the generous expanse of Sunken Gardens Park, this Collegiate Gothic landmark exemplifies City Beautiful–era planning. The symmetrical four-story school with a central seven-story tower is constructed of light manganese brick trimmed in buff terra-cotta. A 1975 gymnasium and a 1978 wing are the most notable additions, along with a more sympathetic 1990s swimming pool and outdoor patio connected by a three-story bridge.

The original plan arranged rooms along subsidiary corridors radiating from a large central corridor and

incorporated natural lighting for all rooms. The main entry is adorned with WPA Federal Art Project murals by Edward Chavez and Jennie Magafan. Flanking the auditorium doors are the 1933 *Golden West* murals of Edmund L. Lambert, a graduate of West High.

SPEER BOULEVARD

HD-2 SPEER BOULEVARD HISTORIC DISTRICT (see Map 2, page 2)

(1907–1918, George Kessler and others), from University Blvd. to Irving St., NRD

Mayor Robert W. Speer hired the nationally prominent parkway planner George Kessler to draw a 1907 Denver park and parkway master plan. Kessler's key diagonal, then called Cherry Creek Drive, followed Cherry Creek from East 1st Avenue to the creek's confluence with the South Platte River and across the river to Federal Boulevard in Northwest Denver. Kessler's imaginative plan transformed the dump-lined, trash-strewn creek into a tree-lined boulevard, renamed Speer Boulevard in 1909. Subsequent planners, most notably landscape architect Saco R. DeBoer and architect-preservationist Paul Foster, have enhanced, expanded, and revived Kessler's plan.

The boulevard's 1988 landmark designation ended the street widening that had reduced its grassy, tree-shaded edges. Restoration of the historic lighting, bridges, and landscaping on Speer stimulated a rejuvenation of the entire parkway and park system along City Beautiful lines. Speer Boulevard was recelebrated during the 1980s with monumental pillars, an arched bridge, and restored plantings. Pedestrian/cyclist ramps off the boulevard access a paved creekside trail to Denver's birthplace, Confluence Park.

One of the loveliest stretches of the Cherry Creek Greenway, a paved bike path and pedestrian trail, is **Creekfront Park** (1992, Robert Karns and Bill Wenk) at Speer Boulevard and Larimer Street, with a water garden and a path under Speer connecting the Auraria campus and Larimer Square.

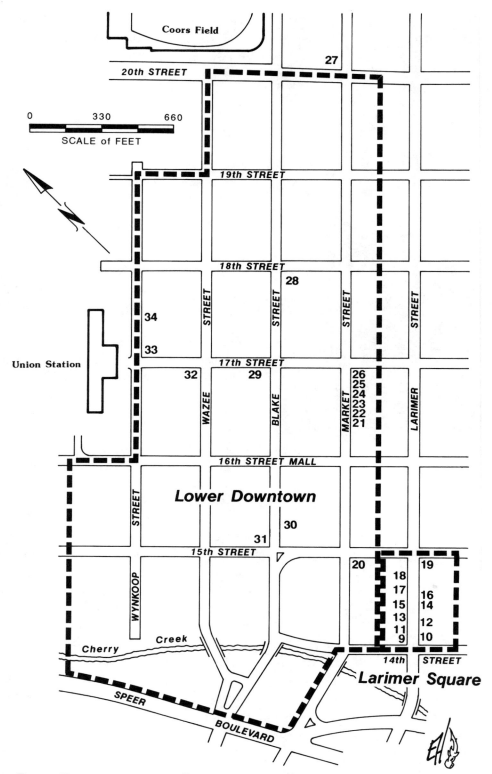

Coors Field

20th STREET

27

0   330   660
SCALE of FEET

19th STREET

18th STREET

28

STREET

STREET

STREET

STREET

34

33

Union Station

17th STREET

32   29

WAZEE   BLAKE   MARKET   LARIMER

26
25
24
23
22
21

16th STREET MALL

Lower Downtown

STREET   WYNKOOP

30

31

15th STREET

20   19

18
17   16
15   14
13   12
11   10
9

Creek

Cherry

14th STREET

Larimer Square

SPEER

BOULEVARD

3. Larimer Square &
Lower Downtown Historic Districts

HD-3 Larimer Square in 1875. (Photo by William G. Chamberlain, courtesy Denver Public Library)

LARIMER SQUARE

HD-3 LARIMER SQUARE HISTORIC DISTRICT

(1870s and 1880s. 1965, Langdon Morris and others. 1990s, Semple-Brown-Roberts), 1400 block of Larimer St., NRD

Larimer Square, like Larimer Street, is named for William H. Larimer, Jr., who founded Denver in 1858. The 1400 block of Larimer Street features a creative adaptation and reuse of antique brick buildings with cast-iron storefronts, metal cornices, and ornamental stonework. The eighteen commercial structures have been opened with cut-throughs, recessed facades, interior courts, and open basements. This effort to spare the block from Denver Urban Renewal Authority bulldozers proved successful enough to inspire the rejuvenation of the rest of Lower Downtown. It also preserves one of Denver's earliest face blocks of commercial buildings, with the oldest structures dating to the 1870s. Langdon Morris, the original preservation architect, was a member of the Denver Landmark Preservation Commission.

9. Gahan's Saloon/Lanktree Hotel

(1889), 1401–1407 Larimer St.

To his groggery, city councilman John Gahan, Sr., welcomed constituents and politicians alike. Both flocked here from City Hall, which once stood across the street on a site now marked by the bell from the old tower. Gahan's switched to soft drinks during Prohibition and was reopened by John, Jr., as a saloon and restaurant after Prohibition was repealed in 1933. Numerous short-lived saloons followed Gahan's before the building became a ladies' clothing shop in the 1980s. This three-story red brick building, which housed the Lanktree Hotel upstairs, boasts red sandstone trim, brick corbeling, and cast-iron columns framing plate glass storefronts.

10. Hotel Hope

(c. 1888), 1404 Larimer St.

A metal frieze atop the third story of this building has a distinctive off-center pediment surmounted by a peculiar curved parapet with a central finial. Numerous storefront businesses and upper-story hotels have occupied the brick structure over the years, the Hotel Hope being its most memorable long-term occupant. A one-story addition (1993, Semple-Brown-Roberts) was made to the southwest side of the building, erasing a parking lot and carrying the structure to 14th Street. The addition's red brick and cast red stone match masonry construction typical of Larimer Square. Its pioneer occupant, The Cadillac Ranch restaurant and bar, likewise perpetuates a liquid tradition on Larimer Street, which once housed some fifty-seven saloons. This 1993 addition is topped by an outdoor deck along the old brick sidewall of the Hotel Hope, giving the public sunshine, fresh air, and views of Larimer Square, the Auraria campus, and the Rocky Mountains beyond.

11. McKibben Building

(c. 1890), 1409–1411 Larimer St.

A bracketed cornice and brick dentils dress up this two-story brick Italianate building with a glass storefront and recessed central entry. It was named for the contractor who worked on the original 1960s Larimer Square restoration.

12. Barnum Building

(1889), 1412 Larimer St.

On the 1860s site of John J. Walley's long-lived pioneer undertaking parlor, this three-story red brick commercial building with stone trim housed various hotels. Changing storefront businesses included a cigar maker, liquor dealer, and plumber.

13. Lincoln Hall

(1887), 1413–1419 Larimer St.

This two-story Second Empire brick building gained a stylish mansard third story in the 1880s, along with a dance floor suspended from cables to provide more bounce. Lincoln Hall became a rowdy, notorious dance hall. To the relief of Denver police, the building was converted in 1891 to the Fred Mueller Harness Shop, which remained until the 1960s. More recently, various boutiques have replaced the saddle shop.

13. Lincoln Hall. (Photo by Tom Noel)

14. Kettle Building

(1873. 1990, renovation by Semple-Brown-Roberts), 1426 Larimer St.

George Kettle's butcher shop, the oldest building in Larimer Square, is only twenty feet wide, with a cut stone facade and a fancy molded cornice. The tiny shop was gutted in 1990 to create an arcade leading to a rear courtyard. Above the new native sandstone interior walls, a vaulted stucco ceiling mural (1988, Evans & Brown) depicts early Denver characters. The San Francisco artists fancifully portrayed General Larimer prospecting with a Greek urn instead of a gold pan.

15. Apollo Hall/Congdon Building

(1870s), 1421–1425 Larimer St.

Libeus Barney, a shrewd and literate Vermont man, built this two-story frame front-gabled building. He kept a saloon downstairs and a hall upstairs that hosted early theater performances and the first meetings of Denver's vigilante city government. Barney, in his posthumously published *Letters of the Pike's Peak Gold Rush,* claimed that he found a small fortune in gold dust by sweeping up his tavern floor. For much of the twentieth century, the two-story 1870s structure that replaced Apollo Hall housed the Schaefer Tent & Awning Company. After its 1960s restoration, the building was renamed for Tom and Noel Congdon, early investors in the Larimer Square project. Since the 1970s, a food market and coffee bar have occupied the street floor. The basement houses a restaurant, and the second story, with its venerable round-arch windows, has been recycled as a nightclub.

16. Sussex Building

(1880), 1430 Larimer St.

This four-story brick structure trimmed in both smooth and rough-cut red-orange sandstone has a cast-iron storefront. It has housed various businesses over the years, with access enhanced by construction of rear courtyards and a rear arcade during the 1960s.

17. Crawford Building

(1875), 1439–1441 Larimer St.

This rare Denver specimen of the Second Empire style was renamed to honor Dana Crawford, who spearheaded Larimer Square's rehabilitation. "I used to go antiquing in the old pawnshops down on Larimer," she explained. "Then one day I noticed that these buildings themselves were fabulous antiques." Opulent detailing includes the ornate cast-iron engaged columns (made by the Union Foundry in Chicago), second-story lintels with scalloped and broken pediments, and a grandiose pressed metal frieze, bracketed cornice, and scalloped parapet.

18. Gallup-Stanbury Building

(1873), 1445–1451 Larimer St.

In the Tambien Saloon, opened on this site by Avery Gallup and Andrew Stanbury, western artist Charles Stewart Stobie raffled several of his landscapes

17. Crawford Building. (Photo by Tom Noel)

and Indian portraits to help pay his bar tab. The false-fronted saloon was replaced by this three-story brick Italianate building decorated with stone and cast-iron pilasters that blossom into metal flowers. The makeshift frame parapet is a duplicate of the original, a typical Gilded Age gimmick to fancify the facade.

19. Clayton Building/Granite Hotel

(1882), 1456–1460 Larimer St.

George Washington Clayton acquired city founder William Larimer's 1858 log cabin in 1859, put a frame false front on it, and opened a general store. In 1882 Clayton replaced his shop with this handsome five-story corner edifice, which he built with his brother, William M. Clayton, the mayor of Denver from 1868–1869. The Claytons are memorialized by the inscribed stone atop the angled entry of this cornerstone of Larimer

18. Gallup-Stanbury Building. (Photo by Tom Noel)

Square. The building was constructed with red-orange sandstone, lighter rhyolite blocks, and gray granite pillars. The Clayton Building was converted to the Granite Hotel and then to shops and offices, but it retains its original skylight, several stained glass windows, and cast-iron columns.

LOWER DOWNTOWN

HD-4 LOWER DOWNTOWN HISTORIC DISTRICT (see Map 3, page 8)

Cherry Creek to 20th St. between Market and Wynkoop Sts.

Before the city designated this historic district in 1988, demolitions were reducing Lower Downtown to little more than parking lots for the Central Business District. Market Street, its southeastern boundary, was Denver's red-light district from the 1870s to 1912. Today, many of the old taverns, bordellos, and warehouses have been rehabilitated. An outstanding example of sympathetic infill is the **Cactus Club** (1990, Peter H. Dominick, Jr.), 1621 Blake Street, which borrows inspiration from the two-story Oxford Hotel addition on Wazee Street.

The **Colorado Bakery & Saloon** (c. 1863, Frederick C. Eberley; 1890; 1989, restoration by Larry Nelson), 1440–1444 Market Street, is a particularly fine revival of what may be Denver's oldest vernacular storefront. Tall, arched second-story Italianate windows, cast-iron fronts, and a bracketed metal cornice typify the first generation of Denver's brick business buildings.

20. Wells Fargo Depot

(c. 1874), 1338 15th St., corner of Market St.

This pioneer stagecoach office is a reminder that Denver became the territory's transportation hub even before the arrival of the railroads. Well-armed guards rode shotgun on the stages leaving here with gold. This much-altered, one-story red brick building on a rusticated rhyolite foundation has unusual pointed-arch portals. Parts of the 1860s stagecoach depot may survive in a structure that received a second story addition (since removed) during the 1870s.

21. Hitchings Block

(1893), 1620 Market St.

Reverend Horace B. Hitchings, a wealthy New Yorker who became pastor (1862–1868) of Denver's St. John's in the Wilderness Episcopal Church, built this four-story brick investment property. The round arches of the fourth floor are topped by an inscribed pedimented parapet. In recent decades, restaurants and nightclubs have occupied the basement and ground floor, with offices upstairs. This is the southwesternmost of a row of six buildings restored in the 1980s as Market Center, a rejuvenated retail and office complex that provides a striking masonry foreground for downtown's newer glass and concrete towers.

21–26. Market Center. (Photo by Roger Whitacre)

22. Liebhardt-Lindner Building

(1881), 1624 Market St.

Gustavus C. Liebhardt built this headquarters for the Liebhardt Brothers Commission Company, which supplied Denver with fresh fruit, as well as flowers from the Liebhardts' thirty-six-acre Rose Acres Farms at 6320 West 26th Avenue. In 1937, the Lindner Packing & Provision Company, a meatpacking facility and wholesale meat market, moved into the Liebhardt Building. Lindner's later became Mapelli's Meats, then Sigman Meats, and ultimately part of Greeley's huge Monfort Meat Company. Handsomely remodeled inside for restaurant use, it retains some of the meat-packing apparatus as interior decor. On the imposing facade, a corbeled frieze is overshadowed by an intricate cornice.

23. McCrary Building

(1889), 1626–1632 Market St.

Napoleon Bonaparte McCrary built this home for his wholesale grocery firm. The third story, with its round-arch windows beneath roundels and a bracketed cornice, may be a later addition.

24. Waters Building

(1888), 1642 Market St.

This three-story red brick Italianate structure is symmetrically divided into three bays, with corresponding upper-story windows and divisions in the bracketed metal cornice with signature parapet.

13

25. Bockfinger-Flint Mercantile

(1885), 1644–1650 Market St.

Stripped of its cornice and less ornate than its sister buildings, this mercantile shop maintains the scale and continuity of a rare intact row of Victorian commercial buildings.

26. Columbia Hotel

(1880, Franklin Goodnow), 1320–1380 17th St., corner of Market St.

Remnants of an ambitious pressed metal cornice, elegant brick corbeling, and stone lintels have survived two fires and much neglect of this four-story red brick edifice. James A. Duff, a Scottish entrepreneur representing British investors organized as the Colorado Mortgage and Investment Company, financed what was originally a stylish Italianate office building. It was converted to a hotel around 1890. Cornices and corbeling separate the four floors, and brick piers further divide the facade into recessed storefronts and bays. After several decades as a flophouse with a first-floor tavern, it was revamped in the 1970s for offices.

27. Mattie Silks House

(1886), 2009 Market St.

Market Street between 19th and 21st Streets was Denver's red-light district from the 1870s until 1912, when reformers closed the district, with its "brides of the multitude." Market Street was so notorious that property owners above 23rd Street and on the Auraria side of Cherry Creek had their segments renamed Walnut Street. Mattie came to Denver in 1876 and reigned as the "Queen of Market Street." She died in 1929 at the age of eighty-three and is buried in Denver's Fairmount Cemetery under the name of Martha A. Ready. Her former brothel, a memorial to Colorado's most notorious madam, is a two-story Italianate house now converted to retail and office use. Mattie Silks, the most prominent and prosperous of Denver's madams, also ran the still-standing, if altered, houses at 1942 and 2015 Market Street. These, together with 2009, are survivors among a vanishing breed of building — the whorehouse.

28. Windsor Stables and Storefront

(1886, John W. Roberts?, 1978, renovation by William Saslow), 1732-1770 Blake St., corner of 18th St.

Here stood a service building and stables for the Windsor Hotel (demolished in 1960), two blocks away at 1800 Larimer Street. John W. Roberts, an architect who worked on New York City's Trinity Church, came to Denver in 1879 to build the Windsor Hotel, and he probably worked on this adjunct structure as well. William Saslow renovated this in 1978 to be one of the first residential/retail units in the then-slummy Union Station neighborhood. Saslow renamed it the Blake Street Bath & Racquet Club after converting the rear stables area to a tennis court and swimming pool for the residents of the units above the storefronts. This symmetrical red brick edifice with stone trim has ten two-story bays divide by piers.

29. Barth Hotel

(1882, Frederick C. Eberley. 1980s, restoration by Long Hoeft Architects), 1514 17th St., corner of Blake St.

Built as the Union Wholesale Liquor warehouse, this structure had become the Union Hotel by 1890. It was revamped and renamed the Elk Hotel in 1905, as a bronze plaque in the sidewalk reminds pedestrians. M. Allen Barth purchased the building in 1931 and renamed it the Barth Hotel. Fifty years later, Senior Housing Options acquired the Barth and restored it in one of the few efforts to retain cheap, subsidized housing for the elderly poor being displaced by gentrification. This four-story red brick edifice features Italianate arched and paired upper-level windows, stone banding and window trim, and a prominent bracketed metal cornice.

30. Barney Ford Restaurant

(1863. 1875. 1889, Frederick C. Eberley?, 1983, restoration by James C. Morgan, Paul Foster, Cab Childress), 1512–1514 Blake St., NR

Only parts of Barney Ford's People's Restaurant, a two-story brick building, survive within this much-altered structure, now three stories with square stone lintels and sills. Barney Ford, Colorado's best-known

31. Constitution Hall, 1920s. (Courtesy Denver Public Library)

African American pioneer, was a successful businessman and a leading spokesman for his people. The child of a slave and a white father, he escaped the South via the Underground Railroad and came to Colorado in 1860. Ford's original 1862 saloon and barbershop on this site was destroyed by the Great Fire of 1863. He replaced it with a new $9,000 structure boasting a basement barbershop, ground-floor restaurant, and upstairs saloon hall. Ford also built the four-story, Second-Empire-style Inter-Ocean Hotel at 16th and Blake Streets, now demolished. Preservation architect James C. Morgan, with assistance from Paul Foster and Cab Childress, restored the exterior and renovated the interior of 1512–1514 Blake in 1983.

31. Constitution Hall Site

(1865. 1870s addition), 1501–1507 Blake St., corner of 15th St.

The original two-story, red brick First National Bank had a street-level arcade matched by second-story arched stone lintels. The Odd Fellows built a mansard third-story addition in the Second Empire mode in the 1870s for use as their lodge hall. Delegates met there to draft a constitution for Colorado statehood in 1876. This landmark later became the Stores Restaurant Equipment Supply Company, which was burned down in 1977 by a disgruntled former employee.

Elephant Corral

(1859. 1902. 1980, renovation by Jay Nold Midyette), 1434–1444 Wazee St.

The Elephant Corral, Denver's pioneer transportation hub, originally occupied much of this block. It included the Denver House, an inn that was the first stop for many arriving argonauts, and corrals for livestock. Horses, mules, and cattle were stabled, bought, sold, and leased here — but not elephants. The name came from an expression popular among fortune seekers of the 1850s and 1860s, who headed west for the mines "to

15

look for the elephant." The term originated with an 1850 song for a San Francisco musical about frustrated gold seekers who found only disappointment. Numerous changes over the years left the current two-story, red brick complex with a full basement. The complex is wrapped around a U-shaped corral that was converted in 1980 to a courtyard for a deluxe office complex.

32. Cruise Room, Oxford Hotel. (Courtesy Amon Carter Museum)

32. Oxford Hotel

(1890–1891. 1902 addition by Frank E. Edbrooke. 1912 annex: Fallis & Willison. 1983, restoration by William Muchow & Associates), 1612 17th St., corner of Wazee St., NR

Denver's oldest operating hotel opened two years before Edbrooke's masterpiece, the Brown Palace Hotel, was completed at the other end of 17th Street. The original five-story red brick structure was built on a U-shaped plan, with a two-story addition (1902) on Wazee wearing the same facade detailing.

To celebrate the repeal of Prohibition in 1933, the Oxford had Denver architect Charles Jaka design a Streamline Moderne cocktail lounge, the Cruise Room (1935). Flowing lines shape the front bar, booths, and even the ceiling. The walls are paneled with beaverboard bas-relief portraits by Denver artist Alley Henson that feature prominent characters from various nations raising toasts in their own languages. The **Oxford Hotel Annex** (1912, Montana Fallis and Robert Willison),

1612–1616 17th Street, is the same height as the hotel, but the entire facade is elaborately detailed white terra-cotta, an echo of the Belle Époque.

33. Denver City Railway Company

(1883. 1892 remodel by Harold Baerresen and Viggio Baerresen. 1994, renovation by Urban Design Group), 1635 17th St., corner of Wynkoop St., NR

The four-story false front of red brick with rhyolite trim exemplifies the architectural ambitions of the Gilded Age. This three-story horsecar barn and corporate headquarters for an early streetcar firm poses as a grandiose stone and brick edifice. For much of the twentieth century, the building served as the home of Hendrie and Bolthoff, one of the world's largest manufacturers of mining machinery. In 1994, a $9 million project brought retail development to the ground floor, with forty-three loft apartments above. Star-shaped tie rods help relate the upper-story, high-tech expansion to the original edifice.

Union Station

(1881, William E. Taylor. 1895, Van Brunt and Howe. 1912, Aaron M. Gove and Thomas F. Walsh), 17th and Wynkoop Sts., NR

Although not a designated landmark, the centerpiece of Lower Downtown (LoDo) is the Beaux-Arts/Italianate apparition at the lower end of 17th Street. New York tycoon Jay Gould and local entrepreneur Walter Scott Cheesman put together a multiblock parcel to build a consolidated train station. William Taylor, a Kansas City architect, planned the original depot, which received a new central section from the Kansas City firm of Van Brunt and Howe in 1895 after a fire. They switched from the Second Empire style to the then fashionable Italianate mode. The 1881 wings remain Italianate, covered in the rusticated rhyolite with limestone trim that sheathed the original depot, which was the largest structure in town.

The 1912 Beaux-Arts Neoclassical expansion and redesign of the central hall was by Gove and Walsh, a Denver firm also responsible for many of the Wynkoop Street warehouses around Union Station. Gove and Walsh used a granite exterior wainscoting that gives way to a terra-cotta skin textured and colored to resemble the granite. Grand round-arched windows flood the main hall with natural light. Amtrak and the Winter Park Ski Train still offer passenger service at this station, whose basement is occupied by a huge model railroad layout.

Union Station anchors 17th Street, the "Wall Street of the Rockies," which since the 1880s has been lined with many of the city's tallest banks, hotels, and office buildings. The depot's great hall still evokes the golden age of railroading and the spiderweb of steel linking Denver to its vast Rocky Mountain hinterland.

34. The Wynkoop Building with its saviors, Joanne and Emanuel Salzman. (Photo by Roger Whitacre)

34. Spice and Commission Warehouse/The Edward W. Wynkoop Building

(1901, Aaron M. Gove and Thomas F. Walsh?), 1738 Wynkoop St.

Dr. Emanuel and Joanne Salzman restored the four-story red brick Spice and Commission Warehouse, renaming it for pioneer sheriff Edward W. Wynkoop,

who also gave his name to the street fronting Union Station. The Salzmans and architect Frank Zancanella remodeled interior spaces in 1980 for offices, the Salzman residence, and a roof garden. "At that time, LoDo was mostly vacancies and vagrants," reports Dr. Salzman, former chief of radiology at Denver General Hospital. "There weren't enough people around to support an honest mugger. Joanne and I were impressed with my brother's loft in SoHo back in New York and decided to try the same thing here in Denver."

J. S. Brown Mercantile/Wynkoop Brewing Company

(1899, Aaron M. Gove and Thomas F. Walsh. 1989, restoration by Joe Simmons), 1634 18th St., corner of Wynkoop St.

The John S. Brown Mercantile warehouse rises in recessed window bays to fifth-story round arches that echo the large street-level windows. Exterior walls of the former wholesale grocery warehouse are red pressed brick with sandstone trim and a quartzite foundation. The original interior was finished in Oregon pine and oak, with maple floors. In 1989 the building was remodeled for Denver's first brew pub, which features a second-floor pool hall. Pressed metal ceilings on the first and second floors help shield upper-level condominiums from the brew pub and pool hall hubbub below.

35. Hose Company No. 1

(c. 1883), 1963 Chestnut St., corner of 20th St.

Volunteer firefighters once tended horses and hose carts in one of Denver's oldest surviving fire stations. The red brick edifice with a corbeled cornice and twin, two-story arched bays is one of the few relics of the once teeming riverside neighborhood known as "the bottoms," where shacks and shanties presented a fire hazard.

36. Moffat Station

(1906, Edwin H. Moorman), 2101 15th St., corner of Bassett St., NR

This Neoclassical Revival brick box trimmed with lighter brick, concrete, limestone, and distinctive metal globe finials is a relic of David H. Moffat's railroad empire. With his Denver, Salt Lake & Pacific Railroad (better known as the Moffat Road), he hoped to give Denver a line west through the mountains to the Pacific coast. This dream earned Moffat the enmity of the Union Pacific and Santa Fe Railroad barons, who did not want competition to erode their lucrative Colorado business. They squeezed Moffat out of Union Station, forcing him to build his own depot. This passenger station was abandoned in 1947 when the Moffat Road was acquired by the Denver and Rio Grande Railroad.

CENTRAL BUSINESS DISTRICT

Today's Central Business District (see Map 2, page 2) began life in the 1870s as a residential area on the southeast edge of the original commercial district between Blake and Larimer Streets. The 1880s boom led to commercial construction that quickly transformed the area from Larimer to Broadway between 20th Street and Cherry Creek. Of the initial residential area, the only remaining single-family residences are the **Byers-Evans House,** 1310 Bannock St., and the **Curry-Chukovich-Gerash House,** 1439 Court Place.

Many demolitions, intensified by the Skyline Urban Renewal Project, erased twenty-six blocks of downtown Denver. These losses inspired the city to create the Denver Landmark Preservation Commission in 1967. The commission and city council have subsequently landmarked some of the surviving antique structures in the Central Business District.

37. Denver City Cable Railway Company

(1889. 1974, restoration by James Sudler Associates), 1215 18th St., corner of Lawrence St., NR

Denver's once extensive cable car network had its corporate offices, car barns, and power plant in this brickmason's tour-de-force. The two-story Romanesque edifice wears a variety of brick patterns, courses, corbeling, and trim. Pairs of round-arched windows occupy round, corbeled insets and echo the two-story recessed entry. Ornate brickwork also characterizes the cornice and the 110-foot smokestack, the top ten feet of which were removed after a lightning strike. Denver architect

James A. Sudler restored the building, which had been converted to an auto garage, adding a white stucco recessed entrance to the upstairs offices of his firm. The first-floor restaurant features a private dining room in an antique cable car.

38. The Twentieth Street Bathhouse, 1908. (Courtesy Denver Public Library)

38. Twentieth Street Bathhouse

(1908, Robert Willison), 1101 20th St., corner of Curtis St.

To scrub away some of Denver's pungent frontier heritage, Mayor Speer built the first municipal bathhouse, which also contains a gym, pool room, and recreation center. The brick building with sparse Neoclassical frosting is still open to the public for a variety of recreational programs. It commemorates the Progressive Era commitment to improving the lives of all citizens, including the unwashed poor.

39. The Daniels & Fisher Tower

(1911, Frederick J. Sterner and George H. Williamson. 1981, restoration by Gensler & Associates), 1601 Arapahoe St., corner of 16th Street Mall, NR

This 372-foot tower is loosely modeled on the campanile of St. Mark's in Venice. The *Denver Times* gloated that, thanks to the flagpole, it was six feet taller than its Italian prototype. The tower was once the beacon for Daniels & Fisher, the city's finest department store. Today it stands alone, having narrowly escaped the urban renewal demolition that erased the remainder of

37. The Denver City Cable Railway Building, 1971, on the eve of restoration. (Tom Noel Collection)

the complex. Mismatched brick indicates where the demolished wings were attached. Blond brick and creamy terra-cotta cover a steel skeleton set on a twenty-four-foot-deep concrete foundation. Protruding cornices set off an arcaded observation deck topped by Seth Thomas clocks with six-foot hands. A two-and-a-half-ton bell occupies the two uppermost stories. Restoration workers found an urn containing the ashes of the dreamer behind this Renaissance Revival apparition, William C. Daniels, the dilettante son of the company's co-founder. David Owen Tryba, an architect with offices in the tower, restored the top in 1995, adding air jets to keep the flag forever fluttering.

40. Central Bank Site

(1911, J.J.B. Benedict), 1100–1108 15th St., corner of Arapahoe St.

This nine-story neoclassically inspired edifice was the only large commercial building of Denver's best Beaux-Arts-trained architect. Benedict gave the brick and terra-cotta building a rounded corner with a round-arched entry fronted by four two-story Corinthian columns. The heroic entry arch was repeated by twelve-foot-high rounded street windows framed in fluted terra-cotta Corinthian engaged columns. Despite the building's landmark designation, Central Bank and its financial partners demolished it in 1989, ignoring wide-

39. The Daniels & Fisher Tower. (Photo by Tom Noel)

40. Central Bank, c. 1920. (Photo by Louis C. McClure, courtesy Denver Public Library)

41. The Denver Tramway Building was under construction in 1911, as was the Daniels & Fisher Tower in the background. (Courtesy Denver Public Library)

spread public protest, including that of Denver Mayor Federico Peña. Subsequently, the landmark ordinance was rewritten to increase the demolition moratorium from ninety days to one year for individually designated landmarks.

41. Denver Tramway Building

(1912, William E. Fisher and Arthur A. Fisher), 1100 14th St., corner of Arapahoe St., NR.

The family of territorial governor John Evans demolished his pioneer home to build the corporate offices of the streetcar monopoly headed by his son, William Gray Evans. Renaissance Revival–inspired trim in white terra-cotta climbs the eight-story red brick tower from the street-front arches to a rooftop frieze with the tramway's T logo. The brass entry lamps hint at

the interior opulence of a lobby with pink Tennessee marble floors, green Vermont marble trim where the walls join the floor, and wainscoting of white Arizona marble. Marble trim, handsome hardwoods, and bronze

42. Denver Municipal Auditorium, c. 1920. (Courtesy Denver Public Library)

fixtures survive throughout the tower. The tower, and the three-story attached streetcar barns, were converted in 1957 to the University of Colorado's Denver campus. After CU-Denver moved out, the interior was remodeled for the Denver Center for the Performing Arts, Auraria Higher Education Center classrooms, and proposed residential units.

42. Denver Municipal Auditorium

(1908, Robert Willison. 1941, G. Meredith Musick and Frederick E. Mountjoy. 1991, restoration by Semple-Brown-Roberts), 920 14th St. between Curtis and Champa Sts., NR

This Neoclassical municipal hall opened on July 4, 1908, to host the Democratic National Convention, the only convention to select a presidential candidate ever held in Denver. Second in size only to New York City's Madison Square Garden at the time, the auditorium was built of beige brick with terra-cotta trim, following the

Neoclassical design of the earlier auditorium in St. Paul, Minnesota. Some seven thousand lightbulbs outline its pediments, domes, dentiled cornice, and quoins. The 12,000-seat hall could at one time be converted to a 3,300-seat theater with a movable proscenium arch and walls lowered from the ceiling. Along with conventions and concerts, the auditorium has hosted everything from opera to auto shows. The auditorium expanded in 1941 to fill the entire block and received a facelift in the early 1990s, when part of it reopened as the Temple Hoyne Buell Theater. Buell, who reveled in architectural escapism, would probably have enjoyed the theater's neon accents and postmodern facade. The remodeling included repair and relighting of the exterior lightbulbs outlining the corner towers with their roundels and rooftop cupolas. A vaulted clear plastic roof now connects the auditorium to a multistory parking garage, making a galleria of what was the 1300 block of Curtis Street.

21

43. Denver Gas and Electric Company. (Courtesy Denver Public Library)

44. Odd Fellows' Hall, c. 1980. (Tom Noel Collection)

43. Denver Gas and Electric Company

(1910, Harry W.J. Edbrooke), 910 15th St., corner of Champa St., NR

With thirteen thousand outlets for lightbulbs in its terra-cotta skin, this is the brightest survivor of the "City of Lights" era, when Denver prided itself on the decorative illumination of its downtown. In this case the illumination also was an attempt to brighten the dark public image of a monopoly that rigged elections to maintain its exclusive franchise. Edbrooke, the son of Willoughby, began his architectural career in the Denver office of his uncle, Frank. A 1990 restoration of what had been remodeled and renamed the Insurance Exchange Building uncovered the original ceiling and relit the dazzling geometric light display. The arched tenth-story windows form an arcade beneath the flared cornice.

44. Odd Fellows' Hall

(1887, Emmett Anthony. 1983, renovation by C. W. Fentress and Associates), 1543–1545 Champa St.

Colorado Union Lodge No. 1 of the International Order of Odd Fellows erected one of downtown's finest stone facades, rendered here with Eastlake trim. It is crowned by a pressed metal roof with ball finials, a scrolled cornice, and a corner mansard tower. A $3.4 million 1983 restoration provided new stone columns and encased in protective Lexan the grand third-story meeting-hall stained glass window incorporating the lodge's motto — the three links of "Friendship, Love, and Truth." Behind a dutiful facade restoration, architects rearranged the interior around a new skylighted atrium with a glass elevator.

45. The Boston Building originally had protruding stone cornices, banding, balconies, and a rusticated base that were shaved off as the sandstone began to decay and bombard pedestrians. (c. 1900 photo by William Henry Jackson, Colorado Historical Society, and c. 1990 photo by Roger Whitacre)

45. Boston Building

(1890, Andrews, Jacques & Rantoul), 828 17th St., corner of Champa St., NR

The Boston firm that designed the Equitable Building also produced this Richardsonian Romanesque eight-story office building. Its red sandstone base supports round-arched bays on alternate floors. These arches are repeated in a narrower version on the top two stories in pairs divided by colonnettes. Weathering of the red sandstone, quarried near Manitou Springs, forced removal of the original cornice, carved stringcourses, and much other trim. The huge rusticated blocks of the base have been shaved smooth to limit spalling. A $16 million loft conversion planned for 1997 will create 130 residential units in this grande dame of 17th Street.

46. Ideal Building

(1907, Montana Fallis and John J. Stein. 1927, William E. Fisher and Arthur A. Fisher), 821 17th St., corner of Champa St., NR

For its headquarters, the Ideal Cement Company erected the region's first major reinforced concrete structure in 1907. The first two floors were faced with large blocks of dressed Colorado travertine in 1927, and upper floors, clad in brick, were stuccoed. A central two-story arch with an eagle keystone frames the entry to what was at one time the Denver National Bank. In conjunction with the 1927 rear addition, the bank redecorated the two-story lobby, whose ceiling is supported by steel columns simulating marble. An Arnold Ronnebeck frieze around the mezzanine illustrates the theme of money in history. Colorado Federal Bank remodeled the building as its home in the 1970s. The bank's huge basement safe has been converted to a private

46. The Ideal Building. (Photo by Roger Whitacre)

47. U.S. Post Office and Federal Building. (Photo by Tom Noel)

dining room within a subterranean restaurant beneath what is now the Women's Bank.

47. U.S. Post Office and Federal Building

(1910–1916, James Knox Taylor. 1922, Tracy, Swarthwout & Litchfield; and Maurice Biscoe. 1963, renovation and restoration by Victor Hornbein and Edward D. White, Jr. 1994, restoration by Michael Barber Associates), 1823 Stout St. between 18th and 19th Sts., NR

In the Neoclassical style favored by the federal government as befitting a vigorous young republic, this five-story Greek temple faced in Colorado Yule marble fills an entire block. On the Stout Street facade of the building, sixteen three-story, fluted Ionic columns form a heroic portico atop a cascading marble staircase. The names of postmasters general and of Pony Express riders are carved into the marble end walls of the vaulted lobby. Gladys Caldwell Fisher, wife of Denver architect Alan Fisher, sculpted the granite bighorn sheep that flank the 18th Street entrance. The Postal Service surrendered this masterpiece to the federal judiciary, which lavished $27 million on a 1994 restoration by Michael Barber for what is now the Byron White Federal Courthouse. Byron "Whizzer" White, a football star for the University of Colorado and a Rhodes Scholar, was appointed to the U.S. Supreme Court in 1962 by President John F. Kennedy. White, a native of Fort Collins, served on the highest court until his retirement in 1993.

48. U.S. National Bank/Guaranty Bank

(1921, William E. Fisher and Arthur A. Fisher), 815 17th St., corner of Stout St., NR

Denver entrepreneur John A. Ferguson replaced his three-story Century Building with this Chicago-style commercial structure. Its Neoclassical elements include paired Ionic pilasters, and quoins cut into the smooth limestone skin. The U.S. National Bank initially occupied the ground floor, with the upper eight stories leased for offices. The U.S. National Bank merged with Denver National to become United (now Norwest)

48. U.S. National Bank/Guaranty Bank. (Courtesy Denver Public Library)

Banks and moved to 17th and Broadway. The old building became the home of the Guaranty Bank & Trust Company. Landmark designation helped rescue this stately, if understated, edifice from the wrecking ball. This onetime haven for bankers and other fat cats was revamped in 1996 as 118 low- and moderate-income lofts.

49. First National Bank of Denver/Holtze Executive Place Hotel

(1911, Harry W.J. Edbrooke. 1962, remodel by James Sudler Associates. 1995, remodel and restoration by Guy Thornton), 818 17th St., corner of Stout St., NR

The First National Bank moved from the Equitable Building in 1911 to this thirteen-story brick high-rise. Frank Edbrooke's nephew and employee, Harry W.J. Edbrooke, was the lead architect. Notwithstanding the Chicago-style steel frame construction, the bank reflected the classical division of a building into a base,

shaft, and capital (the structure of a classical column). The two-story base is clad in concrete, textured and colored to resemble granite, around enormous display windows. The base is separated by a prominent double cornice from the shaft — floors three through nine — which is clad in light brick. The capital, formed by the top four floors, has extensive terra-cotta trim topped by a bracketed metal cornice. As the tallest and largest bank in Colorado, the First National helped confirm 17th Street's status as the "Wall Street of the Rockies."

When the First National had Raymond Harry Erwin design a new twenty-eight-story home at 621 17th Street in 1958, they sold this building to the American National Bank. That bank had architect Jim Sudler add a then-stylish precast concrete sunscreen, which hid the old building. In 1995, this was stripped off and the original Edbrooke exterior restored, as was the original interior light well, returning natural light to what is now a drive-through entry court. Brothers Eric and Steve Holtze completed the $21 million remodel, assisted by the Denver Urban Renewal Authority and the State Historical Fund, converting the bank to a 250-room luxury hotel.

The adjacent five-story parking garage is still clad in the 1962 sunscreen. As a final delight for this splendid reincarnation, the Holtzes reinstalled a large street-corner clock, the traditional symbol with which bankers advertised interest payments and reminded passersby by that "time is money."

50. Equitable Building

(1892, Andrews, Jacques & Rantoul), 730 17th St., corner of Stout St., NR

The Equitable Life Assurance Society of New York erected Denver's premier office building, using the design of a prominent Boston firm that also planned the neighboring Boston Building. This nine-story edifice does not have a steel frame skeleton: the huge Pikes Peak granite blocks of the first two stories support the gray brick walls of the upper seven stories. This Italian Renaissance Revival edifice is enlivened with stone carvings, such as the cherubs adorning the stone balcony of the fifth floor. The back-to-back, double-E plan not only displays the Equitable's logo but also allows light and air into the interior offices.

50. Equitable Building. (Courtesy Denver Public Library)

In the sanctuary-like interior, the marble wainscoting is complemented by the mosaics with Byzantine motifs on the vaulted ceilings. Marble from France, Italy, Vermont, and Tennessee enhances the interior, with a particularly notable, almost translucent Sienna marble reception desk and stairway walls. This marble lobby is illuminated by a tripartite, transomed Tiffany window. This well-maintained landmark has been overshadowed, but not outclassed, by the many bland new skyscrapers of the 17th Street financial district.

51. Neusteter Building

(1924, William E. Fisher and Arthur A. Fisher. 1988, restoration and remodeling by Gensler & Associates), 720–730 16th St., corner of Stout St., NR

Max and Meyer Neusteter incorporated the three-story Hughes Block (c. 1890), where they opened their women's clothing store in 1911, into this sleek 1924 expansion. This stone-sheathed, five-story brick building is given a horizontal emphasis by the wide, bracketed eaves, clearly defined banding, and wide Chicago-

style windows. In 1941, Neusteter's expanded into the neighboring Coronado Building at 1540–1544 Stout Street. In time, this popular and fashionable store acquired the rest of the Stout Street block to build a multistory parking garage at 15th and Stout. The Neusteter family closed their store in 1985. After an exterior restoration by Gensler & Associates and interior remodeling by John Carney & Associates, the building reopened in 1988 with residences on the upper four levels above streetfront retail shops.

52. Denver Dry Goods

(1889, Frank E. Edbrooke. 1898 and 1907, additions by Frank E. Edbrooke. 1994, restoration by The Urban Design Group), 700 16th St., corner of California St., NR

Edbrooke, as the architectural historian Richard Brettell pointed out, was almost single-handedly responsible for downtown Denver's architectural maturity in the late 1800s. Edbrooke's original three-story red brick store at 16th and California for the McNamara Dry Goods Company had limestone trim and nearly solid plate glass storefronts. Edbrooke's 1898 rear addition has a fourth story with round-arched windows, a wide festooned frieze, and bracketed cornice suggestive of the Renaissance Revival mode. In 1907, Edbrooke's second addition extended the building the entire block along California to 15th Street. The 15th Street addition has six stories and wider windows but similar broad-bracketed eaves and classical details. In 1924 one story was added to the original 16th Street structure with a balustraded roof terrace for Denver's famous Tea Room.

The Denver Dry Goods Building is legendary for its commercial and sentimental importance. The firm originated in 1886 with Michael J. McNamara's Dry Goods Company in the Clayton Building at 15th and Larimer Streets. McNamara moved to 700 16th Street at California Street shortly before the Crash of 1893, when the Colorado National Bank foreclosed on and reorganized his business as the Denver Dry Goods Company. Between the 1950s and the 1980s, this thriving store opened eleven branches in shopping centers from Fort Collins to Pueblo. The Denver's longtime rival, May D & F (now Foley's), bought the store in 1987 and closed it. After being restored outside and

52. The Denver Dry Goods building expanded upward and outward from this original core store at 16th and California Streets. (Courtesy Colorado Historical Society)

remodeled inside with the help of the Denver Urban Renewal Authority, the building reopened in 1994 with various new businesses in the grand old department store.

53. Hayden, Dickinson, and Feldhauser Building/Colorado Building

(1891, John W. Roberts. 1909, addition by Frank E. Edbrooke. 1935, renovation by J.J.B. Benedict), 1615 California St., corner of 16th St. Mall

A 1935 Art Deco facelift transformed this red brick Chicago-style commercial building into glistening white terra-cotta with an ornate parapet of alternating pinnacles and pediments. The terra-cotta overlay sparkles with molded geometric and naturalistic designs including mountains and pine trees. Between the 1935 piers, the original spandrels and cast-iron storefronts with acanthus-leaf capitals are still visible. The remodeled Hayden, Dickinson, and Feldhauser building was given a new name, the Colorado Building. The five-story original structure had earlier received an additional two stories designed by Frank E. Edbrooke.

54. Masonic Temple. (Photo by Tom Noel)

54. Masonic Temple

(1890, Frank E. Edbrooke. 1950, W. Gordon Jamieson. 1985, renovation by C. W. Fentress and Associates), 1614 Welton St., corner of 16th St. Mall, NR

Edbrooke, a Thirty-third Degree Mason, clad this temple with a base of Pikes Peak granite and upper levels

55. Paramount Theater. (Photo by Roger Whitacre)

of Manitou red-orange sandstone. Corner bays are connected by a central fifth-floor arcade echoing the ground-floor entry arches. The Welton Street entry is through a fifteen-foot-wide Romanesque arch with engaged columns supporting an extraordinary carved panel. After a 1984 arson fire, a new steel frame was constructed within the buckled walls and new sandstone from the original Lyons quarry was sculpted to resemble

and replace the granite removed in 1950 from the first two floors. With the addition of a hipped roof glass penthouse and interior rearrangements, the temple has been enlarged from five to nine stories. In front of the recessed entry, restoration architects added a sandstone arch that underscores the round-arch openings of this otherwise chunky, vernacular version of Romanesque Revival.

56. The Denver Athletic Club. (Photo by William Henry Jackson, courtesy Colorado Historical Society)

55. Paramount Theater

(1930, Temple Hoyne Buell), 1621 Glenarm Pl., corner of 16th St. Mall, NR

As a member of the firm headed by C. W. Rapp and George Rapp that designed many movie houses across the United States, Buell created this 2,100-seat Art Deco theater. The building is made of precast concrete block sheathed in glazed terra-cotta manufactured by the Denver Terra Cotta Company. The three-story Glenarm facade is divided into twelve bays of paired windows with recurrent rosettes, feathers, and fiddlehead ferns, which also adorn the elaborate Art Deco interior with its twin twenty-rank Wurlitzer pipe organs. Pilasters are capped by fan-shaped frosted glass figures. The sunburst ceiling and the chandelier create a starry effect. The grand, two-story theater entry lobby in the **Kittredge Building** (1891, A. Morris Stuckert) to the west has been lost, and patrons now enter

through the original exit doors on Glenarm Place. Of seventeen theaters once found downtown, the Paramount is the only old-timer extant.

56. Denver Athletic Club

(1889, Ernest P. Varian and Frederick J. Sterner. 1973, addition by Rodney S. Davis. 1984, addition by James Sudler Associates), 1325 Glenarm Pl. between 13th and 14th Sts., NR

The original six-story clubhouse has a pink sandstone and red brick facade atop a sandstone basement and first floor. Recessed spandrels between the third and fourth floors add horizontal emphasis to the paired brick round window arches. The 13th Street athletic facilities addition (1973) and the 14th Street addition (1984) offer modern minimalist reinterpretations of the red brick and architectural lines of the original. Inside, the bar and billiard room, once men's havens but now open to all, are especially venerable spaces.

57. Denver Press Club

(1925, Merrill H. Hoyt and Burnham Hoyt), 1330 Glenarm Pl.

This red brick clubhouse trimmed in white terra-cotta quoins and window surrounds that hint at the Collegiate Gothic mode is more notable for its history than its architecture. The first-floor bar and dining room, basement pool hall, and second-story meeting hall are haunted by the ghosts of prominent journalists such as William Barrett, Paul Conrad, Thomas Hornsby Ferril, Jack Foster, Gene Fowler, Pat Oliphant, Damon Runyan, Lee Casey Taylor, and — after women were admitted in 1970 — Sandra Dallas and Marjorie Barrett.

Although founded in 1884, the Press Club lacked its own home until the completion of this cozy clubhouse, discreetly described by the late cowboy columnist of *The Denver Post,* Red Fenwick: "Back in a lustier but unlamented era of journalism, the Press Club was a friendly island of threadbare public rectitude."

58. Fire Station No. 1. (Photo by Roger Whitacre)

58. Fire Station No. 1

(1909, Glen W. Huntington & Company), 1326 Tremont Pl., NR

Behind the ornate gray brick and light sandstone facade topped by an elaborate dentiled cornice, the original firehouse interior is starkly functional, almost modern. This Neoclassical station with recessed second-story balcony became the Denver Firefighters' Museum in 1980. Visitors can inspect vintage fire trucks and other equipment, as well as the dormitories and fire pole.

59. Denver Public Schools Administration Building/Denver Art Museum Administration Building

(1923, William N. Bowman), 414 14th St., corner of Tremont Pl.

Bowman, who designed many of Denver's public schools, also created this DPS Administration Building. This three-story brick structure is enlivened by terra-cotta trim, including the exclamation marks on the second-story level of the brick piers. In 1937 and 1950, additions were made to this building, which was converted in 1994 to the administrative offices of the nearby Denver Art Museum.

60. Curry-Chucovich-Gerash House

(1888, Fred A. Hale. 1982, restoration by Edward D. White, Jr.), 1439 Court Pl., NR

The solitary remnant of a vanished residential neighborhood, this two-and-a-half-story, side-hall Victorian townhouse now stands alone amid asphalt parking lots on one of the city's original 25-by-125-foot lots. Hale, who started his Denver career with Frank Edbrooke, used rosy sandstone blocks with carved stone trim for the facade of this red brick dwelling. The original wooden cornice with a recessed paneled frieze is capped by a rooftop balustrade above the slate roof. James H. Curry provided rhyolite from his Castle Rock quarry for the foundation, coping, and front steps of his home. Denver's *Western Architect and Building News* hailed the dwelling as "a genuine two-story brownstone" with a "chaste and happy" interior "of fresco and Lincrusta-Walton relief work" with a staircase arch "of intricate arabesque fretwork in oak." Vaso Chukovich, a Yugoslavian immigrant, later bought the house and lived here. Chukovich, who owned and operated various saloons and gambling houses, became Denver's underworld czar. He died in 1933, a real estate magnate and millionaire who left $100,000 to build the children's wing of Denver General Hospital as a memorial to Mayor Robert W. Speer, whose powerful political machine had protected Chukovich's unsavory businesses. In 1982 Denver defense attorney Walter Gerash restored the house inside and out for his law firm's offices. "We even redid the interior stenciling and added the Ten Commandments," Gerash reports, "but in Hebrew so none of my clients would be embarrassed."

61. Brown Palace Hotel

(1892, Frank E. Edbrooke), 321 17th St., between Tremont Pl. and Broadway, NR

The finest work of Colorado's foremost nineteenth-century architect remains Denver's grand hotel. Henry C. Brown, who homesteaded Capitol Hill, commissioned this $2 million palace of red sandstone on a base of Pikes Peak granite. Responding to the triangular site, Edbrooke gave the nine-story hotel three gracefully curved corners. The steel-and-iron frame, clad in terra-cotta and concrete as well as stone, made this one of the United States's first fireproof structures, according to a May 21, 1892, cover story in *Scientific American*.

Repetition of arcaded window patterns; cornices above the first, second, seventh, and ninth stories; and banding around corner curves add horizontal emphasis to what was then the tallest building in town. Stone creatures once swarmed over the exterior, but nearly all were removed after deteriorating pieces began bombarding the sidewalk. Twenty-six carved stone medallions of native Colorado animals by James Whitehouse survive on the top-floor fenestration arcade. The now closed Broadway ogee-arched entrance retains some original stone trim, including a bas-relief bust of Brown.

Interior rooms open to the enormous skylighted atrium. In the lobby, caramel and cream swirls flow through twelve thousand square feet of onyx paneling from Mexico. The especially well-preserved Onyx Room has a ceiling mural of cherubs hovering in a heavenly blue sky. Two later murals by Allen Tupper True depicting the stagecoach and airplane ages adorn the Tremont Place entrance lobby. The Ship Tavern, a celebration of the repeal of Prohibition, was designed by architect Alan B. Fisher, son of William E. Fisher. The tavern sports nautical artifacts, ranging from a crow's nest wrapped around the room's central beam to a collection of ships in bottles. In addition to this splendid saloon and its libations, the hotel is famous for its artesian water well and its high teas. Recent restorations have undone areas of 1950s modernization, returning Denver's grand hotel to its Victorian splendor.

62. The Navarre (Courtesy Denver Public Library)

62. Brinker Collegiate Institute/The Navarre/ Museum of Western Art

(1880, Frank E. Edbrooke. 1983, restoration by C. W. Fentress and Associates, and John M. Prosser), 1725–1727 Tremont Pl., NR

The Brinker Collegiate Institute was erected as a girls' school for $20,000. In 1901–1902, the structure became the Navarre — a cafe, gambling hall, brothel, and Denver's most notorious department store of vice. Subsequently rehabilitated as a legitimate restaurant and jazz club, it was reincarnated yet again in 1983 as the Museum of Western Art. Restoration for the museum removed a century of additions and revisions and resurrected the double-bracketed cornice and distinctive copper-colored cupola. With three stories plus basement, this Italianate structure of red brick is enhanced by full-height bays with pedimented gables. The building is connected by a basement tunnel under Tremont Place to the Brown Palace Hotel, but the passage is a utility tunnel too tiny to have allowed any patronage of the Navarre's *nymphes du pavé.*

63. Trinity United Methodist Church

(1888, Robert S. Roeschlaub. 1982, restoration and expansion by Seracuse, Lawler & Partners), 1820 Broadway, NE corner of E. 18th Ave., NR

The finest building of Colorado's first licensed architect is made of rhyolite from Castle Rock quarries. The light weight of this purplish gray stone allowed Roeschlaub to design a 181-foot-high hexagonal corner

63. Trinity United Methodist Church. (Photo by Tom Noel)

steeple in stone without a single brace. The rough-faced rhyolite is trimmed in purple sandstone, including three horizontal contrasting stripes in the steeple. This allusion to the Trinity is repeated in the triple-arched entry on Broadway and in Gothic windows arranged in sets of three. Except for these Gothic arches, the church might be called Richardsonian Romanesque.

Inside, Roeschlaub created a 1,200-seat sanctuary resembling a theater; a large proscenium arch frames a four-thousand-pipe Roosevelt organ made by Theodore Roosevelt's cousin, Hilbourne Roosevelt. Electric lights on the arch, box seats, and balcony add to the sense of drama. Of many fine stained glass windows, the Resurrection window on the west wall is the grandest.

The solid bronze and oak pulpit commemorates the church's most famous pastor, the Reverend Henry Buchtel, who also served as chancellor of the University of Denver and governor of Colorado.

In 1982 Trinity sold its air rights to a Toronto developer for a $2.7 million endowment and restoration of the church, plus construction of a subterranean office, education, and parking complex beneath a park on the north side of this exquisite edifice. A 1926 addition was lost in the process, and the air rights fortunately remain unused.

CIVIC CENTER

HD-5 CIVIC CENTER HISTORIC DISTRICT, NR (see Map 2, page 2)

Grant to Delaware Sts. between (roughly) Colfax and 13th Aves.

Mayor Robert W. Speer enlisted Charles M. Robinson, a New York planner and author of *Modern Civic Art, or The City Made Beautiful* (1903), to do the initial 1906 plan for a government office park. Robinson used the State Capitol (whose grounds were designed earlier by Colorado's pioneer landscape architect Reinhard Schuetze) as the eastern anchor of a civic mall for city, state, and federal buildings wrapped around a central park. Sculptor Frederick MacMonnies refined the Civic Center plan to include his **Pioneer Fountain** (1911) at the northwest corner of West Colfax Avenue and Broadway. He introduced the semicircles formed by curving Colfax and 14th Avenues between Broadway and Bannock and placed the City and County Building on Bannock opposite the Capitol, anchoring the western end of the civic mall. Frederick Law Olmsted, Jr., also contributed a plan (1912), as did Chicago city planner Edward H. Bennett (1917) and Denver landscape architect Saco R. DeBoer.

Civic Center's north-south axis terminates in two classical structures inspired by the 1893 World's Columbian Exposition. At the north end, the **Voorhies Memorial** (1920, William E. Fisher and Arthur A. Fisher), 100 West Colfax Avenue, is a copy of the exposition's Water Gateway. An arcade of Turkey Creek sandstone curves around a pool with twin fountains of cherubs riding sea lions designed by Denver sculptor

HD-5 Civic Center. (Courtesy Colorado Historical Society)

Robert Garrison. In the lunettes of the arcade are murals by Allen True depicting bison and elk in the style and colors of antique Greek vases. The memorial was funded by banker and mining entrepreneur John H.P. Voorhies, who lived across the street.

The **Greek Theater** and **Colonnade of Civic Benefactors** (1919, Willis A. Marean and Albert J. Norton), West 14th Avenue and Acoma Street, echoes and balances the Voorhies Memorial at the opposite end of the north-south axis. Edward Bennett, the protégé and successor of Daniel Burnham, proposed this arrangement despite local critics who complained, "Why the hell does Denver need a Greek theater? We ain't got that many Greeks here!" The theater's arc responds to the curving wings of the Voorhies Memorial and is constructed of the same Turkey Creek sand-

stone. Two Allen True murals, *Trapper* and *Prospector,* depict pioneer types in wilderness settings. The theater's north side is terraced down into an open semicircular arena seating 1,200.

Plans for a sunken sculpture garden at the center of Civic Center Park solidified around two bronze statues by Denverite Alexander Phimister Proctor, *Bronco Buster* (1920) and *On the War Trail* (1922). On the east side of the capitol is *Closing Era,* a bronze Indian and buffalo crafted for the 1893 World's Columbian Exposition by Preston Powers, who once taught in Denver. Civic Center Park was restored and enhanced in 1991 by Long Hoeft Architects. Civic Center is the heart of Denver's park system and one of this country's better-preserved examples of the standard Progressive Era prescription for improving crowded, ugly urban cores.

Colorado State Capitol

(1886–1908, Elijah E. Myers, then Frank E. Edbrooke), E. Colfax to E. 14th Aves. between Lincoln and Grant Sts.

At the eastern edge of Civic Center, this cruciform four-story building culminates in a gold dome. The brick building is faced with Colorado gray granite from the Aberdeen Quarry in Gunnison County. Similar symmetrical bays characterize all four sides, with a west entrance portico overlooking Civic Center. Triple-arched central entrances on each side are topped by triangular pediments with bas-relief sculptures. Lighter, cheaper, cast iron that matches the granite color is used for the three cylindrical stages of the dome. Colorado mining magnates donated the twenty-four-carat gold leaf for the 272-foot-high dome.

Elijah Myers also designed state capitols for Idaho, Michigan, Texas, and Utah. As in his other statehouses, Myers gave Colorado a Neoclassical design of Renaissance origins. The Capitol Board of Managers dismissed Myers in 1889 to save money. Frank E. Edbrooke, who had placed second in the original architectural competition, completed the structure, basically following Myers's 1886 design. Edbrooke substituted gold for copper on the dome and dropped the allegorical female figure with which Myers had crowned it. Apparently, the legislature, after considerable study of models in various states of dress, could not agree on which was the most shapely.

The interior features Beulah red marble and Colorado Yule marble wainscoting and brass fixtures. Of 160 rooms, the most noteworthy are the old supreme court chambers, the Senate and House chambers, and the first-floor rotunda, whose walls display murals (1938) by Colorado's premier muralist, Allen Tupper True, with captions from Colorado poet laureate Thomas Hornsby Ferril.

Colorado State Museum

(1913, Frank E. Edbrooke), SE corner of 14th Avenue and Sherman St.

For the stately museum on the south side of the Capitol, Edbrooke used Colorado Yule marble on a Gunnison granite base in a Neoclassical style similar to that of the Capitol. As this building shows, Edbrooke made the leap from nineteenth-century Romantic styles to early twentieth-century Neoclassicism. Richard Brettell, in his book *Historic Denver: The Architects and the Architecture, 1858–1893* (1973), eulogizes Edbrooke's final edifice:

> Its plan is symmetrical, clear, and ample. The classical allusions are no longer piece-meal, nor are they tempered by elements of other styles from other architectural pasts. Rather, the classicism is apparently complete and almost archaeological in its effect on the viewer. The building is architecturally pure and its imagery exudes a hardened pomp and grandeur. Its memorial, almost funereal, appearance is appropriate both because it is a museum — a historical society — and because it was Edbrooke's self-consciously last building.

During the 1980s, Pahl, Pahl & Pahl renovated and restored the museum for legislative offices.

State Office Building

(1921, William N. Bowman. 1985 restoration by The Urban Design Group), 201 E. Colfax Ave, NE corner of Sherman St.

Of a half dozen twentieth-century state office buildings clustered around the Capitol within the historic district, this is one of the finest. This Renaissance-Revival-style palace guarded by bronze lions sculpted by Robert Garrison has an exterior of Cotopaxi granite. The exquisite interior features a black-and-white marble checkerboard-floored central court, pink marble walls, and bronze fixtures under a stained glass skylight. After a narrow escape from the wrecking ball, a $4 million restoration preserved this five-story classic as offices for the Colorado Department of Education.

Denver Public Library

(1955, Burnham Hoyt; William E. Fisher and Arthur A. Fisher. 1995, addition by Michael Graves and Klipp Colussy Jenks DuBois), 10 W. 14th Ave. Pkwy., SW corner of Broadway

On the north side of this full-block complex, the 1955 four-story Burnham Hoyt library subtly plays on classical composition, using two-story window bands to represent a glazed colonnade and third-story fenestration arranged like a frieze. A semicircular two-story bay overlooks Civic Center.

Such refinements deferring to the Neoclassicism of Civic Center were lost on Michael Graves, the famed Princeton, New Jersey, postmodernist who, with the

Denver firm of Brian Klipp, produced a seven-story addition to the south of the original building. This addition tripled the size of the library, creating a depository for more than a million books, two million government documents, and a cornucopia of special collections. The massive size of the addition is visually broken up by a variety of rectangles, cylinders, and towers. Copper sheaths the domed entry pavilion of the children's library and serves as accent trim elsewhere on the exterior.

Rejecting the Neoclassicism of the Civic Center Historic District, Graves used clearly articulated masses that express their functions. His drumlike rotunda houses the first-floor reference room, third-floor periodicals room, and fifth-floor Gates Reading Room of the Western History Department. This distinctive drum, Graves's signature shape, is centered in the setback, rectangular massing of the south elevation. Here Graves comes closest to Neoclassical harmony, with a parade of columns along the 13th Avenue facade. German limestone from the fossil-rich Solnhofen quarries covers the south facade in a creamy color matching the Indiana limestone skin of Hoyt's 1955 library on the north side. Other elevations are clad in reddish and greenish cast stone emphasizing the geometrical shapes of a structure that local supervising architect Brian Klipp calls "classically contemporary."

Graves excels as an interior designer. He used warm, golden maple for interior paneling, shelves, and furnishings, as well as for his custom chairs, desks, and lamps in this eye-catching edifice that city librarian Rick J. Ashton calls "library heaven."

City and County Building

(1932, Allied Architects), W. Colfax Ave. to W. 14th Ave. between Bannock and Cherokee Sts.

Balancing the State Capitol and completing a dominant east-west axis for Civic Center, this monument to Mayor Speer's City Beautiful was part of the 1906 Robinson Plan but materialized slowly on its full-block site.

The design was refined and implemented by a coalition of thirty-nine leading locals organized as the Allied Architects, under the leadership of Roland L. Linder and Robert K. Fuller. The Neoclassical facade has three-story travertine Corinthian columns atop a grand

entry staircase. Unusual curving wings that resemble outstretched arms reach toward the Capitol, or, some say, toward taxpaying citizens.

Although Colorado granite forms the base and Colorado travertine is used for the columns and interior, the upper walls are Stone Mountain, Georgia, granite, with *fleur de pêche* marble inserts. The gold eagle and carillon clock tower capping this handsome city hall were donated in Mayor Speer's memory by his widow, Kate. The slender bell tower and the building's relatively low profile preserve mountain vistas from Capitol Hill.

Tremendous bronze doors in the entry portico open to an interior featuring eleven varieties of marble. Colorado travertine panels the main corridors and forms eight nineteen-foot-tall columns on the second floor. A $10 million 1991–1992 refurbishing brightened the interior and restored some features, including the grand lobby, Allen True's mural *The Miners' Court,* and Gladys Caldwell Fisher's life-size bas-relief *Montezuma and the Animals.* The most impressive interior spaces are the fourth-floor city council chambers and the main entry hall with 1993 collages by Denver artist Susan Cooper depicting Denver's architectural heritage.

Carnegie Main Library

(1910, Albert Randolph Ross), 144 W. Colfax Ave.

Denver's first freestanding library is a Neoclassical extension of the north wing of the City and County Building. It was to be paired with an art museum extension of the south wing, but the art museum eventually was built on the other side of West 14th Avenue. This Greek temple in gray Turkey Creek sandstone on a base of Pikes Peak granite is fronted by fourteen Corinthian columns. Converting the old library to City Hall Annex 3 led to unfortunate "improvements."

64. U.S. Mint

(1906, James Knox Taylor, with Gordon, Tracy, and Swarthwout. 1987, additions by Rogers-Nagel-Langhart), 320 W. Colfax Ave. between Cherokee, Delaware, and W. 14th Ave., NR

The fact that one of this country's three federal mints is located in Denver reflects the city's gold rush origins. This federal mint evolved from the private mint of Clark, Gruber & Company. The present-day two-

65. Byers–Evans House. (Photo by Roger Whitacre)

64. U.S. Mint. (Courtesy Colorado Historical Society)

story gray fortress was supposedly inspired architecturally by the Palazzo Medici-Riccardi in Florence. The north entry porch, stairs, and base for the perimeter fence are made of pinkish, black-flecked Pikes Peak granite that contrasts with the Cotopaxi gray granite ashlar above. Marble lunettes crown high, rectangular windows on the first level, with smaller, paired second-

floor windows divided by marble columns and topped by arched marble panels, each inlaid with a single disk. The granite cornice is bracketed above a decorated frieze. Wrought iron is used for the entry lanterns, window grilles, and perimeter fencing. Murals by Vincent Aderente in the main hall portray mining, manufacturing, and commerce. Although James Knox Taylor was the supervising architect in Washington, D.C., the New York City firm of Gordon, Tracy, and Swarthwout designed the mint. Additions have aspired with debatable success to enhance what remains the city's most popular free attraction — although three subterranean floors where gold bars are stored are not open to the public.

65. Byers–Evans House

(1883. 1895–1905, addition. 1989, restoration by Long Hoeft Architects), 1310 Bannock St., NE corner of W. 13th Ave., NR

This two-story Italianate house, a rare remnant of the prosperous residential district that once flourished here, shares the block with the Denver Art Museum.

The dwelling was built by William Newton Byers, founding editor of the *Rocky Mountain News*. In 1889 it became the family home of William Gray Evans, son of Colorado territorial governor John Evans. Different fenestration betrays the 1895–1905 two-story south addition of an entry hall, library, two bathrooms, two bedrooms, a sitting room, and maid's quarters. Restored in 1989 as a house museum containing Evans family furnishings, its exhibits focus on Denver in general, as well as the history of the Byers and Evans clans. In the former servants' parlor and garage, interactive videos portray the development of Denver.

CHAPTER 2
Capitol Hill Area

CAPITOL HILL
QUALITY HILL
HUMBOLDT STREET
MORGAN ADDITION/CHEESMAN PARK
WYMAN ADDITION
CITY PARK
SNELL ADDITION
EAST SEVENTH AVENUE
COUNTRY CLUB

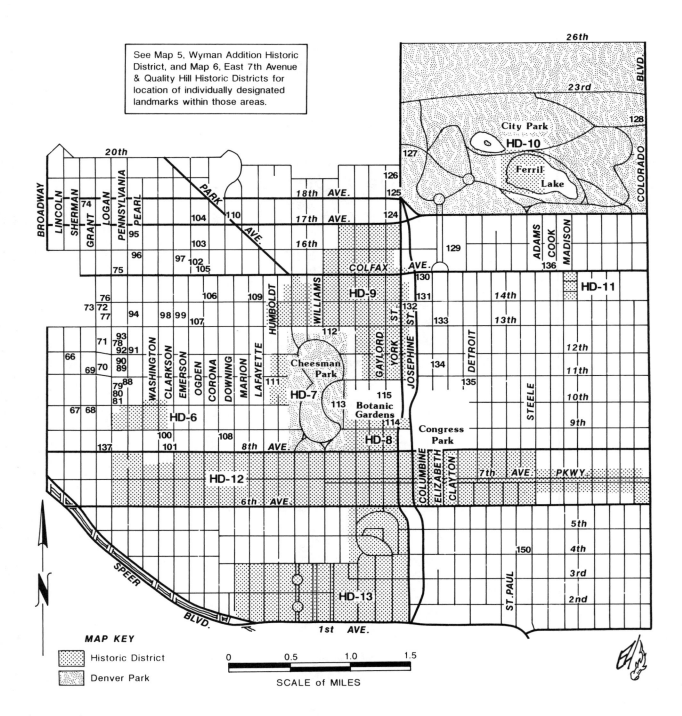

See Map 5, Wyman Addition Historic District, and Map 6, East 7th Avenue & Quality Hill Historic Districts for location of individually designated landmarks within those areas.

MAP KEY

Historic District

Denver Park

SCALE of MILES

0   0.5   1.0   1.5

4. Capitol Hill Area

CAPITOL HILL

Henry C. Brown homesteaded the hill east of Broadway in 1864. To attract land buyers, he donated part of Brown's Bluff in 1868 as the State Capitol site, hoping that the Capitol would be a showplace for an elite residential neighborhood. Although the gold-domed statehouse was not completed until 1908, Brown's hopes were answered: Colorado's movers and shakers began decorating Capitol Hill with their exuberant masonry mansions during the 1880s. These piles flaunted various elements of the Queen Anne, Richardsonian Romanesque, Colonial Revival, and Neoclassical styles. Not only the mansions of the upper crust, but their churches, clubs, and schools arose along the tree-shaded sandstone sidewalks of Capitol Hill.

Greater Capitol Hill, bounded by Broadway and Colorado Boulevard between East 20th and East 1st Avenues, includes nine historic districts and more than fifty-five individual landmarks. Much of the original nineteenth-century construction survives. The key to survival has been the large size of the homes that were the prevalent building type. Many were converted to apartments and tuberculosis sanitaria in the early 1900s, when mining booms fizzled and the health-care industry flourished in the sunny Mile High City. Today many residences have been returned to single-family use or converted to offices. Others have been recycled as the eating, drinking, and lodging establishments that make Capitol Hill hospitable.

66. St. Mark's Episcopal Church

(1890, William Lang and Marshall R. Pugh), 1160 Lincoln St., SE corner of E. 12th Ave., NR

Sister Eliza Barton's Mission of the Holy Comforter, which originally stood on this corner, was replaced by Lang and Pugh's English Gothic edifice of Longmont sandstone. A corner bell tower collapsed, leaving a stubby base amid the protruding buttresses, bays, gables, and miniature roof spire. The interior features clustered columns of red sandstone from which spring black ash ceiling beams that meet in Gothic arches. These high vaults frame an altar with a gold-leaf triptych by Albert B. Olson, a Denver artist. The sanctuary end wall has seven tall Gothic window slits shaped like burning candles.

67. Hill Mansion

(1906, Theodore Davis Boal and Frederick Louis Harnois. 1990, restoration by Peter H. Dominick, Jr.), 150 E. 10th Ave., SW corner of Sherman St., NR

Among the French Renaissance Revival elements of this stately home are the mansard roof and the symmetrical north facade with a trio of pedimented dormers flanked by ocular windows. A two-story east portico with a third-floor balcony is supported by tall Ionic columns. Mrs. Crawford Hill, Denver's society queen, reigned here for decades after her husband's death. After her death in 1955, this mansion became the Town Club before it was restored as offices in 1990. This sparkling show home was built with a Hill family fortune made in the smelting industry, which darkened the skies of Black Hawk and north-central Denver.

68. Henry M. Porter House

(1913, Maurice Biscoe), 975 Grant St.

After coming to Denver in 1859, the versatile and very successful entrepreneur portrayed in Mark S. Foster's book *Henry M. Porter: Rocky Mountain Empire Builder* (1991) built a telegraph, ranching, freight, real estate, mining, and retailing empire. Porter lived until 1937, becoming involved in many aspects of Denver's growth. Some of his fortune built Porter Memorial Hospital. His house, a red brick Georgian, is a study in understated elegance, with modest red brick trim and a red tile roof. Landmark designation rescued the Porter House in 1989 on the eve of its scheduled demolition.

69. Sheedy Mansion

(1892, E. T. Carr. 1975, restoration by Daniel J. Havekost), 1115 Grant St., NW corner of E. 11th Ave., NR

Dennis Sheedy, a rancher, banker, and businessman, had E. T. Carr, a Kansas architect, erect this eclectic red brick residence with generous red sandstone trim. It is notable for fine interior woodwork by carpenter Joseph John Queree. "A love of nature prompted me to furnish

67. Hill Mansion. (Photo by Tom Noel)

68. Henry M. Porter House. (*Denver Post* photo by Orin A. Sealey)

69. Sheedy Mansion. (Photo by Tom Noel)

each room with a distinctive wood," Sheedy explained, "and I carried out the idea to include the furniture." Four years after Sheedy's death in 1923, his home, with its grand music room, became a music school and musicians' boardinghouse known as the Fine Arts Studios. The house and matching carriage house, renovated in the 1970s for business use, retain much original decor, such as sheepskin wall coverings in the foyer and buffalo hide on the breakfast room walls.

Asymmetrical yet harmonious massing embraces porches, towers, balconies, a courtyard, and a porte cochere in this three-story reminder that Grant Street was once Millionaires' Row.

71. Creswell House. (Photo by Tom Noel)

70. Whitehead-Peabody House. (Photo by Tom Noel)

70. Whitehead-Peabody House

(1889, Frank E. Edbrooke), 1128 Grant St.

Dr. William R. Whitehead, a surgeon in the Confederate Army, later became a Denver city councilman and chairman of the Denver Board of Health. James H. Peabody lived here during his term as governor (1902–1904). Peabody used the state militia to crush the Western Federation of Miners, who were striking against mine and smelter owners statewide for an eight-hour workday and a minimum daily wage of $3. Peabody's illegal actions destroyed the union and also his chances for re-election. His scary tactics, and several strange occurrences in his former domicile, have given this house a reputation for being haunted. Several ambitious but short-lived restaurants and nightclubs were ultimately scared out by bizarre happenings. In 1994, this long-neglected, spooky Queen Anne dwelling of red brick and rusticated red sandstone was restored for office use.

71. Creswell House

(1889, John J. Huddart), 1244 Grant St., NR

Joseph Creswell, whose Davis-Creswell Manufacturing Company made architectural steel, iron, and plumbing products, commissioned this vernacular Richardsonian Romanesque family home in red sandstone and gray Castle Rock rhyolite. Red sandstone is a soft rock that erodes quickly but can be carved easily, as demonstrated by the mythical stone beasts perched on the front gable.

72. Scottish Rite Masonic Temple

(1924, William N. Bowman), 1370 Grant St., SE corner of E. 14th Ave.

A grandiose pedimented entry, curved corner, and large dome characterize this three-story Neoclassical monument. The brick and steel structure is clad in white terra-cotta blocks resembling limestone atop a base of Pikes Peak granite. The dome covers an immense interior auditorium with a double-arched stage. Although a relative latecomer, the structure's Neoclassicism complements the classical entourage around the State Capitol. Scottish Rite Masons, who trace their origins to the eighteenth-century Enlightenment in Europe, have been one of Colorado's most prominent fraternal groups.

DENVER LANDMARKS & HISTORIC DISTRICTS

73. The First Baptist Church received its landmark plaque in 1968 from Commissioner Alan B. Fisher, at right. (Photo by Glenn Cuerden)

73. First Baptist Church

(1938, G. Meredith Musick), 230 E. 14th Ave., SW corner of Grant St.

Immense polished red granite columns support the pedimented entry portico of this red brick church trimmed with Indiana limestone. The $253,711 edifice is built in a **T** shape, with the sanctuary and vestibule forming the stem, and classrooms and offices forming the crossbar. Elegant landscaping of the narrow street margins has enhanced the setting of this Georgian Revival church, which has a slender, distinctive spire.

74. El Jebel Temple/Rocky Mountain Consistory

(1906, Baerresen Brothers), 1770 Sherman St., SE corner of E. 18th Ave.

A fanciful Moorish shrine with exotic, onion domes, and a roof balcony, this five-story red brick building has contrasting creamy terra-cotta trim, most notably on the horseshoe-shaped window arches. Harold W., Viggio, Albert T., and William J. Baerresen, sons of a noted Danish designer of ships and shipyards,

established a successful architecture firm in Denver. Between 1884 and 1928 they designed and constructed many of the city's buildings, of which this is their most remarkable. This was the headquarters for Colorado's Shriners, the Thirty-third Degree Masons who belong to the Ancient Arabic Order of the Mystic Shrine, before they moved into a new consistory next to the Willis Case Golf Course in Northwest Denver. Among the inscriptions is one in the ballroom: "The Dream of the Architects — Baerresen Brothers." In 1996 the temple became the home of the Eulipions, an African American theater group.

75. Immaculate Conception Basilica

(1902–1912, Leon Coquard, and Aaron M. Gove and Thomas F. Walsh), 401 E. Colfax Ave., NE corner of Logan St., NR

Denver's finest example of the French Gothic style is clad in gray Bedford, Indiana, limestone above a foundation of Colorado granite. Twin 210-foot bell-tower spires flank a large rose window with stained glass angels playing classical instruments. The exquisitely detailed reredos, thirty feet high, is made of Carrara marble, as are the pulpit, much of the statuary, and the archbishop's chair. Leonardo da Vinci's *The Last Supper* inspired the altar table bas-relief, and Bartolomé Murillo's painting of the *Immaculate Conception* was the model for the central statue above the altar. The stained glass was made by the F. X. Zetter Royal Bavarian Art Institute in Munich. At the top of each interior column, a trinity of ribs springs from a cluster of marble wheat and grapes. These ribs support the Gothic vaulted ceiling, which soars sixty-eight feet over the slightly sloping 1,500-seat nave. The Vatican honored the cathedral by designating it a minor basilica in 1979. A $2.5 million restoration for the 1993 visit of Pope John Paul II added a bronze sculpture, *The Assumption of Mary,* in a meditation garden (1993, John Norris) on East Colfax Avenue, which is more noted for its sinners than its saints.

76. First Church of Christ Scientist

(1901–1906, Frederick J. Sterner), 1401–1415 Logan St., NW corner of E. 14th Ave.

Smooth white rhyolite sheaths this Neoclassical temple with two-story Ionic-columned portico and huge domed copper-clad roof behind a classical cornice.

75. Immaculate Conception Basilica in 1911. (Photo by Louis C. McClure, courtesy Denver Public Library)

76. First Church of Christ Scientist. (Photo by José Dole)

Inside, a sloping floor and huge sanctuary suggest a classical amphitheater. This $163,000 church features a large organ built by the Casavant Frères Limitée of St. Hyacinth, Quebec. In 1928, an adjoining administration building and public reading room were built at 1415 Logan Street in a complementary style.

77. Denver Women's Press Club

(1910, Ernest P. Varian and Lester E. Varian), 1325 Logan St.

George Elbert Burr, one of this country's foremost etchers of natural scenes, built this home and studio after settling in Denver in 1906. His life, landscapes, and nature etchings are discussed in Louise Combes Seeber's catalog *George Elbert Burr, 1859–1939* (1971). After Burr moved to Phoenix, Arizona, in 1924, his home became the clubhouse of the Denver Women's Press Club, which had met in private homes since its 1898 founding. This picturesque English cottage has dark red brick walls with a bracketed hood over the entrance. The entrance hall has a low ceiling and a small open staircase to a balcony overlooking the two-story sky-lighted, vaulted-ceilinged studio.

78. Baker/Plested Cottage. (Photo by José Dole)

78. Baker-Plested Cottage

(1886), 1208 Logan St.

Henry P. Baker, an agent of the Colorado Telephone Company, built and originally occupied the frame house that later became better known as the residence of journalist Dolores N. Plested. She worked for the *Trinidad Chronicle* and the *New York Times* and is a mainstay of the Denver Women's Press Club. Her simple cottage is the only wooden dwelling in a neighborhood of larger masonry structures.

QUALITY HILL

HD-6 QUALITY HILL HISTORIC DISTRICT (see Map 6, page 71)

E. 9th to E. 10th Aves. between (roughly) Logan and Clarkson Sts.

Quality Hill, according to a story in the *Denver Times,* June 26, 1901, was a "most exclusive residential section" bounded by Grant and Corona Streets between East 6th and East 11th Avenues. Although the area is not as grand today, the fragment designated as the Quality Hill Historic District remains amid a variety of single- and multiple-family housing. The landmark district is a smaller area roughly between Logan and Washington Streets from East 9th to East 10th Avenues. The southwestern cornerstone is the **Craig House** (1914, J.J.B. Benedict?), 605 East 9th Avenue, northeast corner of Pearl Street, a trim, Neoclassical two-story townhouse. Dr. Alexander Craig's domicile has a hipped tile roof and broad, overhanging eaves above a dentiled cornice. The offset entry does not upset the generally symmetrical appearance of the stucco walls ascending from a dark brick base.

The Granada Apartments, 607–615 East 10th Avenue, and **The Cardenas Apartments,** 707–715 East 10th Avenue, are both three-story 1925 apartment buildings designed by Walter Rice. They flaunt ornaments loosely based on Moorish and Spanish colonial designs, such as iron balconies, curvilinear parapets, and arched bays whose white plaster contrasts dramatically with the red brick walls. Various other apartment houses and residences, reflecting various styles and time periods, add diversity to this mixed district.

79. Daly House

(1894), 1034 Logan St.

Thomas F. Daly founded the Capitol Life Insurance Company, which built the Renaissance palace of an office building that still stands at 1600 Sherman Street. Daly's own two-story residence of rusticated red sandstone with a central bay thrust forward was restored in the 1970s as offices.

80. Stearns House

(1896, Harry T.E. Wendell), 1030 Logan St.

For one of Denver's first Spanish-style buildings, Wendell used modified Mission Revival elements and symmetrical massing for the home of Joel W. Stearns, president of the Mountain Electric Company. Radiating window voussoirs emphasize the round-arch window and door openings on the first floor. Quoins are of brick, and wrought iron is used for the balcony and gate, providing contrast with the light stucco skin of this three-story brick dwelling under a red tile roof. Converted to apartments in the 1940s, it was restored in 1978 for office use.

81. Brind-Axtens House

(1908, Frederick J. Sterner and George H. Williamson), 1000 Logan St., NE corner of E. 10th Ave.

J. Fritz Brind, an Englishman, presided over the Insoloid Dynamite Fuse Company and held considerable stock in the Butterfly-Terrible Mining Company. His wife, Maria, was a president of the Old Ladies Home and of the Denver Orphans Home. She was also the first woman on the executive board of the Denver Charity Organization, which evolved into the United Way. The Brinds moved from their previous residence, a fine extant stone home at 825 Logan Street, to this dwelling incorporating a variety of Mediterranean and Mission elements. Buff brick is used for the walls and the four tall chimneys that soar over the red tile roof and half-timbered dormers. The open beam timber trim is suggestive of Mission Revival, although the rectangular massing, windows, wrought-iron entry gate, and balconies are more eclectic.

A prolific Denver architect, S. Arthur Axtens lived here from 1956 until 1970 and used this as his studio and office. Among his works are the Streamline Moderne **Dorset House Apartments** (1937) across the street at 1001 Logan Street. Axtens's modernism is reflected in the Art Deco remodeling of the interior of the Brind-Axtens House, although the original marble and wood trim remains.

82. Campbell House

(1891, Ernest P. Varian and Frederick J. Sterner), 950 Logan St.

Like the nearby McNeil House, this was built by broker-speculator Fred A. Thompson and sold to Lafayette E. Campbell. Captain Campbell came to Denver to supervise construction of Fort Logan and stayed to supervise David Moffat's mines. With its red brick and rich white frame trim, including prominent third-story dormers and a round entry porch, this is a good vernacular example of Georgian Revival with its symmetrical massing and sidelighted entry. Campbell House and 940 Logan Street next door were among the first Colonial-

Revival-style dwellings to be built in Denver. "Just before we restored the house for office use," developer-realtor Mary Rae commented in 1975, "this place had become a slummy apartment with seventy-five people living in it, with three old ladies residing on the landing."

83. Clarke House

(1891, Ernest P. Varian and Frederick J. Sterner), 940 Logan St.

A two-story porch with fluted Ionic columns topped by a pedimented gable dominates one of Denver's earliest Georgian Revival dwellings. Note the fan-lighted entry, frieze, and dentiled cornice and the boxy symmetrical composition typical of this colonial Revival type. Horace W. Clarke, vice-president and general manager of the Denver & Rio Grande Railroad, lived here. During the 1940s his residence became a men's boardinghouse that was restored for office use during the early 1970s. Since 1992, this has been the Rocky Mountain International House, a residence for foreign students and professors of the University of Colorado at Denver.

84. McNeil House. (Photo by Tom Noel)

84. McNeil House

(1890, Ernest P. Varian and Frederick J. Sterner?), 930 Logan St.

John L. McNeil, a banker, lived here until 1915, when he sold the home to Lucien Hallet, whose father lived next door. Like many large Capitol Hill homes, it was converted to a rooming house during the Great Depression, then restored as a single-family residence in 1974 and subsequently converted to offices. An unusual combination of elements — a Palladian window, shed-roof dormers, round entry porch, and polygonal bay windows — make this house easy to catalog as eclectic.

85. Hallet House. (Photo by Roger Whitacre)

85. Hallet House

(1892, Grable & Weber), 900 Logan St., NE corner of E. 9th Ave.

Moses Hallet, a chief justice of the Colorado Territorial Court and later of the state supreme court, became judge of the U.S. District Court for Colorado from 1877 to 1906. His Queen Anne residence of red pressed brick is dominated by a wraparound veranda, now enclosed. On the third story, the profusion of shingled gables, dormers, steeply pitched irregular rooflines, and massive smooth chimneys suggest the shingle style. This well-kept home of Colorado's most distinguished pioneer jurist has been an apartment house since the 1940s.

86. Clemes-Lipe House

(1898, Franklin E. Kidder and Thielman R. Wieger. 1915, remodel), 901 Pennsylvania St., NW corner of E. 9th Ave.

Constructed as a red brick home for James H. Clemes in the Queen Anne style with corner towers, this dwelling was radically remodeled, stuccoed, and

expanded in 1915, when it became a duplex for brothers Walter E. Lipe and William C. Lipe, who also shared offices at the Lipe Brothers real estate firm.

87. Taylor House

(1900, Lester E. Varian and Frederick J. Sterner), 945 Pennsylvania St., NR

The "House of Arches" is an eclectic edifice with distinctive porch arches repeated in the second- and third-story windows and the rear octagonal corner tower, as well as in the arches of the octagonal central hall inside. Frank M. Taylor, a mining man, served on the boards of the Denver Museum of Natural History, the Denver Public Schools, and St. Luke's Hospital. In 1974, this residence was purchased and restored as the home of Colorado Outward Bound, part of a national organization that introduces city folk to the spiritual and physical challenges of outdoor recreation.

88. Croke-Patterson-Campbell Mansion

(1887, Isaac Hodgson and Edgar J. Hodgson), 428–430 E. 11th Ave., SW corner of Pennsylvania St., NR

Thomas B. Croke was a schoolteacher who invested in railroads and an irrigated 3,500-acre farm that has become the suburb of Northglenn. His experimental farm proved remunerative enough to pay for this $100,000 mansion. Later the mansion became home to Thomas M. Patterson, owner of the *Rocky Mountain News* and a U.S. senator, whose multifaceted career is examined in *Tom Patterson: Crusader for Change* (1995) by his great-granddaughter, Sybil Downing, and Robert E. Smith. Patterson's son-in-law, Richard C. Campbell, was the next owner-occupant. Several deaths here have inspired persistent rumors that this crumbling red sandstone chateau with its creaky floors and squeaky doors is haunted.

The Loire Valley chateau of Azay-le-Rideau may have inspired the three-story dwelling. The steep slate roof bristles with crockets, finials, roundel dormers, and corner turrets, although much carved sandstone decoration has disappeared on one of Denver's best examples of the French chateau style. The irregular plan includes a Châteauesque carriage house connected to the house by a small courtyard.

89. Butters House

(1890, Frank E. Edbrooke), 1129 Pennsylvania St., NR

Like many a westerner, Alfred Butters grew fat on the cattle business. He bought thousands of Texas longhorns at a few dollars a head, then drove them north to market, where he sold the steers for $30 a head. Butters became a businessman, banker, and state representative who lived in this eclectic dwelling with Neoclassical porch details. Its distinctive Palladian window is a Renaissance device that Edbrooke apparently introduced to Denver in this residence.

90. Fleming-Hanington House served as the Eagle Lodge for Native Americans, who erected this more comfortable summer tipi in the front yard in 1967. (Photo by Tom Noel)

90. Fleming-Hanington House

(1893, Edgar J. Hodgson), 1133 Pennsylvania St., NR

A retardaire two-story Greek portico fronts the foursquare of Josiah M. Fleming, general manager of the Daniels & Fisher Stores. Fleming built this "Greek survival" house, with overscale fluted columns and a classical pediment on the facade, for his daughter. From 1912–1924 this was the home of the family of Charles Hanington, a mining man who later became president of Mountain Motors Company. He was a civic activist who served as president of the Colorado Historical Society, the Museum of Natural History, and the Denver School Board.

91. Dunning-Benedict House

(1889, William Lang), 1200 Pennsylvania St., NE corner of E. 12th Ave., NR

One of the finest houses of Denver's leading nineteenth-century residential architect embodies the heavy asymmetrical massing, rough-faced masonry walls, and chunky stone arches of the Richardsonian Romanesque style. Three stories of rusticated gray rhyolite rise to gabled roofs and into four prominent chimneys. The balustraded entry porch has stout stone posts with foliated capitals. A crenelated parapet on a round corner tower is echoed by the crenelated balcony of a two-story south bay. The use of stained glass is extravagant, especially in the large peacock window on the north wall. The two-story carriage house was connected to the dwelling by a later addition.

Walter Dunning, a realtor, commissioned this house, which illustrates William Lang's exuberance and penchant for eclectic historicist details from various periods. Mitchell Benedict, a state supreme court justice, bought the house in 1898, and his family lived here until the 1930s, when the building was converted to apartments and, more recently, to offices.

92. Keating House

(1891, Reiche, Carter & Smith), 1207 Pennsylvania St., NW corner of E. 12th Ave., NR

This Queen Anne three-story dwelling features rough masonry walls, a conical tower, and recessed porches. The exterior red sandstone with hand-carved trim comes from the Red Rock Canyon quarries near Colorado Springs. Built for businessman and realtor Jeffrey Keating and his wife, Mary, it later was converted, like so many Capitol Hill homes, to a boardinghouse, the Buena Vista Hotel. Following a restoration that returned the original floor plan and interior woodwork, it reopened in 1993 as the Capitol Hill Mansion Bed & Breakfast.

91. Dunning-Benedict House. (Photo by Roger Whitacre)

93. Robinson House

(1906, Willis A. Marean and Albert J. Norton), 1225 Pennsylvania St.

Low-pitched overhanging eaves, half timbering, and a rounded bay window lend Craftsman-style distinction to this two-story brick dwelling, the home of William F. and Mary Byers Robinson. Mary was the daughter of William Byers, founding editor of the *Rocky Mountain News*. Robinson worked for the *News* and then ran the *Leadville Democrat* before opening the Robinson Printing Company, which he operated until his death in 1912. Today's Bradford-Robinson Printing Company is

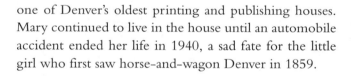

92. Keating House. (Photo by Tom Noel)

95. Guerrieri–DeCunto House. (Photo by Tom Noel)

one of Denver's oldest printing and publishing houses. Mary continued to live in the house until an automobile accident ended her life in 1940, a sad fate for the little girl who first saw horse-and-wagon Denver in 1859.

94. Molly Brown House

(1890, William Lang), 1340 Pennsylvania St., NR

The irrepressible wife of a successful miner from Leadville became the source of legend and of the Broadway play and later movie *The Unsinkable Molly Brown*. Molly was snubbed by Denver society as a vulgar parvenue. Snobs sniffed that the whole family was Irish Catholic and that Molly's mother, who lived with her, smoked a corncob pipe. In response, Molly educated herself and began traveling among the fashionable set in Europe and on the East Coast. She even survived the 1912 sinking of the ocean liner *Titanic*, but, later on, her

house almost perished. After her death in 1932, the house became a bachelors' rooming house, a home for wayward girls, and then a target for demolition, the fate of a twin structure that once stood next door to the north. Historic Denver, Inc., was formed in 1970 to rescue and restore this Queen Anne residence built of quarry-faced pink and gray rhyolite with red sandstone trim. As one of this country's best-known self-made women, Molly would probably be tickled pink to know that her home is now a popular house museum, restored from the anaglypta-covered hallways to the stone lions in front. Interiors are fussy and rich with carved woodwork and a wealth of furnishings from the Brown era. The two-story carriage house has been converted to a visitor center and gift shop selling Christine Whitacre's *Molly Brown: Denver's Unsinkable Lady* (1984), containing testimonials from two actresses who played Molly, Tammy Grimes and Debbie Reynolds.

51

94. Molly Brown House front hall. (Photo by Roger Whitacre)

95. Guerrieri–DeCunto House

(1896, Frank Guerrieri, bldr.?), 1650 Pennsylvania St., NR

Frank Guerrieri, an immigrant from Paladello, Italy, arrived in Denver in 1876 as a violinist, then opened a liquor business with his brothers. In 1896, he built this house and moved in. Another partner, Frank DeCunto, bought the house from Guerrieri in 1901 and lived there until 1919, when he sold it to yet another Italian immigrant with mercantile interests, David Serafini.

This house, now used as offices, is a brick four-square dressed up with an Italianate facade by the Italian immigrants who constructed it and lived here. Arched stone window lintels, wrought-iron balconies, and Corinthian porch columns survive.

96. Temple Emanuel Center. (Photo by Roger Whitacre)

97. German House/Denver Turnverein. (Photo by Roger Whitacre)

96. Temple Emanuel Center

(1899, John J. Humphreys. 1924, addition by Thielman R. Wieger), 1595 Pearl St., SW corner of E. 16th Ave., NR

Ogee arches and other exotic influences in this beige brick building celebrate Judaism's Middle Eastern origins. The facade features minaretlike towers with copper domes. The latter are repeated atop two pavilions on the north and south sides. The central and north towers are octagonal and taller than the south tower, which fronts a 1924 rectangular addition with buttressed corners. Stone trim, striated brick banding, and a red tile roof enhance the composition. Floral and geometric motifs prevalent in Islamic architecture are evident in rows below the eaves, in the door panels, and in extensive stained glass windows, as well as in the interior carved wood paneling and stenciling. This synagogue once housed Colorado's largest Jewish congregation, as Marjorie Hornbein wrote in *Temple Emanuel of Denver: A Centennial History* (1974). It is now owned by the City and County of Denver and used as an events center.

97. German House/Denver Turnverein

(1921, George L. Bettcher), 1570 Clarkson St., SR

Colorado's oldest ethnic club still holds meetings, parties, dances, and German-language performances here. The Turnverein, founded in Prussia around 1811 by Friedrich Ludwig Jahn, cherishes the slogan "A Sound Mind in a Sound Body." *Turner* is the German word for gymnast, and *verein* means union or associa-

tion. Begun as a men's gymnastic club promoting rhythmic exercise (aerobics), sports, and fellowship, it evolved into a social and cultural organization that included women and children. Popularly known as the German House, the club promoted German music, dance, drama, and art, as well as German food and drink. Germans were the largest single foreign-born group in Denver during the late nineteenth century, and this chapter flourished after opening its first hall on Market Street in 1865. A larger clubhouse was built in 1889 at 21st and Arapahoe Streets, and a third one, the Turnhalle, survives as a large theater with a horseshoe-shaped balcony in the Tivoli Brewery on the Auraria campus.

Like other Turnvereins, the Denver German House pushed the idea of physical education. A Denver Turner, Robert Barth, became the first physical education teacher in the Denver Public Schools, and another member, Ruth Drumm Witting, was the first woman to direct exercise sessions over the radio. Although anti-German sentiment during World Wars I and II forced the Turnverein to adopt a much lower profile, it continued to welcome Teutons and promote the German language and culture.

This fourth home of the Turnverein at 16th and Clarkson Streets is a stucco building hinting at the Mediterranean Revival style with its large fanlighted windows, pedimented entry parapet, corner towerettes, and red tile roof. The terra-cotta entablature over the entry features a scantily robed woman dancing with a goat-footed satyr who is playing a lyre. Murals and German inscriptions in the basement rathskeller recall the Old Country. The upstairs hall, with its stage and bandstand, hosts dances, meetings, and fine arts programs. Built as a private social club, the Coronado Club, in 1921, the hall was purchased in 1922 by the Turnverein. Although the landscaping and beer garden have been replaced by the parking lot, this handsome structure commemorates Denver's rich German heritage.

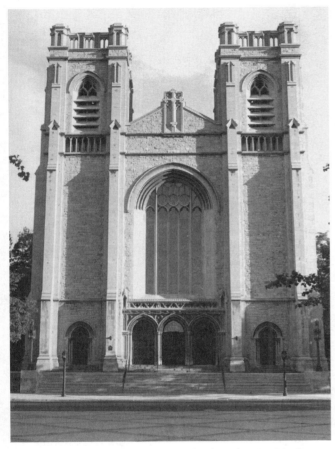

98. St. John's Episcopal Cathedral. (Photo by Tom Noel)

98. St. John's Episcopal Cathedral

(1911, Gordon, Tracy, and Swarthwout), 1313 Clarkson St., between E. 13th and E. 14th Aves., NR

After St. John's in the Wilderness at 20th Avenue and Welton Street was burned by an arsonist, the congregation built this cathedral on a one-block site. Gordon, Tracy, and Swarthwout, the New York City firm that won a national architectural competition, accommodated the surrounding residential neighborhood with a low, generously landscaped English Gothic Revival design clad in random-coursed Indiana oolitic limestone. A carillon of fifteen bells is housed in twin square, castellated towers flanking the north entrance. The fifty-one stained glass windows range in style from Gothic Revival to contemporary. A rosebush was added to the Adam and Eve window to provide cover for Eve, whose seductive form proved distracting to churchgoers. The altar, rood screen, and reredos, all carved from Salonica oak, were salvaged from the earlier burned church. A taller central tower, transepts, and south additions included in the original design were never completed. The attached St. Martin's Chapel, a 1928 Gothic Revival design from Merrill Hoyt and Burnham Hoyt, has a fine wooden reredos by Denver sculptor Arnold Ronnebeck.

99. Morey Middle School

(1921, Arthur A. Fisher and William E. Fisher), 840 E. 14th Ave. between Clarkson and Emerson Sts.

This Beaux-Arts, Italian Renaissance—style school features a central fountain court, round-arched windows, and a red tile roof. In addition to the two exterior entry murals, other murals by Louise Ronnebeck are in the auditorium, along with Robert Garrison's three polychrome statues *Athena, Bust of a Youth,* and *Bust of a Girl.* This school, which includes a tiled basement swimming pool, indoor track, and a library with a vaulted ceiling and fine oak woodwork, was named for businessman and school board member Chester Morey. One of the first junior high schools constructed in Denver, it was executed in the City Beautiful tradition evident in the building's generous one-block landscaped site and grand architecture incorporating art to edify students and the public.

100. Kistler-Rodriguez House

(1920, J.J.B. Benedict), 700 E. 9th Ave., SE corner of Washington St., NR

William H. Kistler, founder of the Kistler Stationery Company, lived here until his death in 1936. Dr. Rene Alvarez Rodriguez, a prominent physician and civic activist, became the house's second owner. Dr. Rodriguez served as the consul for his native country, the Dominican Republic, and converted his residence to that country's consulate. He served as a leading spokesperson for Denver's Latin American community. This two-story brick house in the eclectic style has become even more eclectic with rear additions.

101. Cass House

(1899, Willis A. Marean and Albert J. Norton), 733 E. 8th Ave., NW corner of Clarkson St.

The stepped gable and dormer ends distinguish this as a rare Denver example of the Dutch colonial style. The tightly laid, pressed red brick is trimmed with sandstone accents and banding. Generous windows, the conical corner tower, and distinctive, slender chimneys provided residential ambience for the home of Emogene Cass, widow of Dr. Oscar David Cass, a pioneer physician and gold broker who settled in Denver in 1860. Dr. Cass was a founder of the Hinckley Express Company and the Exchange Bank, two investment houses. His home became an Episcopal commune in the 1960s before its conversion to law offices in the 1980s.

102. Zang Townhouse

(1889, William Lang), 1532 Emerson St., NR

Adolph J. Zang, who presided over Colorado's largest pre-Prohibition brewery, commissioned this tall, narrow, three-story townhouse. Its rough-faced rhyolite facade climbs to a steep front gable and a slender corner oriel window with a steep conical roof. The parapeted front gable is topped by a carved stone griffin that adds a Gothic shiver to the asymmetrical, dramatically vertical facade. Three more of William Lang's townhouses (1889–1890) survive two blocks west in the 1600 block of Washington Street, including his own residence at 1626 Washington, whose facade sports a stepped gable.

103. Flower-Vaile House

(1889, Robert H. Balcomb and Eugene R. Rice), 1610 Emerson St., NR

The Queen Anne style is expressed by the whimsical massing and exuberant ornamentation of this three-story dwelling. Pressed brick with stone trim is sugar-coated with vergeboards that dramatize the gables and dormers, especially at the octagonal entry porch. Here, the elaborate turned spindle porch posts spring into

102. Zang Townhouse. (Photo by Tom Noel)

arches, a pattern repeated overhead on the second-story porch. Heavily rusticated stone trim on the window surrounds competes for attention with the double-decker porch on this hyperactive facade. This weighty show of opulence was restored in 1981 and converted from an apartment house to law offices.

John S. Flower, a prominent Denver realtor and strong supporter of Mayor Robert W. Speer's City Beautiful schemes, sold the house in 1890 to attorney John F. Vaile. Vaile's wife, Charlotte, authored children's books, including *The Orchard Girls, The Truth About Santa Claus,* and a fictional account of Colorado mining, *The M.C.C.*

Balcomb and Rice also designed the Bouvier-Lathrop House (1890) next door at 1600 Emerson, another fussy facade that bulges beyond its rectangular plan and rusticated stone corseting.

103. Flower-Vaile House. (Photo by Tom Noel)

104. Edbrooke House. (Photo by Glenn Cuerden)

104. Edbrooke House

(1893, Frank E. Edbrooke), 931 E. 17th Ave. near Ogden St.

Denver's style-setting architect of the late nineteenth century designed not only grand commercial edifices but also splendid residences, including this one, which he built for himself. This asymmetrical Queen Anne is given a fine sense of proportion by the repeated rooflines and details such as the grouped columns on the first- and second-story porches. Windows are trimmed with raised brick courses that accentuate the arches. Stone banding at the sill level is skillfully incorporated into the porch balustrade, and a second-story band becomes the common sill of three windows that paraphrase Andrea Palladio. The 1896 Edbrooke-designed house next door at 941 East 17th Avenue has been converted to the Merritt House Bed and Breakfast.

105. Ogden Theatre

(1917, Harry W.J. Edbrooke), 935 E. Colfax Ave. at Ogden St., NR

After Thomas Edison and George Eastman developed motion picture film, the golden age of movie houses arrived in the 1910s and 1920s. Even small neighborhood theaters like the Ogden put on architectural airs. Otherwise a simple, functional, two-story brick box, the Ogden wears a fanciful facade framed by twin octagonal towers complete with false windows, a geometric frieze, and corner roof caps. The terra-cotta cherubs, garlands, swags, and other Beaux-Arts details suggest the visual escapes that the movies inside provided. John Thompson hired Frank Edbrooke's nephew and protégé, Harry, who gave the edifice its vaguely Mediterranean flair.

A 1993 exterior restoration was accompanied by a remodeling of the interior to include nightclub tables and seating, three bars, and a dance floor. The original forty-five-foot oak stage and domed ceiling stayed. The original stenciling, Neoclassical terra-cotta trim, and

105. These two unidentified hipsters are among the young people patronizing the Ogden Theatre since its 1993 conversion to a live theater and night club. (Photo by Glenn Cuerden)

Corinthian columns have been restored to preserve a grand setting worlds away from the bleak shoeboxes of modern multiplex theaters.

106. Emerson School/Ralph Waldo Emerson Center

(1884, Robert S. Roeschlaub), 1420 Ogden St., NE corner of E. 14th Ave.

The most impressive feature of this school, as Francine Haber, Kenneth R. Fuller, and David N. Wetzel note in their book *Robert S. Roeschlaub*, is "a windowless wall consisting of nothing more than band courses and a large white Indiana limestone sundial within an ornamental arch." As in other Roeschlaub schools, the central public court allows easy inspection of the classrooms

angled off it. This two-story red brick school rises into a steeply pitched roof punctuated by dormers, gables, elaborate chimneys, and cresting. Since its restoration during the 1980s, the school has housed the Ralph Waldo Emerson Community Center.

107. The Cornwall

(1901, Walter E. Rice), 921 E. 13th Ave., NW corner of Ogden St., NR

William T. Cornwall built and lived in this stylish apartment house, whose Mediterranean Revival mode is reflected in the column capitals, cornices, architraves, friezes, wrought iron, and terra-cotta trim. Walter Rice, a developer, engineer, and inventor as well as an architect, built his own terra-cotta studio in the basement. There he made the trim and the tiles covering the corner towers of the roof garden, which had open promenades. This handsome, stylish, and striking structure was turned into condominiums during the 1970s.

108. Corona School/Dora Moore School

(1889, Robert S. Roeschlaub. 1993, restoration and additions by Stanley Pouw Associates), 846 Corona St., NR

In 1975, when the school board announced plans to demolish this elementary school, students helped persuade the Denver Landmark Preservation Commission and the Denver City Council to declare this Romanesque Revival gem the first locally landmarked school. Roeschlaub, Colorado's leading institutional architect of the nineteenth century, designed at least a dozen Denver schools, including three other Denver landmarks: Emerson Elementary at East 14th Avenue and Ogden Street, Stevens Elementary at 1140 Columbine Street, and Wyatt Elementary at 3620 Franklin Street.

Symmetrical composition, generous exterior detail, and the interior court plan distinguish this as Roeschlaub's most beautiful school. The square corner entry towers are topped by bell-shaped domes with nipple finials. The brick walls blend into rich layers of stone and terra-cotta trim that include cherubs as role models for schoolchildren. Two large additions, each reflecting its own era, complement the original without crowding the

108. Corona School/Dora Moore School. (Photo by Tom Noel)

one-block site. Originally called the Corona School, it was renamed in 1938 for a longtime principal.

109. Wolcott School

(1898, Frederick J. Sterner?), 1400–1414 Marion St., NE corner of E. 14th Ave.

The Wolcott School for Girls, once an elite Capitol Hill private academy, reflects the Renaissance Revival mode with balconies and groupings of pointed- and round-arched windows, as well as the alley arch connection to the 1906 auditorium addition. Miss Anna Louise Wolcott, sister of U.S. Senator Henry R. Wolcott, founded the school for the offspring of Denver's power elite. Miss Wolcott became the first woman regent of the University of Colorado in 1910 and was active in musical, educational, and social circles. After her marriage to Frederick J. Vaile, the Wolcott School was run by Miss Mary Kent Wallace. She left to open the Kent School for Girls in 1922. Shortly afterward, the Wolcott School closed and was turned into apartments.

110. Rosenzweig House

(1882, Charles L. Dow, bldr.), 1129 E. 17th Ave. and Park Ave. between Downing and Marion Sts., NR

Charles L. Dow, a contractor, built numerous other Denver houses and briefly lived in this one. Leopold Rosenzweig, a Russian Jew who moved to Denver for his health, later occupied the house. His daughter Frances became a Wagnerian soprano who performed under the name of Frances Rose. When she retired, she lived here until her death in 1956. Publisher Charles Cleworth has restored this and neighboring residences, including the tiny, steep-roofed 1882 cottage at 1732 Downing Street, and converted them to a distinctive office complex.

The two-and-a-half-story structure has an Eastlake-style porch at the west-side entrance, a dentiled frame cornice, and bracketed eaves under a hip roof. Also on the site are a gabled barn and a coal shed.

HUMBOLDT STREET

HD-7 HUMBOLDT STREET HISTORIC DISTRICT, NRD (see Map 4, page 40)

On the west side of Cheesman Park, twenty-six large homes constitute the residential enclave often called Humboldt Island. Built between the 1890s and the 1920s, the dwellings vary in style, but nearly all were architect designed. Langdon Morris, in his book *Denver Landmarks* (1979), contends that this district reflects "that unfortunate period when architects were timidly seeking new forms" and lacks "the vigor and design sense of the preceding High Victorian era." If most of these homes lack daring, they do exemplify the conservative tastes and interest in fine craftsmanship of Denver's monied elite.

The Dencla-Walker-White House (1898, Harry T.E. Wendell) is a distinctive Georgian Revival with a walled garden and second-story eyebrow dormers. At 1510 East 10th Avenue, on the southeast corner of Humboldt Street, the imposing mansion of Frederick G. Bonfils was demolished in 1969 and replaced by a fifteen-story apartment house, Cheesman Gardens. After public protest failed to stop this high-rise, Denver passed an ordinance to protect Cheesman Park's mountain view from further encroachments. Bonfils, a former Kansas City con man, and Henry H. Tammen, a former bartender whose Tuscan villa (1907, Edwin Moorman) is at 1061 Humboldt, made *The Denver Post* the most lucrative — and sensational — newspaper ever published in the Rockies. These two self-made millionaires and the Stoibers, a wealthy mining family, gave Humboldt Island a reputation as the address for Denver's nouveau riche.

Stoiber-Reed-Humphreys Mansion

(1907, Willis A. Marean and Albert J. Norton), 1022 Humboldt St., NR

In the Humboldt district parade of homes, the showiest of all has a two-story-high glass atrium shedding sunlight on the basement swimming pool. Lena Stoiber's twelve-foot-high stone wall makes it difficult to see the formal Renaissance Revival mansion built by her husband, Edward G. Stoiber. He struck it rich at Silverton's Silver Lake mine and, like so many other mining millionaires, gravitated to Denver. The high wall, at least in legend, was Lena's way of spiting snooty neighbors who gossiped about her past in Silverton's notorious red-light district, Blair Street. After her husband's death, she married Hugh Rood, who perished on the *Titanic* in 1912. Lena then sold the thirty-room mansion to Mrs. Verner Z. Reed. When Mrs. Reed built her Tudor mansion at 475 Circle Drive, she sold the Humboldt Street mansion to Ruth Boettcher Humphreys, who succeeded Mrs. Crawford Hill as the queen bee of Denver society.

Thompson-Henry House

(1905, Baerresen Brothers), 1070 Humboldt St.

Palladian windows and a grand semicircular portico with fluted Corinthian columns front this beige brick Georgian Revival dwelling trimmed in white terracotta. A second-story pedimented porch door and third-story Palladian-influenced dormer further distinguish one of the first Denver homes erected with steel beam construction. On the north side, immense two-story Ionic columns support a third-story balustraded porch beneath an ocular window. Inside, an oval entry hall and octagonal dining room have elaborate ceiling

moldings and a Romeo and Juliet stained glass stairway window. Realtor Alonzo H. Thompson, the original owner and occupant, was followed by Arthur Henry, a president of the Colorado Bar Association and a Colorado legislator from 1929–1932.

111. Sweet House

(1906, Frederick J. Sterner and George H. Williamson), 1075 Humboldt St., SW corner of E. 11th Ave.

Colorado Governor William E. Sweet, a Progressive, unsuccessfully took on the Ku Klux Klan, who ousted him from office in 1924. The governor's two-and-a-half-story Georgian Revival home, where his widow lived until her death in 1962, is distinguished by an expansive front porch with a balustraded balcony and by a variety of Palladian windows. Kent Miller, an attorney, purchased the home in 1984 and restored the classical interior elements such as fluted columns, arches, and ceiling moldings.

Brown-MacKenzie-McDougal House

(1903, Eugene R. Rice), 1100 Humboldt St.

Eclectic design pairs an oriel window and a double-arch window with a wrought-iron balcony over an unrelated entry canopy added later. Nearly every window is a different size and design, and the massing is irregular, as if Rice set out deliberately to provide an alternative to the foursquares from which his plan derives. His unpredictable composition is unified by the heavy tile roof and the dormers and gables sharing the same hipped roof pitch and knob finials. Since 1940, attorney Robert McDougal and his family have owned the house built by Lymon B. Brown, a broker.

112. Tears-McFarlane House

(1896, Frederick J. Sterner), 1290 Williams St., SE corner of E. 13th Ave., NR

Daniel W. Tears, an attorney with offices in the Equitable Building, commissioned this Georgian Revival dwelling on the north edge of Cheesman Park. Third-story pedimented dormers behind a balustrade distinguish this red brick house whose rounded entry porch, supported by paired columns, is topped by a balcony.

113. Cheesman Park Memorial Pavilion, c. 1920. (Photo by Humphreys Aviation, Tom Noel Collection)

After Tears died in 1922, this became the home of William and Ida Kruse McFarlane, a prominent Central City family. She taught English at the University of Denver, co-founded the Central City Opera House Association with Anne Evans, and started a dance academy in the basement of this large home. On the northside stairway landing the big stained glass window is attributed to the firm of Louis Comfort Tiffany. The Capitol Hill Community Center moved into the mansion in 1978 and added the large south-side meeting room.

113. Cheesman Park Memorial Pavilion

(1910, Willis A. Marean and Albert J. Norton), 1000 High St. in Cheesman Park, NR

This Colorado Yule marble memorial commemorates pioneer business tycoon Walter Scott Cheesman with a viewing platform reminiscent of the Greek Parthenon. Surrounded by formal gardens and a reflecting pool, the classical-columned pavilion crowns the hill at the east end of **Cheesman Park** (1898, Reinhard Schuetze). Once the city cemetery, this urban park features curvilinear walks and drives and perimeter trees bordering an expanse of lawn that carries the eye to the mountain view. Cheesman Esplanade, as the full-block

grassy median strip between Williams and High Streets is called, connects the park with East 7th Avenue Parkway.

MORGAN ADDITION/CHEESMAN PARK

HD-8 MORGAN ADDITION HISTORIC DISTRICT (see Map 4, page 40)

E. 9th Ave. to E. 8th Ave. between Cheesman Park and York St.

Samuel B. Morgan subdivided what had been the south edge of the Catholic section of City Cemetery. Between 1910 and 1930, some of the city's most prominent and wealthy families constructed grand homes here on the south side of what is now the Denver Botanic Gardens. The forty-five homes showcased in this district, mostly revival styles by leading architects, are purer and more confident than the eclectic homes of Humboldt Island across Cheesman Park.

Sullivan House

(1926, J.J.B. Benedict), 801 Race St.

The unusually stark, almost abstract 8th Avenue facade of this house contrasts with the building's colonnaded west facade and with Benedict's more typical Renaissance Revival palace at 817 Race Street, the **Neusteter-Chenoweth House** (1921).

Livermore-Benton House

(1911, Maurice Biscoe and Henry H. Hewitt), 901 Race St.

This red brick Colonial Revival house has white-painted wood trim that includes fluted pilasters and a fine Georgian entry. The second-story balustrade once extended around all four sides below dormered third-story servants' quarters. Variegated brick end walls rise into large double chimneys. The formal house hides an underground garage and has Cheesman Park as its backyard. Built by Richard L. Livermore, an army officer, it has been the residence of prominent attorney and school board member Ed Benton since 1964. Other specimens of the Georgian Revival are the neighboring **Dines House** (1931, Harry James Manning), 900 Race Street, and the **Daniel Millet House** (1920, William E. Fisher and Arthur A. Fisher), 860 Vine Street.

114. Denver Botanic Gardens House

(1926, J.J.B. Benedict), 909 York St., NW, corner of E. 9th Ave., NR

Elements from several styles enhance this eclectic show home, whose irregular massing, stucco walls, oriel and grouped windows, and steeply pitched roof make it one of Benedict's rare excursions into the Tudoresque. The house sits behind a tree-shaded garden and courtyard at the southeast corner of the Denver Botanic Gardens. Exquisitely furnished, it boasts the usual Benedict hallmark, a carved stone fireplace. The main staircase, with its wrought-iron balustrade, winds gracefully up from the entry. A second stairway, hidden behind shelves in the library, leads down to the wine cellar and up to the master bedroom. Constructed for Richard C. Campbell, this mansion was later purchased for the Denver Botanic Gardens for use as their headquarters by Mrs. James J. (Ruth Porter) Waring, who lived next door at 910 Gaylord Street in an exquisite 1924 Beaux-Arts house also by Benedict.

115. Boettcher Conservatory, Denver Botanic Gardens

(1964, Victor Hornbein and Edward D. White, Jr.), 1005 York St.

Despite the convention that landmarks should be at least fifty years old, the Denver Landmark Preservation Commission designated this futuristic structure only nine years after its completion. The Boettcher Conservatory is made of faceted plexiglass panels between interlaced concrete arches in an inverted catenary curve that arcs fifty feet above tropical gardens. Some six hundred horticultural species are cultivated amid waterfalls and pools constructed in a sloped, naturalistic environment. The Boettcher Foundation, whose money came in large part from Charles Boettcher's Ideal Cement Company, funded this complex and encouraged use of concrete throughout. Even the lampposts in the surrounding walks and gardens are concrete "trees" with globe lights posing as fruits.

WYMAN ADDITION

HD-9 Wyman Addition Historic District

E. 17th to E. 11th Aves. between York and Race Sts. and (roughly) E. Colfax to E. 13th Aves. between Humboldt and Race Sts.

This local landmark district of 547 structures covers approximately the same area as John H. Wyman's original 1882 addition to the City of Denver. Wyman paid $3,000 for his fifty-one-block tract in 1866 and sold it twenty years later for $300,000. The main artery began as a dirt trail known as the Kansas City Road. It was renamed Colfax Avenue in honor of U.S. Representative Schuyler Colfax, who supported Colorado statehood and subsequently became vice president under Ulysses S. Grant. Colfax resigned after publicity about his role in Grant administration scandals. Colfax Avenue, too, has had its share of scandals.

Streetcars originally enabled Denverites to move out of downtown and build fine homes in the Wyman Addition. This section of Capitol Hill attracted mansion-builders such as Senator Lawrence C. Phipps, Sr.,

115. Boettcher Conservatory, Denver Botanic Gardens. (Photo by José Dole)

probably the richest man in Colorado. Streetcars later pushed beyond the Wyman Addition to the Cheesman Park, Country Club, Park Hill, and Montclair neighborhoods, carrying wealthy homeowners with them. Many of the old large homes were converted to boardinghouses or tuberculosis sanitaria.

Only five of the many original Colfax Avenue mansions survive today, and four of these are hiding behind storefronts. The 1400 blocks of High and Vine Streets and the 1300 and 1500 blocks of Race Street still exude opulence with their stout and merry Victorians. New tree plantings and restorations of old landmarks are reviving the entire Wyman district. Notable rebirths such as the Castle Marne Bed & Breakfast, the Milheim House, and the Holiday Chalet Victorian Hotel have inspired the rehabilitation of other antique houses for single-family residences or offices. Designation as a Denver landmark district in 1994 led to district guidelines and incentives that have furthered the dramatic turnaround in this riches-to-rags-to-riches neighborhood.

116. Pope-Thompson-Wasson House

(1894, Harry T.E. Wendell), 1320 Race St.

Gatepost pineapples, a symbol of welcome and hospitality, give this eclectic Mediterranean-style residence its nickname, the Pineapple House. The distinctive diamond-pane front window is arched, as is the doorway. Broad sheltering eaves and a second-story balcony also reach out to welcome passersby to this smiling yellow brick home.

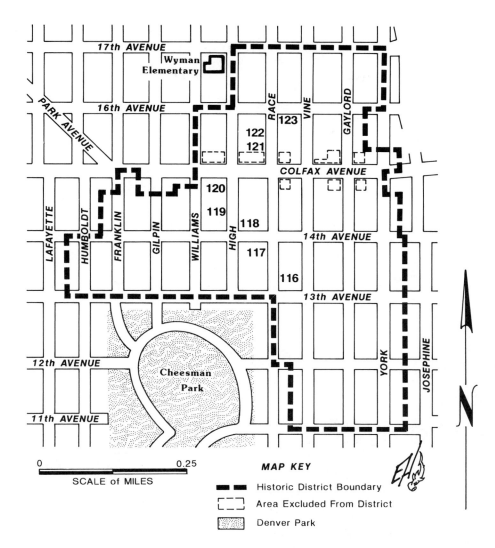

5. Wyman Addition Historic District

117. Adams-Fitzell House

(1892, Franklin E. Kidder and John J. Humphreys), 1359 Race St.

This rare Denver example of a Shingle-style cottage wears a conical cap on the corner tower. A polygonal dormer, recessed entry porch, square oriel window, and steep-pitched roof also distinguish this dwelling. The rustic stone base extends upward into the tall chimney and the porch posts for the overhanging second floor.

Note the stone detail, such as the radiating door and window tops, the irregular polygonal chunks of rhyolite in the skin, and the pedestrian bench built into the sidewalk steps. Craftsman elements include the "question mark" wrought-iron fence, the sawtooth hemline to the second-story shingling, and the exposed porch roof beams. George H. Adams, a cattle and mining man, originally owned the house, which is still occupied by a daughter of Grant R. Fitzell, the second owner.

118. Sykes-Nicholson-Moore House. (Photo by Roger Whitacre)

118. Sykes-Nicholson-Moore House

(1897, Ernest P. Varian and Frederick J. Sterner), 1410 High St.

Reverend Richard E. Sykes, the minister of the First Universalist Church, built this two-story brick Georgian Revival mansion. A second owner, Meredith Nicholson, wrote his mystery novel *The House of a Thousand Candles* (1905) using the house as a setting. This novel became the basis of a Broadway play and two movies. The house received a later addition on the

south side, a semicircular two-story solarium that echoes the curve of the columned entry porch on the west. The well-preserved interior is notable for its many six-over-six windows and golden oak woodwork. The oak mantelpiece is carved with words from Ralph Waldo Emerson: "Ye ornament of ye house is ye guest who frequents it." After stints as the residence of cattleman John C. Moore, as a rooming house, and as a halfway house, the building was restored during the 1980s as a school for maids and butlers.

119. Watson House

(1894, Frederick J. Sterner), 1437 High St.

Ionic columns and pilasters and a third-story Palladian window distinguish the subsequently remodeled Colonial Revival home built for George H. Watson, Jr. This block of High Street has many architectural treasures. The **Clarence H. Olmsted House** (1892, David W. Dryden?), 1460 High Street, has a large gambrel gable, and the **Bohm Mansion** (1895, Colorado Realty & Construction), 1820 East Colfax Avenue at the southwest corner of High Street, has been recycled as the Holiday Chalet Victorian Hotel.

120. McCourt House

(1896, Colorado Realty & Construction), 1471 High St., NR

A two-story porch with full-height Ionic columns fronts this brick foursquare with Colonial Revival ambitions. The facade is fancified by balustraded second- and third-story balconies. Peter McCourt, brother of Elizabeth McCourt "Baby Doe" Tabor, managed the Tabor Grand Opera House for his brother-in-law, Horace Tabor, and orchestrated the Silver Circuit, which brought national theater companies to mining-town opera houses. In McCourt's own home, the interior boasts golden oak woodwork, a Tiffany chandelier, and an electric lamp borne by a statue of Mercury, not to mention the gilded claw feet of the bathtub.

121. Milheim House

(1893), 1515 Race St.

John Milheim, a Swiss immigrant, opened the still-standing Colorado Bakery and Saloon building at 1444

Market Street. Until her death in 1930, his wife, Mary, lived in this house. The exterior embellishments and exquisite original woodwork look back to the Queen Anne era. Shortly before its scheduled demolition in 1989, this two-and-a-half-story, red pressed brick four-square was moved from 1355 Pennsylvania Street. Ralph Heronema acquired the house for next to nothing but spent $400,000 to transport the 583-ton structure seventeen blocks and replant it on its new foundation.

122. Chappell House

(1895, Frank S. Snell?), 1555 Race St., NR

Reflecting the shift from Victorian exuberance to more cautious, Neoclassical styles after the silver crash of 1893, this two-and-a-half-story red brick domicile has a symmetrical massing asserted by a corner tower. Allen Delos Chappell's dwelling, with its dignified interior featuring original hardwood trim, has been home since 1936 to the Unity Temple of Practical Christianity.

123. Raymond House/Castle Marne

(1890, William Lang), 1572 Race St., SE corner of E. 16th Ave., NR

William Lang's flowery stone detailing is exemplified in this three-story rusticated pink and gray rhyolite residence. The trim is Indiana limestone, which is much easier to carve than rhyolite. A novel and fanciful, if superfluous, colonnette supports the keystone of the transom arch on the parlor window beside the carved golden oak front door. On the north side, in another typical Lang detail, stone trim frames a round, stained glass window above two round-arched portals whose awkward junction is disguised with a Baroque limestone bouquet. Exquisite stonework characterizes even the nine limestone chimney pots. Rough-hewn stone balustrades crown the porch and the southwest pentagonal corner tower.

Real estate developer Wilbur S. Raymond built this Richardsonian Romanesque edifice on three lots for $40,000. After a two-story 1920 addition, the house was converted to the Marne Apartments. James Peiker and his family bought it in 1988 for $184,000 and spent $300,000 lovingly restoring and refurnishing it as a bed and breakfast, the Castle Marne. This spectacular Revival, which encompasses the matching carriage

house, helped spark the renaissance of the Wyman Addition.

124. Baerresen-Freeman House. (Photo by Glenn Cuerden)

124. Baerresen-Freeman House

(1904, Baerresen Brothers), 1718 Gaylord St.

This Dutch Colonial house with a plethora of Neoclassical elements was designed by the Baerresen brothers for the oldest of the four siblings, Harold. Harmony was achieved by topping the pairs of three Ionic entry columns with pairs of three balcony balusters that are a diminutive version of those on the front-porch balustrade. The domicile's second owner, William R. Freeman, gained fame as the man who salvaged the Denver, Salt Lake & Pacific Railroad after the death of its president, David Moffat.

125. Smith Mansion

(1902, William E. Fisher and Daniel Riggs Huntington), 1801 York St., NW corner of E. 18th Ave., NR

High chimneys, ornate roundel dormers in a steep-pitched roof, and ornate voussoirs give a French flair to this three-story $45,000 mansion built by Frank L. Smith, a mining man. Gray brick over a steel frame is ornamented with white terra-cotta under tiled hip roofs. The interior boasts fine woodwork. The letter *S* appears repeatedly in the plasterwork, making it clear that the family wanted to be remembered. One of a row of notable residences along the west edge of City Park,

125. Smith Mansion. (Photo by Glenn Cuerden)

this Beaux-Arts mansion and its prominent carriage house served a long stint as a boardinghouse before a 1980s restoration as offices.

126. Pearce-McAllister Cottage

(1899, Frederick J. Sterner), 1880 Gaylord St., NR

Harold V. Pearce, one of many British investors in Colorado railroads, mining, and smelting, married the daughter of Dr. William A. Bell, vice president of the Denver & Rio Grande Railroad. The couple occupied the house until returning to England in 1907. Henry McAllister, general counsel for the D&RG, purchased the house, and his family lived there for decades before donating it to the Colorado Historical Society in 1971, along with many furnishings. It is now a house museum, with the Miniatures, Dolls & Toys Museum upstairs.

Sterner used the Dutch Colonial mode for this two-and-a-half-story brick house, which Pearce had built as a wedding present for his bride. The plan is a modified T, with a two-story servants' wing at the rear. The wood-shingled gambrel roof with three evenly spaced shed dormers overhangs a full-length balustraded entry porch. The offset doorway is flanked by sidelights and pilasters. A glazed conservatory was added to the southeast corner around 1926. A cast-iron cat still prowls the roof ridge, scouting a stately residential neighborhood.

127. Graham-Bible House

(1892–1893), 2080 York St. in City Park, NRD

This modest house, which displays both Queen Anne and Shingle styles in its ornamental vergeboards and curving shingled porch, was built as the official residence of the superintendent of City Park. Superintendent Alexander J. Graham first moved into the dwelling, which later housed longtime park superintendent James A. Bible.

CITY PARK

HD-10 CITY PARK PAVILION HISTORIC DISTRICT (see Map 4, page 40)

(1882, Henry F. Meryweather. 1890s, Reinhard Schuetze), York St. to Colorado Blvd. between E. 17th and E. 26th Aves., NR

City Park, Denver's largest (317 acres) and most elaborate park, contains notable buildings, striking sculpture, a zoo, and the Denver Museum of Natural History. Harry Meryweather, a city civil engineer, laid out the park in the Olmsted tradition, using a romantic, informal plan of looping drives and walks around man-made lakes. Reinhard Schuetze, Denver's first landscape architect, further refined the plan, which ranges from dense tree planting and shrub massing to grassy expanses. George Kessler, the Olmsted Brothers, and Saco R. DeBoer also had a hand in shaping City Park. The **Pavilion** (1896) and the **Floating Bandstand** (1896, William E. Fisher; 1929, Charles F. Pillsbury) at the west end of Ferril Lake were designated a historic district and restored in the 1990s.

128. Fire Station No. 18/Denver Police Gang Unit

(1912, Edwin H. Moorman), 2205 Colorado Blvd., NE corner of E. 22nd Ave.

On the east edge of City Park, this fire station is disguised as a bungalow to blend in with the residential architecture of the Park Hill neighborhood across the boulevard. Edwin Moorman's design bristled with porticos, pergolas, gabled projections, and extended, bracketed Craftsman rafter ends. The simpler building actually erected retains the dark red Harvard brick, columned pergola, Palladian window, and many Craftsman details. During the 1980s a new Station 18 was built elsewhere, and this was converted to an office for the Denver Police Gang Unit.

129. East High School. (Photo by Tom Noel)

129. East High School

(1925, George H. Williamson), City Park Esplanade, 1545 Detroit St., corner of E. Colfax Ave.

Sited next to City Park, East High exemplifies the City Beautiful dream of showcasing public schools on parks and parkways. The school buildings themselves taught lessons in fine design. A seven-story bell tower vaguely reminiscent of Philadelphia's Independence Hall distinguishes this landmark. Mottled red brick trimmed with pale gray terra-cotta sheathes this eclectic adaptation of the English Jacobean style. The four-story, **H**-plan building is remarkable for its 25 percent wall-to-window ratio, designed to allow natural light. Minimal

interior remodeling has left in place the gray Ozark marble of the main lobby, as well as the statue of East High's mascot — an angel — and a replica of Michelangelo's statue *David.*

130. Austin Apartments

(1904, Audley W. Reynolds. Later additions. 1996, rehabilitation by Rod Lane and Cheryl Spector Architects), 2400–2418 E. Colfax Ave., SE corner of Josephine St., SR

This faint echo of the Italian Renaissance Revival style is a three-story brick building with round-arch, top-floor windows and recessed balconies. Pharmacist Frank A. Austin erected the structure and opened his drugstore in the storefront. A $1 million 1996 rehabilitation restored the commercial storefronts and the upstairs apartments as affordable housing, retaining the vintage oak woodwork and skylights.

131. Bosworth House. (Photo by Tom Noel)

131. Bosworth House

(1899, William Lang?), 1400 Josephine St., NE corner of E. 14th Ave.

From 1902 to 1947 this was the home of Mrs. Leora Bosworth, widow of Joab Bosworth, who founded the Denver Fire Clay Company, a leading supplier of decorative masonry trim. Mrs. Bosworth, a civic and social activist, founded the Monday Literary Club. She bequeathed the home in 1947 to the Denver Branch of the American Association of University Women. The AAUW sold the house in 1966 to the Assistance League of Denver, a local chapter of a national charity, which in 1990 restored the house for its offices. The red sandstone Queen Anne is asymmetrical but unified by evenly pitched roofs of dormers and gables with ornate vergeboard.

132. Gates House. (Photo by José Dole)

132. Gates House

(1892, H. Chaten), 1375 Josephine St., SW corner of E. 14th Ave.

One of Denver's best examples of the Richardsonian Romanesque style, this house drew inspiration from the work of Henry Hobson Richardson, who practiced in New York State and Brookline, Massachusetts. It has the typical massive chunks of stone, enormous Romanesque arches, shingled upper stories, oriel and recessed windows, and asymmetrical plan. Rhyolite is used for both the building's first floor skin and the sixty-foot-high chimney.

Russell Gates founded the Russell Gates Mercantile Company, which had stores throughout east-central Colorado. Gates, who ran as a Republican mayoral candidate in 1897, built the house for $16,000. The building became Castle Apartments from the 1920s until the 1970s, when it was restored as an office and residence. In 1995, the 6,313-square-foot dwelling went on the market for $680,000.

133. Benson–Orsborn House

(1890 and 1893, Lorenzo Benson, bldr.), 1305 Elizabeth St., NW corner of E. 13th Ave.

Builder and owner Lorenzo Benson constructed the brick barn (now the garage) in 1890 and the main house in 1893 but disappeared shortly thereafter. George E. Orsborn and Jeannette B. Orsborn, who lived here from 1922 until 1953, practiced medicine as a husband-and-wife firm and were also active in civic circles.

This Queen-Anne-style residence sparkles after a 1990s restoration. The grand entry porch is topped by a second-story open balcony and a third-story closed octagonal tower. Generous bay windows with distinctive flattened arches adorn three sides of the building, which has a second-story oriel window on the east side. The red brick house has red sandstone trim that is outshone by the splendid exterior wooden trim — the vergeboard, the paired Tuscan porch columns, and the geometric shingle work above the tower and oriel windows. The interior retains much fine original woodwork and second-story beveled glass windows.

134. Stevens Elementary School. (Photo by Tom Noel)

134. Stevens Elementary School

(1900, Robert S. Roeschlaub. 1994, remodel by Charles Nash), 1140 Columbine St.

This last of many schools designed by Roeschlaub is relatively modern in its simplicity and the generous banks of windows that flood the interior with light.

136. Bluebird Theater. (Photo by Tom Noel)

This multigabled building is buff brick with sparse Neo-classical stone trim. Opened as the George Washington Clayton School, it was renamed in honor of its first principal, Eugene E. Stevens. Charles Nash remodeled the school, adding attic decks and skylights to reopen it as a condominium complex that retains the chalkboards, playground, and other souvenirs of its school days.

135. Fire Station No. 15

(1903, John J. Huddart), 1080 Clayton St., SE corner of E. 11th Ave.

To the dismay of the neighborhood, the Denver Fire Department announced that they were abandoning this handsome Beaux-Arts, residential-scale firehouse in 1985 because of its deteriorating condition. To the rescue came Nathaniel and Kathleen Fay, who bought and restored it with the help of architect Ron Abo as a private residence with a king-size garage. In undertaking this project, the Fays were the first to use a 1991 state income tax credit that allows owners of designated land-marks tax credits for restoration expenses up to $50,000. In 1995, the Fays restored the classic tin cornice, tuck-pointed the blond brick walls, and made structural repairs.

"We love living in this firehouse and keeping it a part of the neighborhood," reports Kathy Fay. "Our two kids love it, too, especially since we bought our bright red 1949 Ford-Pirsch fire truck. They can slide down the fire pole to breakfast or to sit in the truck. After the kids are grown and gone, we hope to open a bed and breakfast here, The Firehouse Inn."

136. Bluebird Theater

(1914, Harry W.J. Edbrooke), 3315–3317 E. Colfax Ave. between Adams and Cook Sts., SR

Flying away from a pornographic past, the Bluebird has been restored in more ways than one. Originally built as the Thompson Theater, its blond brick Beaux-Arts Mediterranean Revival facade has urn-shaped lamp

69

135. Fire Station No. 15. (Courtesy Denver Public Library)

finials and a prominent marquee culminating in a sil-houetted bluebird. As in many theaters, the fanciful facade is flanked by the plain brick side and rear walls. Denver theater tycoon Harry Huffman acquired the theater in 1922 and renamed it the Bluebird. Ralph Batschelet, who managed the neighborhood theater for Huffman, promoted Depression-era patronage with "Bank Night" and "Deluxe Country Store" giveaways of cash and commodities. The Bluebird turned to skin flicks in 1974 and, to the relief of protesting neighbors, closed in 1987. With city and neighborhood aid, Christopher C. Swank restored the theater as a cabaret so that the Bluebird is once again swanky, with both films and live performances. Inside, the stage was extended to cover the orchestra pit, but the proscenium arch survives, along with its fresco of cherubs admiring a cartouche reading "JET" for the original builder, John E. Thompson.

SNELL ADDITION

HD-11 SNELL ADDITION HISTORIC DISTRICT (see Map 4, page 40)

E. Colfax to E. 14th Aves. between Cook and Madison Sts.

Frank Snell, a Denver native, was never licensed as an architect but was nevertheless an active builder. His Snell Addition (1905–1911) consists of twenty-five houses. Most are foursquares with varying brick colors and detail. The one-block development with two alley streets (Colfax Avenue A and Colfax Avenue B) and "backyard" houses is a rare Denver experiment in small lots and higher-density housing.

Arps House (c. 1905, Frank Snell), 3422 Colfax Avenue A, is typical of the district's scheme of large houses on tiny lots. It was the home of Denver historian Louisa Ward Arps, whose thoroughly researched, well-written books include *Denver in Slices* (1959). The architect-developer built **Snell House** (c. 1905, Frank Snell), 3421 Colfax Avenue A, for himself, with dormer windows on three sides of the third floor. Snell maintained that large yards were undesirable "junk catchers." He contended that many people would rather not spend their time caring for large lawns, an idea ahead of its time. Not until the 1980s did many Denver home buyers begin showing a preference for smaller lots.

EAST SEVENTH AVENUE

HD-12 EAST SEVENTH AVENUE HISTORIC DISTRICT

The district centered on 7th Avenue between Logan Street and Colorado Boulevard, bounded for the most part by East 6th and East 8th Avenues, is Denver's largest historic district. It comprises 927 buildings, from grand mansions and apartment houses on the west end to modest bungalows on the east end. At least seventy-nine different architects produced designs for residences in this district, which includes Albert J. Norton's own 1900 residence at 661 Humboldt Street, Montana Fallis's 1909 domicile at 622 Ogden Street, and Aaron Gove's 1911 house at 750 Marion Street.

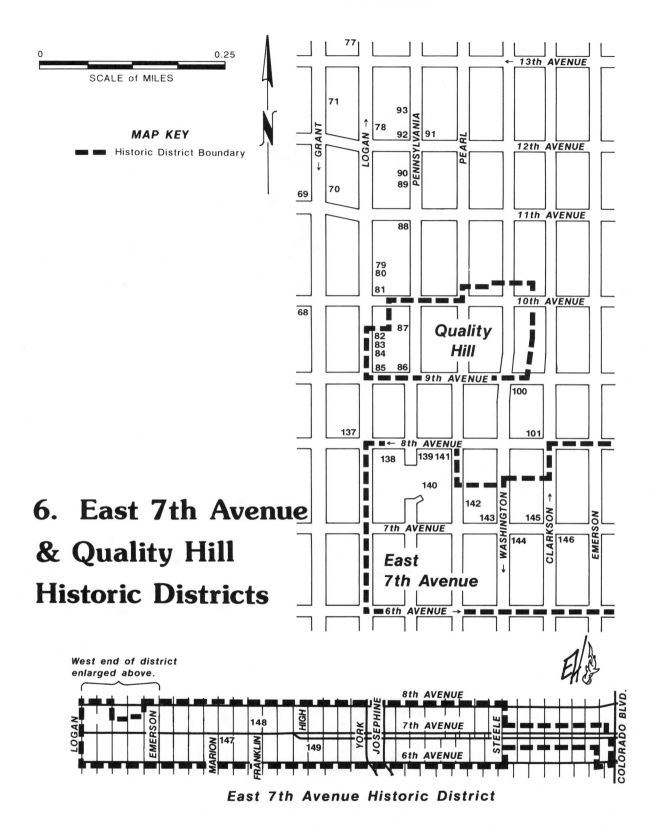

6. East 7th Avenue & Quality Hill Historic Districts

East 7th Avenue Historic District

East Seventh Avenue Parkway

(1914, Saco R. DeBoer), Williams St. to Colorado Blvd., NRD

Seventh Avenue Parkway's uniform tree lawns and setbacks tie together this district of well-landscaped homes. Parkway median plantings range from larch trees to floral extravaganzas, and the planting strips border a variety of houses ranging from J.J.B. Benedict Beaux-Arts villas to Craftsman bungalows.

137. Sayre's Alhambra

(1892, Hal Sayre?), 801 Logan St., NW corner of E. 8th Ave.

Hal Sayre came to Colorado in 1859 and adopted the long hair and buckskin suit typical of westerners. As one of the first mining engineers, he did well in Central City, a gold-rush town that he helped lay out. Sayre was a president of Central City's Rocky Mountain Bank and fought with the Colorado Volunteers at Sand Creek. Supposedly after a trip to Spain, he designed or helped design this twenty-five-room yellow brick house distinguished by ogee-arched transom cutouts inspired by the Spanish Alhambra. The south-side front porch has an arabesque arched arcade. Turquoise accent tiles adorn the exterior and interior of this house, which had a fireplace in each room. Inside, the Moorish theme is continued in the cherry woodwork and in the paneling containing the hand-carved Sayre family crest and the initial *S*. Sayre, a fancier of fast horses, which he stabled in the rear carriage house, lived here until his death at age ninety-one in 1926. His wife, Elizabeth, stayed in the house until her death in 1937. Unrestored and little altered, Sayre's Alhambra in the 1990s became one of the more dignified shelters for Denver's homeless, Providence House.

138. Governor's Mansion

(1908, Willis A. Marean and Albert J. Norton. 1980s, restoration by Edward D. White, Jr.), 400 E. 8th Ave., SE corner of Logan St., NR

Walter Scott Cheesman, a real estate tycoon and businessman, died before he could move into his Georgian Revival mansion. The twenty-seven-room house became the home of his widow and of his daughter, Gladys, and her husband, John Evans II. Later, Claude Boettcher, who ran the huge industrial and commercial

138. Governor's Mansion. (Courtesy Denver Public Library)

empire assembled by his father, Charles, bought the house. After his death, the Boettcher Foundation donated the dwelling to the state in 1958 for the governor's mansion, whose first floor is open to the public for free Tuesday tours.

A wrought-iron fence with cannonball finials on brick entry posts guards this formal Georgian Revival dwelling. Deep red brick walls are almost lost amid rich white wooden frosting under a hip roof with prominent gabled dormers. The pedimented, dentiled cornice provides a strong shadow line. Massive two-story fluted Ionic columns guard the west side portico. The stately entry has grouped columns supporting a porch that becomes a balustraded second-story balcony. Inside, the semicircular Palm Room conservatory has a marble floor and stone columns that match those on the portico that leads into the extensive yards and gardens bordered by Governor's Park.

139. Malo Mansion

(1921, Harry James Manning), 500 E. 8th Ave., SE corner of Pennsylvania St.

One of the city's finest Spanish Colonial Revival mansions, this twenty-three-room, two-story stucco villa exults in finely crafted detail, such as the wrought-iron balconies and hand-painted rosettes on the overhanging

140. Grant-Humphreys Mansion. (Photo by Roger Whitacre)

eaves. Oscar L. Malo, a president of the Colorado Milling and Elevator Company, had the architect include rose patterns in stained glass throughout. A 1980s rear addition does not detract from this refined specimen.

140. Grant–Humphreys Mansion

(1902, Theodore D. Boal and Frederick L. Harnois), 770 Pennsylvania Street, NR

Denver's best-known Neoclassical residence has a monumental semicircular portico supported by four two-story fluted Corinthian columns. Georgian balustrades for the first- and second-story porches and terraces are echoed by a rooftop balustrade. Built for James

B. Grant, a smelter owner and Colorado governor (1883–1885), the peach-hued brick house employs lavish terra-cotta trim in the window surrounds, balustrades, cornices, corner pilasters, and frieze. This early use of terra-cotta as a substitute for decorative stonework set an example widely copied by other local architects and builders. Interiors are on a grand scale, featuring exotic woods, plaster trim, and a sunroom addition. The second owner, Albert E. Humphreys, an oil tycoon who later became embroiled in the Teapot Dome scandal, added a two-story, ten-car garage complete with a car wash and gas pump for his fleet of Rolls-Royces. His son, Ira, donated the house in 1976 to the Colorado Historical Society, which uses it as a house museum and rents it out for special events. Splendidly sited on the southwest corner of Capitol Hill, it has an extensive lawn that flows west across a grassed-over block of Pennsylvania Street into Governor's Park.

141. John Porter House

(1923, Ernest P. Varian and Lester E. Varian), 777 Pearl St., SW corner of E. 8th Ave., NR

This house is a rare Denver example of the Jacobean style, a Tudor variant characterized by gables that rise to the parapet and hide the roof behind. Tudor features include the flattened pointed arches in the prominent entry porch, the triple window groupings, a steep-pitched roof, and the tall, ornate paired chimneys. John Porter was a successful businessman like his father, the tycoon Henry M. Porter. His tapestry red brick house became the residence of Catholic archbishop Urban J. Vehr, who installed a private chapel and elaborate rose garden. It has since been converted to offices.

142. Foster-McCauley-Symes House

(1905, Frederick J. Sterner and George H. Williamson), 738 Pearl St.

This Georgian Revival variant has a rounded front porch and double-pitched central Palladian dormer. Alexis C. Foster of the Causey Foster Securities Company built this three-story dwelling later owned by Vance McCauley and then by U.S. district court judge J. Foster Symes. After use as the French Consulate, this residence was converted to private offices.

143. Wood-Morris-Bonfils House

(1909–1911, Maurice Biscoe and Henry H. Hewitt. 1987, renovation and expansion by Daniel J. Havekost), 707 Washington St., NW corner of E. 7th Ave. Pkwy., NR

A grand formal garden on East 7th Avenue was sacrificed for the 1987 addition of twenty-three condominiums, whose stucco walls, red tile roofs, balconies, and flattened arches echo the Mediterranean mode of the original dwelling. The distinctive two-story residence with balustraded terraces leading to the gardens was built for Gulliford Wood, who made a fortune in Cripple Creek gold mines. Subsequently, it became the home of *Denver Post* owner Helen Bonfils. She and

others have made substantial additions to what is now the Mexican Consulate.

144. Ferguson-Gano House

(1896, Theodore D. Boal and Frederick L. Harnois), 722 E. 7th Ave. Pkwy., SE corner of Washington St.

This two-story Mediterranean-style residence was built as the guest house for the estate of John A. Ferguson, whose even larger, now demolished mansion (also by Boal and Harnois) stood at 700 Washington Street. George W. Gano, a prominent businessman involved in the Gano-Downs Clothing Store, bought the guest house in 1909 and had Boal and Harnois remodel it.

145. Zang Mansion. (Photo by Sandra Dallas, courtesy Denver Public Library)

145. Zang Mansion

(1903, Frederick C. Eberley), 709 Clarkson St., NW corner of E. 7th Ave., NR

After outgrowing his townhouse at 1532 Emerson Street, Adolph J. Zang, the son of the founder of the Zang Brewery, built this $108,000 Neoclassical Revival show home. A monochromatic mansion, its sedate gray brick and gray stone trim seem to snub more ostentatious neighboring residences. The two-story, semicircular portico that announces the main entrance is supported by two massive Ionic columns. The front segmental-arched dormer in the hip roof gives access to a small terrace from the third-floor ballroom. Behind

146. Mitchell-Schomp House. (Photo by Thomas H. Simmons)

splendid oak doors, the fantastic interior features painted and gilded ceilings, five ornate fireplaces, a Tiffany chandelier, and twelve varieties of beautifully carved woodwork. Look for Adolph Zang's monogram in the front double doors, the leaded glass windows, and the upstairs stained glass window with a scene from Shakespeare's *The Merchant of Venice*. The house and matching carriage house have been converted into offices.

146. Mitchell-Schomp House

(1893. 1915, addition by George L. Bettcher. 1973, remodel by Daniel J. Havekost), 680 Clarkson St., SE corner of E. 7th Ave.

John C. Mitchell, president of Denver National Bank, built this two-and-a-half-story house known as "Trail's End" in an eclectic Mediterranean style. With a complementary 1915 wing by George L. Bettcher and landscaping by Jane Silverstein Ries, this large home retains its elegance. Various additions and disparate architectural elements have further contributed to its eclectic appearance. The Mitchells owned the house until 1945. Kay Schomp, who moved into the carriage house in 1949, subsequently acquired the main house. She explains, "We were sick about seeing so many Capitol Hill mansions destroyed. So we landmarked this one and had architect Daniel Havekost remodel it in 1973 with apartments to get full use out of its 13,000 square feet."

147. Brown-Garrey-Congdon House

(1921, J.J.B. Benedict. 1987, restoration by Edward D. White, Jr.), 1300 E. 7th Ave. Pkwy., SE corner of Marion St.

This narrow, one-hundred-foot-long chateau-style townhouse is one of the finest of many splendid homes in the East Seventh Avenue Historic District. A steep, tiled roof with roundel dormers caps the two-story stuccoed masonry walls above a brick base. Brick trim accentuates tall, narrow window bays. A two-story semicircular conservatory bay overlooks the walled backyard garden.

Carroll T. Brown sold his house to mining heiress Anne Reynolds Garrey and her husband George H. Garrey. Another legendary mining man, Tom Congdon, and his wife, Noel, later acquired this long, narrow landmark and found that "Living in a house that's only eighteen feet wide is a bit like living on a bus. We love it!"

148. Jane Silverstein Ries, a leading landscape architect, has surrounded her landmark house at 737 Franklin Street with unusual and profuse plantings. (Tom Noel Collection)

148. Jane Silverstein Ries House

(1935, Henry Eggers and Stanley Morse), 737 Franklin St.

Jane Silverstein Ries, a prominent Colorado landscape architect since the 1930s, transformed this house with her all-encompassing garden. Her campaign to replace lawns and "useless" banks with terraces and walled gardens is reflected in much residential landscaping in the area, as well as in her own home.

149. Kerr House

(1925, J.J.B. Benedict), 1900 E. 7th Ave. Pkwy., SE corner of High St.

John G. Kerr, who once owned the travertine quarry at Wellsville near Salida, used its cream-colored stone to trim this red brick Georgian. A carved travertine entry leads to an interior with travertine floors. Kerr also owned a rhyolite quarry in Kerr Gulch near Howard in Fremont County that produced the extraordinary stone used to build another Denver landmark, the First Church of Christ Scientist, of which Kerr was a member.

Standart–Cleworth House

(1925, Merrill H. Hoyt and Burnham Hoyt), 2025 E. 7th Ave. Pkwy., NW corner of Vine St.

This beautifully proportioned Italian Renaissance Revival residence displays that style's low hipped tile roof, symmetrical front facade, and upper-story windows accented by small classical columns. The Hoyt brothers, in lengthy specifications for the brick home of insurance man Frederick W. Standart, required that the stucco have "one bushel of cattle hair per 100 square yards of plastering." They specified Bedford, Indiana, limestone for the entry surround and window trim. Inside, round archways connect well-proportioned, generally symmetrical rooms adorned with painted glass and wrought-iron fixtures. Charles and Sheila Cleworth, owner-occupants since 1975, have maintained both the exterior and interior in near-original condition. "Thanks to the Hoyts' careful specs," noted Charles, a publisher and historic preservationist, "we've never even needed to repair or paint the stucco because it has all that hairy reinforcement!"

COUNTRY CLUB

HD-13 COUNTRY CLUB HISTORIC DISTRICT (see Map 4, page 40)

E. 1st to E. 4th Aves. between Downing St. and University Blvd.

This residential district contains some of Denver's grandest homes by leading early twentieth-century

HD-13 Country Club, 4th Avenue gates of the Denver Country Club neighborhood. (Photo by Tom Noel)

architects. William and Arthur Fisher collaborated with Frederick Law Olmsted, Jr., to design Country Club Place (1909), which stretches from Franklin to Race Streets between East 1st and East 4th Avenues. This subdivision has extra-long blocks with landscaped medians. For the entry gateways on East 4th Avenue, Fisher used stucco and red barrel tile suggestive of Spain. The Fishers maintained that the Spanish Colonial Revival style was most appropriate for Denver, with its dry, sunny climate. Subsequent subdivisions are Park Club Place (1905), from Franklin to Downing Streets between East 4th and East 1st Avenues, and the Circle Drive area (1930s) between East 4th and East 6th Avenues from University Boulevard to Race Street.

Burnham and Merrill Hoyt's versatility is evident in their impressive Tudor-style **Donald Bromfield House** (1927), 100 Gaylord Street, and the Châteauesque **Charles S. Thomas II Mansion** (1926), 380 Gilpin St., as well as Burnham's fine International-style **Maer House** (1940), 545 Circle Drive. J.J.B. Benedict

designed various Beaux-Arts-influenced, revival-style houses, including the **Arthur House** (1932), 355 Gilpin Street; **Ellis House** (1912), 1700 East 3rd Avenue; the **Huff House** (1912), 120 Humboldt Street; and the **McFarland House** (1927), 476 Westwood Drive. Temple H. Buell designed the Châteauesque **Bard House** (1929) at 100 Vine Street. Many Country Club residences are architect designs, including modern homes by and for architects such as Paul Atchison at 160 Humboldt Street (1956), James Sudler at 180 High Street (1976), and Robert Fuller at 2244 East 4th Avenue, southwest corner of University Boulevard (1977).

Reed Mansion

(1931, Harry James Manning), 475 Circle Dr.

Colorado's grandest Tudor Revival mansion is a towering composition of steep-pitched slate roofs, four immense ornate chimneys with multiple clay pots, and numerous dormers and gables. The glazed tapestry brick walls with limestone trim and half-timbered gable ends soar above two-and-a-half acres of walled gardens, with a separate garden house designed by Saco R. DeBoer. A greenhouse, terrace, fountain, swimming pool, and interior elevator were added in 1955–1956. Mary Reed commissioned the house shortly after the death of her husband, Verner Z. Reed, who made fortunes in both Cripple Creek gold and Salt Creek, Wyoming, oil. The high-style Tudor Revival design helped popularize vernacular Tudor Revival. Marketed as "English bungalow," this mode became one of the most popular local styles of the 1930s. Other large Tudor types by Manning are the nearby dwellings at 150, 160, and 210 Vine Street.

Bridaham House

(1905, Frederick J. Sterner and George H. Williamson), 350 Humboldt St.

Greek Revival went out of style by the 1860s but continued to be used on retardaire banks, churches, and post offices. This rare Colorado residential example of "Greek survival" sits on three lots behind an iron fence with brick piers topped by concrete cannonball finials. Behind an entry court balustrade, the two-story portico is supported by six large Tuscan columns and has triglyphs on the frieze.

Biscoe House

(1908, Maurice Biscoe), 320 Humboldt St.

Maurice Biscoe, a Beaux-Arts-trained architect, came to Denver to represent the New York firm of Gordon, Tracy, and Swarthwout in the construction of St. John's Episcopal Cathedral. He stayed in the Mile High City to design fine residences, including his own, a two-story, L-plan house in Mediterranean Revival style with modest but pleasing detail. Biscoe also designed the **Sinsheimer House** (1917), 190 High Street, an Italian Renaissance Revival villa. Biscoe later joined the Boston firm of Andrews, Rantoul & Jones, where he eventually became a partner.

Speer House

(1912, Willis A. Marean and Albert J. Norton), 300 Humboldt St.

Mayor Robert W. Speer was involved in developing the Country Club area, along with Frederick Ross and others. He lived in this expanded Foursquare with curvilinear pediments announcing entries on both Humboldt Street and East 3rd Avenue. Kate Speer, the mayor's widow, lived here until her death in 1954.

William E. Fisher House

(1910, William E. Fisher), 110 Franklin St.

Architect William Fisher designed his own house in the Spanish style, which he and his brother, Arthur, considered appropriate for Denver's climate. The two-story Spanish Colonial Revival abode, with stucco walls and a red tile roof, is oriented toward the south-side garden with a pillared and pilastered entry. The Fishers ran Denver's most prolific architectural firm from 1905 until William committed suicide in 1937 in this house. The Fisher firm planned the large blocks, wide medians, and tree lawns in the part of the Country Club neighborhood where many other Fisher designs were built, including Arthur Fisher's own 1909 residence at 128 Gilpin Street.

150. Harman Town Hall/Greenleaf Masonic Temple. (Photo by Tom Noel)

150. Harman Town Hall/Greenleaf Masonic Temple

(1891, Franklin E. Kidder and Ida I. Humphreys), 400 St. Paul St., NE corner of E. 4th Ave.

Edwin Preston Harman and his wife, Louisa, purchased a 360-acre tract in 1871 between University and Colorado Boulevards and East Sixth Avenue and Cherry Creek. As Denver boomed during the 1880s, the Harmans incorporated their farm as the town of Harman in

1886. Their little country town erected this town hall to oversee its municipal police force, fire department, dog-catcher, and school. After Harman was annexed to Denver in 1895, this building became a Denver police and fire station. In 1934, the Lawrence N. Greenleaf Masonic Lodge purchased the two-story brick building for its neighborhood temple. Bulges created by the stone banding and trim can be seen under the later stuccoing. Round-arch second-story windows and a bracketed cornice remain, although the first-story elongated Italianate windows have been remodeled.

CHAPTER 3
Northeast Denver Area

CURTIS PARK
CLEMENTS ADDITION
LAFAYETTE STREET
EAST PARK PLACE

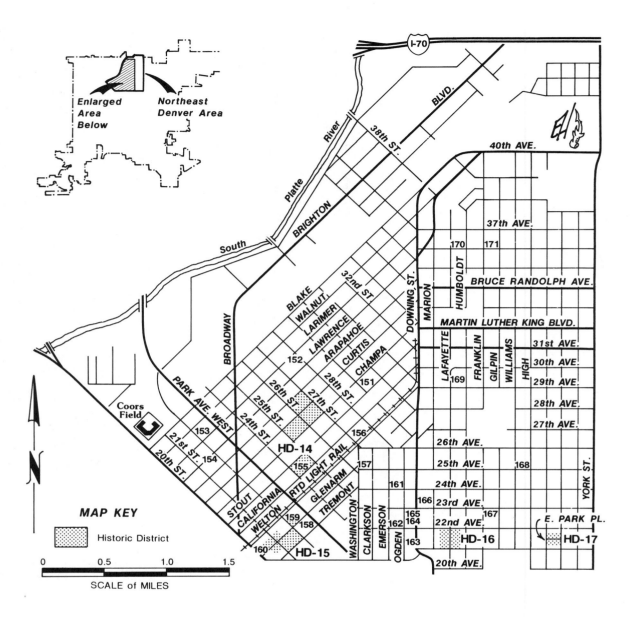

7. Northeast Denver Area

CURTIS PARK

HD–14 CURTIS PARK HISTORIC DISTRICT

(1868), roughly 24th St. to Downing St. between California and Arapahoe Sts., NRD

Within the much larger National Register Historic District, four blocks between 27th and 24th Streets and California and Arapahoe Streets constitute the smaller Curtis Park Denver landmark district. The neighborhood is named for Denver's first municipal park, Curtis Park (1868), located at 30th to 32nd Streets between Arapahoe and Champa Streets. This park, renamed Mestizo-Curtis Park in 1990, was a donation from real estate developer Samuel S. Curtis. As Denver's first streetcar suburb, Curtis Park blossomed after the 1871 completion of the horsecar line from downtown along Champa. Streetcars offered fast and cheap connections to downtown jobs, shopping, and amusements, coaxing Denverites out to what was then suburbia.

Initially a haven for those with the means to afford the suburbs, Curtis Park evolved into a core city working-class neighborhood during the early 1900s, then attracted minorities by the 1920s. This neighborhood has been Denver's melting pot, where African, Anglo, Asian, German, Irish, Jewish, Japanese, Mexican, and Scandinavian Americans have all established homes and businesses.

The **David Crowell House** (1873; 1977, restoration by Brian Congleton), 2816 Curtis, is a small frame cottage and perhaps the oldest structure in the area. Other clapboard dwellings may be found at 2915 Curtis and 2826 and 2828 Stout Streets. At 2445 California Street is one of Denver's rare Second Empire designs, with a mansard roof and hooded and pedimented dormers. Typical of the larger Italianate homes is that of department store founder John Jay Joslin (1880), 2915 Champa Street. A more typical Italianate house belonging to Dr. Justina Ford, a prominent black physician, was moved to 3091 California Street and restored as the Black American West Museum. Since the 1970s, this Victorian neighborhood has been rejuvenated. The Curtis Park face-block project rehabilitated forty-one houses in the district, winning a national AIA Honor Award for Historic Denver, Inc., and preservation architects Gary Long and Kathy Hoeft. The project rescued two nineteenth-century brick workers' cottages by moving them to 28th and Curtis Streets, renovating the interiors, and selling them to low-income buyers. Determined neighborhood residents and the preservationists have even restored the sandstone sidewalks and tree lawns in this unusually intact and livable neighborhood within the shadows of downtown skyscrapers.

151. Anfenger House. (Photo by Roger Whitacre)

151. Anfenger House

(1884), 2900 Champa St.

Louis Anfenger, a Bavarian-born Jewish pioneer, became a state representative and a founder of National Jewish Hospital and Temple Emanuel Synagogue. He built this large house, where he raised eight children. Louis's son Milton was a state senator and prominent attorney who helped establish Denver's early professional baseball club, the Denver Bears. Louis's grandchildren include historian Marjorie Hornbein. The Anfenger House has a low hipped roof with wide eaves, a two-story bay, and long narrow windows with lintels, making it a good example of the Italianate style that prevails in Curtis Park. After condemnation and a narrow escape from the wrecking ball, the house was restored both outside and inside, where there are seven fireplaces and a large third-floor attic. Since the 1980s this has been the home of Dana Crawford, grand dame of Colorado preservationists.

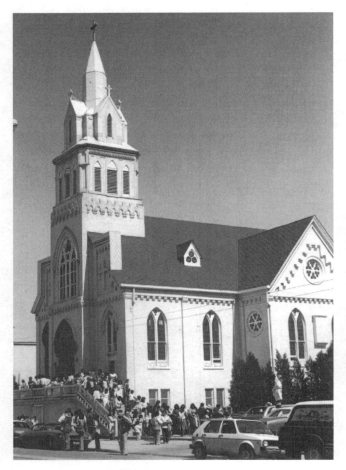

152. Sacred Heart Catholic Church. (Photo by Tom Noel)

152. Sacred Heart Catholic Church

(1880, Emmett Anthony), 2760 Larimer St., NR

Anthony used Carpenter Gothic woodwork to enhance the brick exterior of a traditional cruciform church whose tall steeple is centered above the Larimer Street entrance. A poor immigrant congregation of Irish and Italians used wood trim instead of stone, even on the windows. The octagonal masonry tower has been replaced by a diminutive wooden steeple.

Carlota Espinosa painted the large ceiling mural, which hides the scar where a skylight collapsed. By such creative solutions, a congregation that is now largely Hispanic has kept Sacred Heart alive as the oldest ecclesiastical edifice in Denver used regularly for religious services.

Father Edward Barry, S.J., the third pastor of Sacred Heart Church, was an amateur architect who allegedly designed **Sacred Heart School** (1890), 2840

Lawrence Street. This two-story brick school has large well-lighted classrooms clustered around a two-story auditorium. A brick parapet hides the flat roof. Round transoms atop the windows echo the round-arch entry under a round niche for a statue of the Sacred Heart of Jesus. The high school closed in 1939, although the elementary school remained open until 1978. The similarly styled convent next door at 2844 Lawrence Street is now a shelter for homeless families and single women.

153. Burlington Hotel. (Photo by Tom Noel)

153. Burlington Hotel

(1890, Frank E. Edbrooke), 2201 Larimer St., corner of 22nd St.

By the 1960s, this three-story red brick Romanesque Revival hotel had become Denver's deadliest skid-row flophouse, where men were killed for spare change and the last drops of cheap booze. A narrow U-shaped design gives this hotel a central light well. Developer Rick Borman pursued landmark designation in 1994 as the first step in a proposed rehabilitation of this long-neglected but still salvagable mainstay of upper Larimer Street.

154. Savage Candy Company

(1910, Wilmott & Stoddard?), 2158–2162 Lawrence Street, SE corner of 22nd St.

The Nathan W. Savage Candy Company, founded in Pueblo in 1888, built this Denver factory where some sixty-five employees made a complete line of candy ranging from children's penny treats to chocolate extravaganzas. The typical two-story red brick commercial building with storefronts is distinguished by fancy brickwork, including a corbeled brick parapet and an angled corner beneath a roofline pediment. The building was rehabilitated in 1995 for use by the Phoenix Concept, an institution "dedicated to the resurrection and renewal of lives gone shabby and dissolute."

155. Lydon House. (Photo by Roger Whitacre)

155. Lydon House

(1891, John J. Huddart), 2418 Stout St.

Cole Lydon was a conductor for the Denver & Rio Grande Railroad. Like many other Curtis Park pioneers, he moved to Capitol Hill when it became the more fashionable neighborhood. Lydon's house was purchased in the early 1990s by William A. West, a University of Colorado at Denver professor of Victorian literature. West's interest in all things Victorian led him to Curtis Park and its huge inventory of nineteenth-century homes. He wrote a book on the area, *Curtis Park* (1980), and became the "father" of the Curtis Park Historic District, where his other restorations include the Italianate cottage and gardens at 2826 Curtis Street.

John Huddart, a prolific nineteenth-century Denver architect, was trained in England as an engineer. He designed the Lydon residence in his typically eclectic style. Stepped Dutch side parapets and steep shingled gables, a second-floor oriel window, and a third-story dormer give this narrow house a picturesque verticality further enhanced by the finials. Red pressed brick, carved and smooth stone trim, fish-scale shingles, and floral bas-relief in the gables and oriel window are among the notable details. Another picturesque Huddart composition is nearby, the **Kinneavy Terrace** (1889), 2700–2714 Stout Street.

156. Douglass Undertaking Parlor. (Photo by Tom Noel)

156. Douglass Undertaking Parlor

(c.1891. 1916, remodel by Merrill H. Hoyt and Burnham Hoyt), 2745 Welton St.

Neoclassicism was more than an elitist style for grand public buildings. Here, it shines in an old cottage that the Hoyt brothers converted to a classy storefront with a pedimented and pilastered facade. The urn recessed in the tympanum was the logo of a black businessman whose undertaking parlor was bought in 1957 and converted to a livelier use — a billiard hall. From across the street you can see that this business, like most of its neighbors, is a storefront added to an old house.

157. Fire Station No. 3

(1931, C. Francis Pillsbury), 2500 Washington St.

Reflecting a trend that attempted to blend fire station design with the surrounding residential architecture, this corner building has Spanish Revival elements

157. Fire Station No. 3. (Photo by Tom Noel)

in variegated brick with terra-cotta trim. Fire Station No. 3 was Denver's all-black station from its dedication in 1931 until desegregation of the fire department in 1958.

158. Ebert Elementary School

(1924, Frederick E. Mountjoy and Frank W. Frewan), 410 Park Ave. at Tremont Pl.

This two-story Renaissance Revival building of light yellow brick is enlivened by concrete moldings with lion heads, human heads, garlands, and a floral frieze. Congenial additions have not detracted from this unusually elegant, symmetrical school named for Frederick J. Ebert, a pioneer mining engineer, forester, rancher, surveyor, and state senator. In the library, polychromatic terra-cotta tiles around the fireplace depict fairy-tale characters.

CLEMENTS ADDITION

HD-15 CLEMENTS ADDITION HISTORIC DISTRICT, NRD (see Map 7, page 82)

From roughly 20th to 22nd Streets between Tremont and Glenarm Places, this DLPC district contains a Ralph Adams Cram church amid restored houses and row houses of the 1880s. Vulnerably sited on the fringe of the Central Business District, this is one of Denver's oldest intact residential remnants. **Kingston Row** (1890, Arthur S. Miller), 401–415 21st Street, corner of

Tremont Place (NR), is an ornate three-story red brick terrace with a Queen Anne front and simpler "Mary Jane" rear. At either end of the six row houses are units incorporating round towers topped with slate roofs and finials. Fussy facade fenestration includes round-arched windows, diamond-paned dormers, and curved glass in the tower windows.

159. Clements Row House

(1884), 2201–2217 Glenarm Pl., NR

In Denver, a wide-open western town with plenty of room to grow, multifamily attached housing is rarer than in most cities. Even in the poorest neighborhoods, single-family detached houses are the norm. An exception is this splendid two-story brick Italianate row house with two-story bays, Eastlake incised stone window trim, and an elegantly bracketed and mansarded cornice.

Thomas House

(1883, William Quayle), 2104 Glenarm Pl., NR

This house was built by William Quayle for Hugh H. Thomas, who, with partner George A. Gano, owned the Gano & Thomas Furniture Store. The house was treated to a 1975 restoration by owner-occupants Kay and Bill James, who highlighted Quayle's fine detail work, from the elaborate brick chimneys to the sandstone belt coursing, from the wooden columns of the three porches to the carved stone lintels of windows grouped in twos or threes. The first-floor rooms boast Eastlake woodwork and thirteen-foot-high ceilings.

Quayle, who opened a Denver office in 1880, later worked with brothers Charles and Edward. In 1900, Quayle moved to San Diego, where his work became more prominent. Like many other Quayle houses and schoolhouses, this home reflects his eclectic combination of stylistic elements.

160. St. Andrews Episcopal Church

(1908, Ralph Adams Cram), 2015 Glenarm Pl., NR

Ralph Adams Cram, a high-church Anglican and devotee of John Ruskin, was a leading exponent of the

HD-15 Clements Addition homes. (Photo by Roger Whitacre)

Gothic Revival. This nationally prominent Yankee architect, whose initial partner was Bertram G. Goodhue, designed this small Gothic Revival church on an L plan, using a skin of dark red Harvard brick with limestone trim and a slate roof. The interior, dominated by tall brick Gothic arches, has a timbered ceiling and diamond-paned windows with leaded amber glass and wooden Gothic tracery. The only Colorado work of Cram, it resembles his much larger St. George's Chapel in Newport, Rhode Island. Works of art inside include an Edwardian reredos by Albert Bryan Olson and a Byzantine Revival statue of the Virgin by Margaret

159. Clements Row House. (Photo by Tom Noel)

160. St. Andrews Episcopal Church. (Photo by Thomas H. Simmons)

Buchanan. J.J.B. Benedict designed the 1928 parish house next door at 2013 Glenarm Place.

161. Zion Baptist Church

(1893, Frank H. Jackson and George F. Rivinius), 933 E. 24th Ave., NW corner of Ogden St.

Colorado's first black congregation, Zion Baptist, was established by former slaves in 1865. In 1911, that flock bought this edifice, originally built as Calvary Baptist Church. Reverend Wendell T. Liggins, pastor from 1941 until his death in 1991, was a famed orator and civic activist who made this a popular and influential church. A rusticated rhyolite structure trimmed in the same gray stone, this church exemplifies the Richardsonian Romanesque style. Inside, distinctive stained glass windows brighten an interior dominated by dark ceiling beams and woodwork.

161. Zion Baptist Church thrived under Reverend Wendell T. Liggins, shown here cutting an anniversary cake for Colorado's first black congregation. (Photo by Burnis McCloud, courtesy Denver Public Library)

162. Scott Methodist Church/Sanctuary Lofts. (Photo by Tom Noel)

162. Scott Methodist Church/Sanctuary Lofts

(1892, Franklin E. Kidder. 1995, renovation by Norman Cable), 2201 Ogden St., NR

Built as Christ Methodist Episcopal Church, this structure was renamed for a pioneer black Methodist bishop, Isaiah B. Scott, after an African American con-gregation bought the church in 1927. Gothic arches prevail on a structure whose bulky massing and rusti-cated stone skin are otherwise more Romanesque. Gray rhyolite walls are trimmed in red sandstone on an elabo-rate exterior where the pressed metal crockets and finials have been painted red to match the sandstone. The sim-pler interior sanctuary has little ornament other than the colored glass windows in floral and geometric pat-terns and the cast-iron support columns. The 190-foot-tall wooden steeple, the tallest in town when erected, was removed from the stone corner bell tower after 1976 wind damage. In 1995 this landmark church, whose congregation built a new church at 2880 Garfield Street, was rehabilitated as the Sanctuary Lofts.

163. Thomas Hornsby Ferril House

(1889, Franklin Goodnow), 2123 Downing St., NR

Thomas Hornsby Ferril, Colorado's poet laureate, lived here from 1900 until his death in 1988. His great-aunt, Mrs. John Palmer, built this typically eclectic red brick Victorian house with geometric Eastlake trim.

163. Thomas Hornsby Ferril House. (Photo by Thomas H. Simmons)

Ferril's poetry, however, is far from typical in capturing Colorado's past, with its fragile communities and vanishing landmarks, as these lines from "House in Denver" demonstrate:

> In the morning I could stand
> A long time watching my father disappear
> Beyond the sunflowers which you noticed farther
> In the morning. Now tall buildings interfere
> In piles of shining masonry, but are there
> Walls yet to come no more secure than these?
> My city has not worn its shadows long
> Enough to quiet even prairie bees.

164. McBird House

(1880, Matthew John McBird? 1994, renovation by Christopher Craven and Charles and Kathleen Brantigan), 2225 Downing St.

This Victorian house with a distinctive three-story mansard tower was moved to this site in 1993 from 2023

Lafayette Street to accommodate expansion of the hospital district. Architect Matthew John McBird presumably designed this house, where he lived from 1880 until his death in 1903. Later owners Charles and Kathleen Brantigan renovated the brick abode to revive Second Empire elements such as the keystone-arch double windows and pedimented dormer windows of what is now a medical office.

165. Gebhard-Smith-Brantigan House

(1884, Henry Gebhard?), 2253 Downing St., SW corner of E. 23rd Ave., NR

This Italianate domicile with a two-story bay and decorative brick chimneys was restored in the 1980s by Dr. Charles Brantigan for his medical offices. The porch has ornate columns and bracketed eaves. Other larger brackets along the eaves of the truncated hip roof divide the facades into window bays, with different lintel treatments on each story. Incised geometric patterns distinguish both the ornate wooden trim and stone lintels. This is one of many historic structures in the San Rafael National Register Historic District, which extends from East 20th to East 26th Avenues between Clarkson and Downing Streets.

166. Holmes House

(1893, James Murdoch), 2330 Downing St.

Dr. Clarence F. Holmes, Denver's most prominent African American dentist, was a spokesperson for his people and spearheaded formation of a Denver chapter of the National Association for the Advancement of Colored People (NAACP). Holmes and his family lived here from 1943 to 1970. This boxy eclectic Victorian anticipates the flatter-roofed Foursquare style.

LAFAYETTE STREET

HD-16 LAFAYETTE STREET HISTORIC DISTRICT (see Map 7, page 82)

Lafayette St. between E. 21st and E. 22nd Aves.

The 2100 block of Lafayette Street includes residential offerings from the Baerresen Brothers, Henry

Dozier, and William Lang. The **Foster-Brantigan House** at 2105 Lafayette (1890), a William Lang design, is a two-and-a-half-story Queen Anne with vergeboard and shingle trim, highlighted in a 1980s restoration by Kathy and Charles Brantigan. The house once again sparkles, with the rejuvenation of its curved, leaded, and stained glass windows, the original tile on all three fireplaces, cast-brass doorknobs, anaglypta wall coverings, and picture moldings. Henry Dozier planned the 1890 Queen Annes at 2115 and 2123 Lafayette Street. The Baerresen Brothers designed the **John Crook House** (1891), 2150 Lafayette, a Queen Anne structure with third-story pedimented and eyebrow dormers. More modest one-story brick Queen Anne cottages at 2122 and 2126–2128 Lafayette add diversity to this block, whose district designation became the first firm boundary between an antique residential neighborhood and the ever-expanding hospital district.

167. Walters-Brierly House

(1888), 2259 Gilpin St., SW corner of E. 23rd Ave.

John Walters, a sheepman who founded the Standard Meat Company, built this two-and-a-half-story house with matching carriage house. His family lived here until the 1940s. The windows with hooded lintels, the Eastlake-style front porch framing, and the symmetrical composition suggest the Italianate style. The steep-pitched roof, however, is more Queen Anne in flavor and may be a later addition.

168. Miller House. (Photo by Tom Noel)

168. Miller House

(1902), 2501 High St.

Byron L. Miller, a businessman and realtor who became a building inspector, built this house and lived here for at least three decades. Paired round arch windows recessed in rusticated rhyolite walls distinguish this eclectic-style house. The stonework is notable, especially on the entry porch with its paired polished stone columns atop the stone porch wall.

EAST PARK PLACE

HD-17 EAST PARK PLACE HISTORIC DISTRICT (see Map 7, page 82)

E. Park Pl. between Vine and Race Sts. and E. 21st and E. 22nd Aves.

The 2000 block of East Park Place contains eight single-family homes, of which seven are foursquares. Four of these classic foursquares were designed by Denver architect and developer Frank S. Snell. Here at East Park Place, as in the Snell Addition Historic District, Snell experimented with smaller yards and denser housing patterns. Snell hoped to build sixteen homes in this block but went out of business in 1907. The block is notable for its ethnic diversity, with a Chinese family arriving in 1949 and black families since 1952.

169. Cody House

(1892, Arthur Hughes, bldr.), 2932 Lafayette St.

William F. "Buffalo Bill" Cody, the most famous Coloradan of all, died here in his sister's house on January 10, 1917. Cody had an illustrious career as a Pony Express rider, army scout, Indian fighter, and buffalo-meat supplier for railroad construction teams. Buffalo Bill became even better known for his Wild West Show, which toured the United States and Europe, delighting millions with re-enactments of western adventures. This two-story red brick Queen Anne with a two-story front porch is a less impressive tribute than the Buffalo Bill Grave and Museum atop Lookout Mountain in a Denver mountain park.

170. Annunciation Catholic Church. (Photo by James Baca)

171. Wyatt School. (Photo by Roger Whitacre)

170. Annunciation Catholic Church

(1907, Frederick W. Paroth), 3601 Humboldt St., NW corner of E. 36th Ave., NR

This Romanesque Revival cornerstone of the Cole neighborhood is the heart of a parish compound that includes a school, convent, and rectory. Since 1970, the Capuchins (the Franciscan Order of Friars Minor) have staffed this parish. They worked with parish volunteers to give the church a facelift, acquired the corner grocery at 38th Avenue and Humboldt Street as a parish center, and replaced the old school with low-income apartments. A projected massive steeple atop the corner bell tower never materialized, but this red brick church with its glorious rose window over a triple-arched entry is still an inspiring sight. Inside, Annunciation is wonderfully old-fashioned, with stained glass windows from the Franz Mayer Company of Munich and a twenty-foot-high Carrara marble high altar guarded by six-foot-tall angels. The nave is adorned with golden oak pews and scagliola columns that burst into florid capitals supporting ornate arches that carry the ribs of the high vaulted ceiling.

171. Wyatt School

(1887, Robert S. Roeschlaub), 3620 Franklin St. between E. 36th and E. 37th Aves.

The Hyde Park Elementary School was renamed for George W. Wyatt, a longtime principal, after his death in 1932. This three-story Richardsonian Romanesque edifice is more playful and less symmetrical than most Roeschlaub schools. The steep-pitched, billowing roof and the bell-cast corner entry tower framed by an eccentric tall chimney and round tower distinguish this red brick school with generous red sandstone and red terra-cotta trim. Closed in 1982, it awaits new use.

CHAPTER 4
Northwest Denver Area

OLD HIGHLAND (15TH STREET)
STONEMEN'S ROW (WEST 28TH AVENUE)
POTTER HIGHLANDS
WITTER-COFIELD

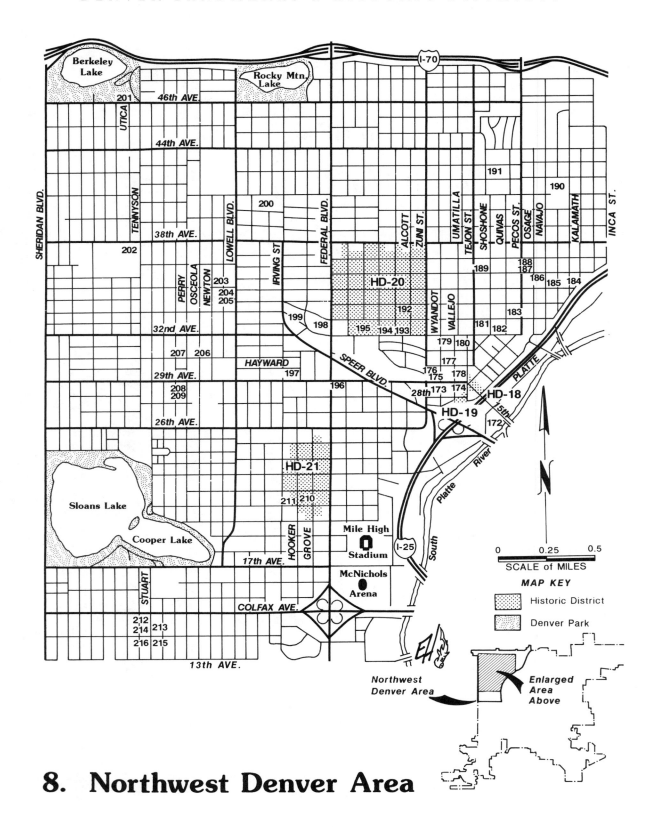

8. Northwest Denver Area

172. Denver Tramway Company Powerhouse/Forney Transportation Museum. (Photo by Glenn Cuerden)

Northwest Denver traces its origins to December 14, 1858, when Denver founder William H. Larimer, Jr., waded across the South Platte River to stake out "Highland" on the bluff northwest of the newborn town. Separated from the rest of the city by the South Platte River and, after 1870, by railroad tracks, Northwest Denver did not flourish until the 1880s.

The initial wave of English, Scottish, and Irish settlers began after General William J. Palmer and Dr. William A. Bell of the Denver & Rio Grande Railroad platted the Highland Park Addition in 1875. Curving streets with Scottish names still characterize this National Register Historic District also known as Scottish Village. Between the 1890s and 1920s, North Den-

ver experienced a high tide of Italian immigrants. They turned part of the area into Little Italy, but Hispanos became the most numerous new ethnic group after 1940. The ethnic peoples of Northwest Denver have given it a colorful collection of churches, cafes, commercial blocks, and dwellings. Here one still gets a feel for nineteenth-century neighborhoods, with their corner stores, churches, schools, and other essentials within walking distance.

Spared the intense development of Lower Downtown, the Central Business District, and Capitol Hill, Northwest Denver retains many original structures. Church spires, not high-rise apartments and office towers, still crown the skyline.

95

172. Denver Tramway Company Powerhouse/ Forney Transportation Museum

(1901, Stearns Rogers Co.), 1416 Platte St.

This Neoclassical temple of technology bordering Confluence Park has red brick walls with roundel windows and corbeled arches. This coal-fed power plant generated electricity to move Denver's trolleys. Converted to a transportation museum by J. Donovan Forney in 1968, it now houses automobiles, trucks, buses, railway rolling stock, and streetcars. This building survived the 1965 South Platte River flood, whose devastation inspired a cleanup of the Platte and the 1976 opening of Confluence Park at the junction of the South Platte River and Cherry Creek. This park and the greenway of trails leading to it have sparked a renaissance in the area surrounding the power plant.

OLD HIGHLAND (15TH STREET)

HD-18 OLD HIGHLAND HISTORIC BUSINESS DISTRICT (see Map 8, page 94)

15th St. between Central and Boulder Sts.

Fires and demolitions have erased much of the original north Denver commercial district that arose along the first streetcar line to cross the river and the railroad tracks. These brick and stone relics represent sturdy nineteenth-century neighborhood commercial complexes. Robert A. Wilson, a civil engineer, helped design the now gone **Marquis Block** (1889), 2501–2509 15th Street, and the **Slockett Block** (1890), 2535 15th Street.

STONEMEN'S ROW (WEST 28TH AVENUE)

HD-19 STONEMEN'S ROW HISTORIC DISTRICT (see Map 8, page 94)

(1891–1893), W. 28th Ave. between Vallejo and Umatilla Sts., NRD

Stonemasons who prospered in Denver's 1880s building boom erected the nine structures in this district for their own families. They were designed by several

architects. Balcomb and Rice created 2753–2755 Umatilla and 2112–2114, 2118–2120, and 2140 West 28th Avenue; Baerresen Brothers designed 2122 West 28th Avenue; and J. H. Barnes planned 2128 West 28th Avenue. These flat-roofed dwellings share a repetition of Richardsonian elements, such as triangular roof pediments, yet have enough variety of texture and materials to avoid monotony. Smooth and rusticated sandstone and rhyolite, combined with the weight of Romanesque Revival elements, make these small brick units seem larger. They overlook the Platte Valley from a bluff offering a grand vista of downtown.

173. Horan House. (Tom Noel Collection)

173. Horan House

(1892, Soloman A. Layton and Frank P. Fryburger, bldrs.?), 2839 Wyandot St.

William P. Horan, a native of Greenfield, Massachusetts, who came to Denver in 1887, resided here with his wife, Elizabeth, and children from 1896 to 1908. The Horans bought the house from the original occupants, the Corine family. Horan, a graduate of the Egyptian School of Embalming, opened a mortuary in

1890 in downtown Denver. He climbed to the top of the trade with state-of-the-art funeral practices such as motorized hearses, which he introduced to Denver in 1912. Horan served for many years as Denver city coroner and presided over the Colorado State Funeral Directors Association and the Colorado chapter of the National Council of Catholic Men. Some charged that Horan, a devout Democrat, helped maintain the list of "dead names" that the political machine of Mayor Robert W. Speer relied on in close elections. Horan supposedly replied, "These people were good Democrats. Why should they be denied the vote just because they're underground?"

After Horan's death in 1930, his children continued to run what became W. P. Horan and Sons, which survives to this day as the Horan & McConaty Funeral Service. The Horan House, a survivor of a block of similar 1890s residences, commemorates one of Denver's best-known Irish Catholic businessmen.

Rectangular-cut, quarry-faced ashlar red sandstone and an ornate tin parapet front the two-story red brick townhouse. It retains some of the original interior woodwork, including the oak staircase.

174. Wheeler Block. (Photo by Thomas H. Simmons)

Wheeler Block

(1894, Louis M. Wood), 2114–2152 W. 29th Ave., SE corner of Vallejo St.

This large five-story corner commercial block has a grand parapet and sunburst nameplate in the pediment. The sandstone-trimmed brick edifice has distinctive arches below the elaborate pressed metal frieze, parapet, and central pediment. Charles A. Wheeler, who lived

nearby at West 28th Avenue and Wyandot Street, was an accountant and railroad official. He built this as a home for societies such as the Daughters of America and the Knights of Pythias. After a 1902 foreclosure, the Wheeler Block became the Mountain View Apartments and ninety years later was restored as offices.

175. Tallmadge & Boyer Terrace

(1889), 2925–2947 Wyandot St.

Realtors Charles E. Tallmadge and John C. Boyer built the two-story 1889 terraces in the Queen Anne style with wavy walls of red brick and Eastlake spoolwork on the gabled porch entries. They are set back from the attached corner store and have their own residence lawns. In 1996, the eight terrace units were renovated for residential use.

Tallmadge and Boyer also commissioned the **Tallmadge & Boyer Block** (1891, Wenzel Janisch and Edwin Miller) at 2926–2942 Zuni Street (NR). Elaborate red brick and red sandstone characterize this commercial block. Rising three stories to a triple-bracketed cornice and wide frieze, the block has both arched and parapeted corbeling over the top-floor windows. Among many other businesses, the block housed a neighborhood newspaper, *The Highlands Chieftain*.

176. Romeo Block

(1889, Baerresen Brothers. 1995, restoration by David Fox and Larry Arbuthnot), 2944–2958 Zuni St., SE corner of W. 30th Ave., NR

A corner oriel bay window crowned with a flattened dome dramatizes this two-story red brick stone-trimmed commercial structure, as do second-story bay windows, recessed first-floor entry bays, and handsome transoms. The Romeo Block was named for liquor dealer Louis M. Weiner's son, Romeo S. Weiner, who built it with his partner, Sam Barets. Barets brought in Denver's largest shipment of whiskey — nine thousand gallons of "Quaker City" rye whiskey — in 1899. This corner commercial block was elegantly restored as a fourteen-unit apartment and retail complex in 1995 by developers David Fox and Larry Arbuthnot. Their $1 million project removed a stucco facade, replaced a rear wall, and repaired or replaced brick, stone, and tinwork to resurrect an unusually fine edifice.

176. Romeo Block. (Photo by Thomas H. Simmons)

177. Asbury Methodist Church

(1890, Franklin E. Kidder and John J. Humphreys), 2215 W. 30th Ave., NW corner of Vallejo St.

On a prominent hillside visible from downtown, this $75,000 edifice of rusticated gray rhyolite was named for Bishop Francis Asbury. The church is reminiscent of Henry H. Richardson's Trinity Church (1879) in Boston with its arched entry at the base of a square corner bell tower with four turrets, now amputated. The tower's narrow, arched openings are divided by stone pilasters grouped at the corners. Round-arched, tripartite window bays center the street elevations. Horizontal red stone bands and arches contrast well with the gray sandstone and visually hold the large expanses together. Inside, the renovated pipe organ (1875) is said to be the oldest in continual use in Colorado. Reflecting the ethnic evolution of North Denver, the original Scotch-Irish flock has been replaced most recently by a Korean congregation.

178. Fager Residence. (Photo by Thomas H. Simmons)

178. Fager Residence

(c. 1884), 2947 Umatilla St.

Charming simplicity radiates from this tiny clapboard, front-gable cottage with a central brick chimney. The frame porch gingerbread includes squared columns and decorative brackets. This rare example of frame

174.

177. Asbury Methodist Church. (Photo by Thomas H. Simmons)

179. All Saints Episcopal Church/Chapel of Our Merciful Savior. (Photo by Thomas H. Simmons)

construction within the Denver city limits has two tiny rear additions. Sarah J. Fager, a fifty-nine-year-old widow from Tennessee, bought the land and built this house around 1884. Later owners added the porch and a chicken coop to this dignified, little-altered, working-class residence.

179. All Saints Episcopal Church/Chapel of Our Merciful Savior

(1890, James Murdoch), 2224 W. 32nd Ave., SE corner of Wyandot St., NR

A soaring steeple on a buttressed corner bell tower and steep gable roof distinguish this red brick Gothic Revival chapel with adjacent rectory. Built as All Saints Episcopal Church, it was renamed after that congregation moved to a larger church at 3650 Yates Street in 1961. Rusticated rhyolite trims the entrance centered beneath a rose window. Inside, the original carved

wooden statues, pulpit, baptismal font, and pews survive under hammered ceiling beams set in a herringbone pattern. The marble angel holding a scalloped holy water basin was sculpted by Elsie Ward Hering, a Denver student of Augustus Saint-Gaudens.

180. Cowie House

(1888, Alexander J. Cowie, bldr.?), 3147 Umatilla St.

Alexander Johnstone Cowie, a Scottish stonemason and city sidewalk inspector, probably built his own brick cottage. Its polychromatic stone facade features a rhyolite base and quoins with floral medallions carved into the stone door frame. Fishscale shingling adorns the front bay window and gable. Originally, this two-lot site was part of the Acacia Cemetery, established in 1866 by the Denver Masons and Order of Odd Fellows. That cemetery, bounded by West 29th and West 32nd Avenues between Tejon and Zuni Streets, was vacated in the early 1880s and the bodies removed so the boneyard could be developed for livelier residential purposes.

181. Cole-DeRose Apartment House

(1895, Linus C. Cole, bldr.), 1940–1946 W. 33rd Ave., SE corner of Tejon St.

Linus C. Cole, a New Yorker who came to Denver in 1892, constructed this red brick apartment house, where he also lived. The Tuscan-columned front porch and a central dormer suggest an elongated foursquare. Cole also built and operated an adjacent corner grocery store. The Cole complex was purchased in 1916 by the DeRose family, a prominent North Denver clan, who lived here and operated the grocery. The grocery disappeared in the 1970s and was replaced by a garden.

182. Fox-Schlatter House

(1888), 3225 Quivas St.

Edward L. Fox's typical one-story brick cottage gained fame in 1895 when Francis Schlatter made it the center of his ministry of public healing. Schlatter lived with the Foxes and stood on a makeshift platform in their front yard to treat hundreds who flocked there daily. During his two-month ministry, Schlatter attracted some eighty thousand people. Trainloads of sick people came to Denver on special Union Pacific Railroad trains. They disembarked at Union Station to board a special North-Denver-bound Denver Tramway Company trolley car marked "This Car for the Healer." Schlatter disappeared as quickly and mysteriously as he came on the night of November 13, 1895. Rumors slowly drifted back to town that his skeletal remains had been found in Mexico, where he may have died of starvation. The Fox house is all that survives of Schlatter's amazing ministry, which brought sensational national newspaper coverage to this modest North Denver dwelling.

John Varone bought the house from Fox's widow, Mary, in 1912 and built his grocery store on the southwest corner of West 33rd Avenue and Quivas Street. The typical house and corner grocery survive, made famous by the brief appearance of Colorado's most spectacular faith healer.

183. St. Patrick's Catholic Church

(1907–1910, Harry James Manning and Francis C. Wagner), 3325 Pecos St., NW corner of W. 33rd Ave., NR

As Colorado's first Irish parish, St. Patrick's promoted Celtic culture and Denver's now-huge St. Patrick's Day Parade. That parade began in the 1880s as a parish festival that included mass and musical entertainment. The festival was held in collaboration with the Daughters of Erin and the Ancient Order of Hibernians.

Father Joseph P. Carrigan built this parish complex inspired by his tour of eighteenth-century California missions. The fine Mission-style design in smooth-dressed light brown stone with a red barrel tile roof features a curvilinear parapet and copper-domed towers. The inner courtyard is rimmed by the church, sacristy, a two-story rectory, and a small library with stucco walls, ceiling beams, and other Mission-style touches. Although Carrigan was dismissed for insubordination, his church stands, recently restored. In 1989 the parish was closed and became Our Lady of Light Monastery for Capuchin Poor Clare nuns, noted for their twenty-four-hour prayer vigils and their heavenly cookies. A block away at 3233 Osage Street, the original red brick Romanesque St. Patrick's Catholic Church (1883) was converted to the parish school and then to the Original Mexican Cafe.

184. Our Lady of Guadalupe Catholic Church

(1948, John K. Monroe), 3559 Kalamath St., SW corner of W. 36th Ave.

Begun as a storefront mission, this ministry has evolved into a parish complex whose murals and architectural details honor both the Spanish and the Aztec traditions. Spanish-speaking Theatine priests named the church for the patroness of Mexico, whose dark-complexioned, life-size statue occupies the niche over the arched doorway. John K. Monroe, who followed his mentor J.J.B. Benedict as the Roman Catholic archdiocesan architect, designed this $66,500 church. Spanish Mission Revival style is apparent in the blond brick masonry construction, red tile roof, prominent curvilinear parapet, domed bell tower, round arches, and arcaded courtyard. The 1990 south wing of the church,

183. St. Patrick's Catholic Church. (Photo by Tom Noel)

184. Our Lady of Guadalupe Catholic Church. (Photo by Roger Whitacre)

seating 180, reflects the growing congregation and prominence of what was once a tiny mission chapel.

Carlota Espinosa painted the interior mural (1975) of Nuestra Señora de Guadalupe, who appeared to a poor Indian boy, Juan Diego, on a hill near Mexico City in 1531. Juan Menchaca painted an older series of murals depicting the stations of the cross. This church has been a center for economic, political, and social activism to improve the lot of Denver Hispanos. It also perpetuates mariachi masses, the Christmastime Las Posadas ceremony, and other traditional rituals.

185. Hannigan-Canino Terrace

(1890), 3500 Navajo St. and 1421–1439 W. 35th Ave., NR

Although single-family housing has always dominated even the poorest neighborhoods in Denver, perhaps a hundred terraces such as this were built in working-class neighborhoods. Ten two-story apartments are divided by basement-to-parapet brick fire walls. The rhythmical composition of red brick is topped with a flat roof and a corbeled cornice. Ten recessed bays are separated by pilasters, and door and window openings all have segmental arches. Each apartment contains a living room and small kitchen on the first floor, with a closed stairway leading to upstairs bedrooms. Built without bathrooms and central heat, the units have been individually remodeled to include these conveniences.

Irish immigrant Frank Hannigan built these units when many of his compatriots were coming to Denver. The corner unit was remodeled as a storefront and small apartment by Joseph Canino in 1935 to accommodate his meat market and family. Second owner Canino represented a later wave of Italian immigrants. These two ethnic groups slowly improved their economic conditions and moved on, to be succeeded by Hispanos.

186. Our Lady of Mount Carmel Catholic Church. (Photo by Thomas H. Simmons)

186. Our Lady of Mount Carmel Catholic Church

(1904, Frederick W. Paroth), 3549 Navajo St., SW corner of W. 36th Ave., NR

Still reigning over the neighborhood once known as Little Italy, Mount Carmel was Colorado's first Italian parish church. The Romanesque Revival design in brick has prominent twin towers capped by rectangular-based copper domes. A large rose window is centered in the front gable above raised brick courses that circle the window and form arches above the entry niche for the

white marble statue of Our Lady of Carmel. A one-thousand-pound bell, the heartbeat of Italian North Denver, once regulated neighborhood life, as church bells did in the Old Country. The interior is decorated with marble statues brought from Italy and with ceiling and wall murals. From the alley behind the church, craftsmanship can be seen in the red brick chimneys with blond brick insets in the shape of a cross. The cornerstone honors the founding pastor, Father Mariano Felice Lepore, who was mysteriously murdered a year before his church opened.

187. Damascio House. (Photo by Thomas H. Simmons)

187. Damascio House

(1895, Frank Damascio), 3611–3615 Osage St.

Frank Damascio, one of Colorado's many Italian stonemasons, helped build the Brown Palace Hotel, the Cathedral of the Immaculate Conception, and other Denver landmarks. In his eclectic family home, he used alternating courses of rusticated granite and smooth red sandstone. Expansive Roman arches frame a recessed porch. Small decorative turrets frame each side of the front facade. Stone posts reinforce the wrought-iron fencing around this double house later converted to a convalescent hospital by Frank's daughter, Elisa Damascio Palladino.

188. Cerrone's Grocery

(1893, Frank Damascio), 3617 Osage St.

Frank Damascio, with his partner Horace Palladino, opened the North Denver Mercantile Company in this

188. Ottey Cerrone is famous for meats at his neighborhood grocery, a landmark at 3617 Osage Street. (Photo by Roger Whitacre)

building of his own design, a single-story brick rectangle with fifteen-foot ceilings. Fluted pilasters rise above the roof to bracket a corbeled cornice. Since the 1920s, the Cerrone family has operated one of Denver's last old-fashioned neighborhood groceries, with its original flagstone entry, hardwood floor, wooden display cabinets, and a meat chopping block guarded by a statue of the Blessed Virgin.

189. Fire Station No. 7

(1909, Glen W. Huntington), 3600 Tejon St., NE corner of W. 36th Ave.

This fire station's predecessor, with slits in its medieval corner watch turrets, survives at West 32nd Avenue and Erie Street. It became the Tivoli Terrace Night Club and, later, the Denvue Apartments. This replacement Denver Fire Station No. 7 by Glen Huntington is pressed red brick with light stone trim. North Denver native and politician Dennis Gallagher recalls that the

189. Fire Station No. 7. (Photo by Thomas H. Simmons)

firefighters here used their horse-drawn wagon to take Mother Frances Cabrini, the first U.S. citizen to be canonized by the Vatican, and her nuns on Sunday picnics. "My dad," Councilman Gallagher adds, "and other old-time smoke eaters told me that whenever they were out with the nuns, North Denver was miraculously protected from any kind of blaze." After the fire company moved to newer quarters in 1975, the firehouse was rehabilitated as a home and art gallery. It retains an extravagant corbeled frieze with broad bracketed eaves, and twin pedimented garage doors.

190. Horace Mann Middle School

(1931, Temple H. Buell. 1956, addition by Temple Hoyne Buell. 1994, addition by Hoover-Berg-Desmond), 4130 Navajo St.

Horace Mann was a Massachusetts legislator and Antioch College president who became a nationally noted advocate of free coeducational schools for all. He also championed better training and pay for schoolteachers. Denver honored Mann with one of its more unusual schools, a brickmason's tour de force with beige bricks that seem to grow out of the structure organically, like ivy. Architect Buell claimed that "I dreamed up Horace Mann sitting one day on my porch watching sun and shadows on brick work. For this school, we employed only brick and all the effects we could create with it — classical, Gothic, Renaissance, and modern." Buell also employed the Art Deco style, as reflected in the vertical brick stacks, stepped massing, and crenelated roofline. The **H**-plan school occupies a full block, with generous landscaping and recreation facilities.

191. Smedley Elementary School

(1902, David W. Dryden. 1911, addition by David W. Dryden), 4250 Shoshone St. between W. 42nd and W. 43rd Aves.

Dentist William Smedley was an early school board president whose residence is a Denver landmark in Auraria's Ninth Street Park. He gave his name to this two-story red brick school characterized by a quiet Neoclassicism. David Dryden, who also designed North High and many other Denver schools, planned both the 1902 original building and the 1911 addition. Straight window lintels and relatively sparse Neoclassical ornament typify this early twentieth-century idea of a modern school building. Faced with plans to demolish and replace Smedley Elementary, teachers, students, and neighbors rallied in the early 1990s to pursue landmark designation and a sensitive 1994 addition that has made the school young again.

POTTER HIGHLANDS

HD-20 POTTER HIGHLANDS HISTORIC DISTRICT (see Map 8, page 94)

Roughly Zuni St. to Federal Blvd. between W. 32nd and W. 38th Aves., NRD

Reverend Walter M. Potter, who established the First Baptist Church of Denver in 1864, bought a 320-acre North Denver site. He died in 1866 and willed the property to the Baptist Home Missionary Society, which sold it to various developers of Potter Highlands. This venerable neighborhood, now a large historic district of 667 buildings, is a fairly intact ensemble of late Victorian dwellings. Tree lawns and flagstone sidewalks front evenly set-back homes. Large Victorian residences, like the **Mouat House,** now the Lumber Baron Bed and Breakfast (1890; 1994, restoration by David Anderson), 2555 West 37th Avenue, and the **Sayre-Brodie House** (1886), 3631 Eliot Street, advertised Mouat's lumber company and Brodie's Lyons sandstone businesses with the materials of their construction. Interspersed are plainer Queen Anne examples, as well as foursquares, classic cottages, and bungalows.

The Edbrooke Foursquares (c. 1904, Frank E. Edbrooke), 2501, 2511, 2519, and 2525 West 32nd Avenue, were constructed as a family complex for John W. Prout, a mining man and geologist in the first graduating class of the Colorado School of Mines. The small rear yards were joined and had a common carriage lot and driveway, which helps explain the lack of garages. These early foursquares, with little ornamentation other than the Tuscan porch columns and bracketed cornices, represent Edbrooke's shift from embellished Victorian designs to Neoclassicism. One of the more modern homes is **Milton House** (1916, Glen W. Huntington), 3400 Federal Boulevard, a Prairie-style residence with a flat roof, overhanging eaves, window bands, and ribbon windows.

192. Mackay House. (Photo by Thomas H. Simmons)

192. Mackay House

(1891, Hugh Mackay, bldr.), 3359 Alcott St., SW corner of W. 34th Ave.

Hugh Mackay, a Scottish immigrant involved in mining and construction, used rough-faced rhyolite for his sturdy house. The second story hunkers down under broad sloping eaves, and its small windows squint into Colorado's brilliant sunshine, which dazzled immigrants from grayer, wetter places. A Scottish thistle is carved into one first-floor window lintel, and the interior has fine turned woodwork and stained glass. The steep-pitched roof and prominent dormers are repeated in the matching carriage house. Anne Mackay, daughter of the builder, kept the house and barn in near original shape for decades after his demise.

193. Foster House

(1874), 2533 W. 32nd Ave.

Henri R. Foster, who helped develop the town of Highlands and served as the first town clerk, built this show home for the new Denver suburb that stretched from Zuni Street to Sheridan Boulevard between West Colfax and West 38th Avenues. Foster also helped develop adjacent Highland Park, with its curvy streets with Scottish names. Highland Park, also known as Scottish Village, is a residential National Register Historic District bounded by Zuni on the east, West 32nd Avenue on the north, Clay Street on the west, and West Dunkeld Place on the south. Foster led the fight against annexation of Highlands and Highland Park, but financial problems related to the 1893 depression led voters to approve annexation by Denver in 1896.

Foster was a director of Riverside Cemetery, a trustee of the State School for the Mute and Blind in Colorado Springs, and an organizer of the now demolished Boulevard Congregational Church. His house has tall, paired Italianate windows, but the steep, double-pitched roof and newer porch on this L-plan house cloud the issue of style on one of the oldest dwellings in North Denver.

194. Lee House

(1890), 2653 W. 32nd Ave., NE corner of Clay St.

Henry Lee, as a state senator and state representative, first introduced legislation to create Sloans Lake Park and City Park. A pioneer who came to Denver in 1864, he established the Pioneer Seed Company and a farm implement firm offering chilled-steel plows capable of breaking the tough prairie sod. He experimented with these plows on his large farm, which is now part of Crown Hill Cemetery. On a spacious site, his large Queen Anne house is distinguished by vergeboards accenting the steep-pitched front gable and fish-scale shingle trim. A wraparound entry porch displays the red sandstone used to trim this pressed red brick domicile.

194. Lee House. (Photo by Thomas H. Simmons)

195. St. Elizabeth's Retreat Chapel

(1897, Frederick J. Sterner), 2825 W. 32nd Ave.

This wonderful Georgian Revival chapel is reminiscent of Christopher Wren's London churches, which Sterner admired. It was built for the Oakes Home, a tuberculosis sanitarium. The Poor Sisters of St. Francis acquired the site in 1943 and converted it to a retirement home. Adjacent Neoclassical buildings of the Oakes Home were demolished to build newer housing for the elderly, including a fourteen-story 1988 high-rise and a garden for a senior residence rechristened the Gardens at St. Elizabeth's.

196. Queree House

(1888, Joseph John Queree), 2914 W. 29th Ave.

Joseph Queree, a Scottish immigrant remembered as one of Denver's finest carpenters, adorned his own brick house — as well as many Denver mansions — with his exquisite woodwork. This small, one-story, flat-topped cottage is distinguished by an octagonal

195. St. Elizabeth's Retreat Chapel. (Photo by Thomas H. Simmons)

196. Queree House. (Photo by Thomas H. Simmons)

tower entrance with a bell-cast roof. Red brick corbeling and arches provide sedate trim. Queree's daughter, Pearl, lived here for many years while working as a teacher and principal in the Denver Public Schools.

197. House With the Round Window

(1890, William W. Monetelius and Raymond J. Walker, bldrs.), 3240 W. Hayward Pl.

This story-and-a-half Queen Anne brick cottage has an eccentric round window in the front gable. Fish-scale, diamond-pane, and square shingles trim the round window gable and also a higher gable hovering over it. Sandstone trim on the brick walls and fine stained, beveled, and leaded glass add to this romantic scenario. Oscar L. Edgecomb, a clerk for the Denver & Rio Grande Railroad, originally owned this residence, which has been restored by current owner Henry L. Cato.

198. Woodbury Branch Library

(1912, J.J.B. Benedict. 1992, restoration by David Owen Tryba), 3265 Federal Blvd.

This is a beautifully proportioned Italian Renaissance villa in miniature at the northeast corner of Highland Park. Roger W. Woodbury, first president of the Denver Public Library Board, suggested the Florentine style for this branch library, where his portrait hangs above one of two original fireplaces. The library sits atop a full basement and is sheathed in beige brick trimmed with elaborate terra-cotta pilasters and medallions. Triple arches grace the central entry. The ceiling's ornately carved open trusses and silver birch decking shine after a 1992 restoration that undid many "improvements" to resurrect the original inspired design. Tryba, a Denver architect, added a rotunda at the rear that opens to an outdoor stage. In this addition, he used the same large-arch portals that distinguish the original facade of this early branch library funded, in part, by the Andrew Carnegie Foundation.

199. Bosler-Yankee House

(1875, John G. Weller), 3209 W. Fairview Pl.

This once elegant but often remodeled Italianate has lost its dominant square entry cupola but has kept much of its other ornament. Ambrose Bosler, who established and operated the Union Ice Company at Rocky Mountain Lake, built this huge home for $14,000. William H. Yankee, vice president of the North Denver Bank, bought the house in 1888. In

197. House With the Round Window. (Photo by Thomas H. Simmons)

198. Woodbury Branch Library. (Photo by Tom Noel)

200. Skinner Middle School. (Photo by Thomas H. Simmons)

1915, it became a sanitarium where Dr. John H. Tilden prescribed diets and bed rest as a cure for everything from tuberculosis to obesity. Yankee began remodeling, and Tilden continued the process, which has diminished a one-time mansion as well as its once expansive gardens. A recent restoration has resurrected the generous original porches.

200. Skinner Middle School

(1922, W. Harry Edwards. 1992, addition by Murata Outland Associates), 3435 W. 40th Ave. between Irving and King Sts.

A simplified Collegiate Gothic style characterizes this **E**-plan school, which retains some of Saco R.

DeBoer's original landscaping and arboretum. On the dark red brick, two-story structure, light terra-cotta dramatizes the roof parapet, half-arch entry transom, and the foliated **S** shields. Among many surviving original interior features are a large oak buffet with a beveled glass mirror for a home economics classroom where students practiced formal entertaining. Miss Elizabeth Hope Skinner was the charismatic oratory and drama teacher for whom this school is named. A 1992 east wing, designed by Kevin Sullivan of Murata Outland Associates, used similar brick, window treatments, and detailing to complement the original edifice.

201. Smiley Branch Library

(1918, Park French of Mountjoy, French & Rewe. 1994, restoration by David Owen Tryba), 4501 W. 46th Ave. at Utica St. in Berkeley Lake Park

Akin to surrounding homes, this English-cottage-style branch is a one-story, residential-looking library. Decorative patterns enhance glazed red brick under a red tile roof. The buttressed corners are highlighted by angled brick courses, and the round-arch of the entry is repeated in the fanlighted windows. A notable triple-stack chimney for the restored fireplace confirms that master masons erected this library, and perhaps the cobblestone restrooms nearby in the park.

202. Elitch Gardens Theater

(1890, Charles Herbert Lee and Rudolph Liden), W. 38th Ave., SW corner of Tennyson St.

This rustic wooden theater is one of the few surviving structures of the Elitch Gardens Amusement Park, which occupied the site bounded by West 38th and 36th Avenues between Tennyson and Wolff Streets until 1995. John and Mary Elitch opened the park and theater in 1890. John, a handsome vaudeville actor and athlete, made the theater his main concern until his 1891 death on a vaudeville tour in San Francisco. Afterward, Mary Elitch ran the theater and gardens with the help of her second husband, Thomas Long, until her death in 1936.

Elitch's, Denver's oldest, largest, and best-known amusement park, moved to a new Auraria site in 1995.

The Mulvihill-Gurtler family, owners since 1936, left the theater behind on its original site. This unusual frame playhouse claimed to be this country's oldest continually operating summer-stock theater when it closed in 1987. Among the hundreds of nationally prominent actors and actresses to tread its stage were June Allyson, Sid Caesar, Douglas Fairbanks, Jr., Jose Ferrer, Tammy Grimes, Julie Harris, Van Johnson, Grace Kelly, Myrna Loy, Jane Powell, Vincent Price, Lynn Redgrave, Debbie Reynolds, Ginger Rogers, and Mickey Rooney.

Architecturally, the theater is a rare example of frame construction combining stick- and shingle-style elements. It evolved over the years from the original circular frame building into an octagon two stories high with a tent-shaped shingle roof crowned by a flagpole. The sides, each measuring forty-three feet wide, are of wood drop siding painted gray with white trim. A two-story addition (c. 1900) forms a vestibule or outer lobby with two enclosed stairways to the balcony. Quaint and unique, this remarkable landmark awaits creative reuse.

203. John Brisben Walker House

(1885, David Cox, Sr.), 3520 Newton St.

Reversing the standard Denver pattern of brick houses trimmed with stone, this gray rhyolite stone house is trimmed in red brick. Asymmetrical Queen Anne massing includes an angled southeast bay facing downtown Denver. Neighborhood stonemason David Cox built this two-and-a-half story residence for John Brisben Walker, a Northwest Denver developer who also owned Red Rocks and sold the land to the city for use as an amphitheater and mountain park. Walker later moved to New York City, where he owned *Cosmopolitan* magazine before selling it to William Randolph Hearst.

204. Cox Gargoyle House

(c. 1889, David Cox, Sr.), 3425 Lowell Blvd.

Stonemason David Cox, Sr., designed and built his two-story home and decorated it with fanciful carved creatures. Constructed of alternating broad and narrow courses of rusticated sandstone block, the dwelling is notable for Cox's craftsmanship. Note the

204. Cox Gargoyle House. (Photo by Thomas H. Simmons)

206. Heiser House. (Photo by Thomas H. Simmons)

stone balustrade of the porch, the grouped porch columns with carved capitals, the carved stone of the gable panel and finial, the floral friezes and dragon downspouts, and the faces topping the window spandrels.

205. Cox House

(1903, David Cox, Sr.), 3417 Lowell Blvd.

Next door to the Gargoyle House is another Cox creation, a foursquare with eighteen-inch-thick wall panels of dressed buff sandstone erected by Cox for his daughter. Decorative stone stringcourses circle the structure at sill levels, with the first-floor course intersecting the cap of the solid porch balustrade.

206. Heiser House

(1893), 3016 Osceola St., NE corner of W. 31st Ave.

Herman H. Heiser, a custom saddler, placed his monogram in the front porch tiles of his two-story Queen Anne residence. Particularly impressive is the entry porch, with flanking leaded glass sidelights and transom and second-story balcony. A tower rises at the southwest corner to a bellcast roof. Interior woodwork, paneling, and doors are beautifully matched, with different woods in each room. A 1989 restoration added a

three-car garage, detailed to match even the narrow mortar joints of the house. Compare this show home with the tiny clapboard cottage (1885) nearby at 2972 Osceola. The diversity of housing types in North Denver has promoted a healthy economic diversity.

207. Moses House

(1895), 4001 W. 30th Ave., NW corner of Perry St.

William E. Moses, an attorney and realtor, selected a fine hilltop site for his Queen Anne residence. This unusual design has a third-story ballroom opening onto a steep-capped balcony tower. The flared edge of the roof is echoed in the single front dormer in an otherwise asymmetrical plan with a prominent second-story oriel window wearing zinc Adamesque garlands. The generous round-arch entry is highlighted with a stone band. This red brick dwelling with crisp stone and frame trim is shaded by one of the largest and oldest red oaks in Denver. Moses, a Civil War veteran and active officer of the Colorado-Wyoming chapter of the Grand Army of the Republic, died in this house in 1929.

208. Lobach House. (Photo by Thomas H. Simmons)

208. Lobach House

(1894, Joseph Vetter, bldr.?), 2851 Perry St., SW corner of W. 29th Ave.

209. Woodbury House

(1894, Joseph Vetter, bldr.?), 2841 Perry St.

Lobach and Woodbury houses are nearly identical twins; they share the same plan, rich vergeboard, and gables framing elaborate second-story Palladian-inspired windows. They differ in the Adamesque trim decorating the gables and pedimented entries to wraparound porches supported by clusters of Tuscan columns. Rough stone foundations and window banding also adorn these one-story Queen Anne brick cottages, which even have similar stained glass sidelights and transom lights in their elaborate front windows. Reflecting a now obsolete custom of families living in proximity, these were built for the intermarried families of Eugene Lobach and Frank Woodbury. Frank ran the *Denver Evening Times* after buying it from his father, Roger

Woodbury. Frank also organized the Rocky Mountain Savings Bank and helped found the Denver Athletic Club. His wife, Grace Lobach Woodbury, was a concert pianist, composer, and music teacher.

WITTER-COFIELD

HD-21 WITTER-COFIELD HISTORIC DISTRICT (see Map 8, page 94)

Federal Blvd. to Irving St. between W. 20th and W. 25th Aves.

Of 216 buildings in this Denver Landmark District, most are single-family 1880s residences in a neighborhood named for the two men who platted it, attorney-developer Daniel Witter and developer Joseph B. Cofield. Queen Anne dwellings, ranging from cottages to large, elaborate homes, reflect the most common architectural style. Homes built after 1910 are mostly modest bungalows.

210. Neef House

(1886), 2143 Grove St., SW corner of W. 22nd Ave.

Frederick Neef of the Neef Brothers Brewing Company built this exquisite Queen Anne that is the finest gem of the Witter-Cofield district. Eastlake vergeboard on the entry porch is repeated on the two-story front bay and in the main front gable of this asymmetrical brick house. Among the exuberant and varied details are an attic oriel window tucked under the front gable and stained glass transoms in a variety of ornate window surrounds.

211. Half-Moon House

(c. 1892), 3205 W. 21st Ave., NW corner of Hooker St.

This dramatic Queen Anne is named for the half-moon openings in the porch woodwork. A third-story front gable with an oriel window sweeps down to frame the second-story balcony and become a roof for the wraparound corner porch. The profuse wooden trim in Eastlake patterns and the unusual asymmetry distinguish the well-preserved house of Stanley M. Barrows, a real

HD-21 Witter-Cofield Historic District. In this district, the 2100 block of Gove Street reflects the residential ambience and mix of big and little houses. (Photo by Bill Sagstetter)

estate developer specializing in Jefferson County farmlands. Timothy Wirth and his wife, Wren, restored the house and matching carriage house in the 1970s before he moved to Washington, where he served as a U.S. representative and, later, senator.

212. Voorhees House

(1890, William Lang and Marshall R. Pugh), 1471 Stuart St., NR

Ralph Voorhees, a real estate developer and state legislator, commissioned William Lang and his partner, Marshall R. Pugh, to design picturesque show homes at 1389, 1390, 1435, 1444, and 1471 Stuart Street for his West Colfax subdivision. Rusticated rhyolite, elegant shingling, deeply recessed sets of round and rectangular ribbon windows, irregular massing, and the heavy stone arches and lintels add distinction to these residences.

211. Half-Moon House. (Photo by Larry Life)

111

210. Neef House. (Photo by Bill Sagstetter)

Most are asymmetrical and culminate in third-story towers, steep-pitched gables, and rustic stone chimneys. Voorhees's own $25,000 three-story house at 1471 Stuart Street, which hides behind a three-story front bay, has been restored by Dr. John Litvak as his medical offices.

213. Spangler House

(1888, William Lang and Marshall R. Pugh), 1444 Stuart St., NR

This splendid shingle-style home is covered by shingles on the top two stories. Jane Spangler, the widow of Arapahoe County sheriff Mike Spangler, lived here, next door to her sister, Mrs. Ralph Voorhees.

214. Smith House

(1890, William Lang and Marshall R. Pugh), 1435 Stuart St., NR

Frank W. Smith bought this rusticated rhyolite Romanesque Revival dwelling with varied and deep-set windows. A three-story tower, finials, and minarets give

214. Smith House. (Photo by Tom Noel)

it a churchlike verticality. South-side window slits follow the interior staircase.

215. McNulty House

(1892, William Lang and Marshall R. Pugh), 1390 Stuart St., SE corner of W. 14th Ave., NR

Elizabeth McNulty, a teacher at nearby Glen Park School, lived here with her two aunts for many years. Displaying architectural versatility, William Lang and his partner designed a Queen Anne alternative to the Richardsonian Romanesque and shingle styles they employed for neighboring homes. Like many other large homes, the McNulty home became an apartment house during World War II, when housing was in short supply.

216. Bliss House

(1892, William Lang and Marshall R. Pugh), 1389 Stuart St., SW corner of W. 14th Ave., NR

Dr. Gerald Bliss, a Civil War veteran and member of the honor guard for President Lincoln's funeral, lived here for almost fifty years. For his dwelling, William Lang and Marshall Pugh departed from their usual Richardsonian Romanesque proclivities in this shingle-style dwelling. A northwest corner tower incorporates a third-story covered porch, and a southwest bay sweeps downward to shelter the recessed entry porch.

216. Bliss House. (Photo by Tom Noel)

CHAPTER 5

South Denver Area

SOUTH DENVER (NORTH OF ALAMEDA AVENUE)
WASHINGTON PARK/CITY DITCH
SOUTH DENVER (SOUTH OF ALAMEDA AVENUE)

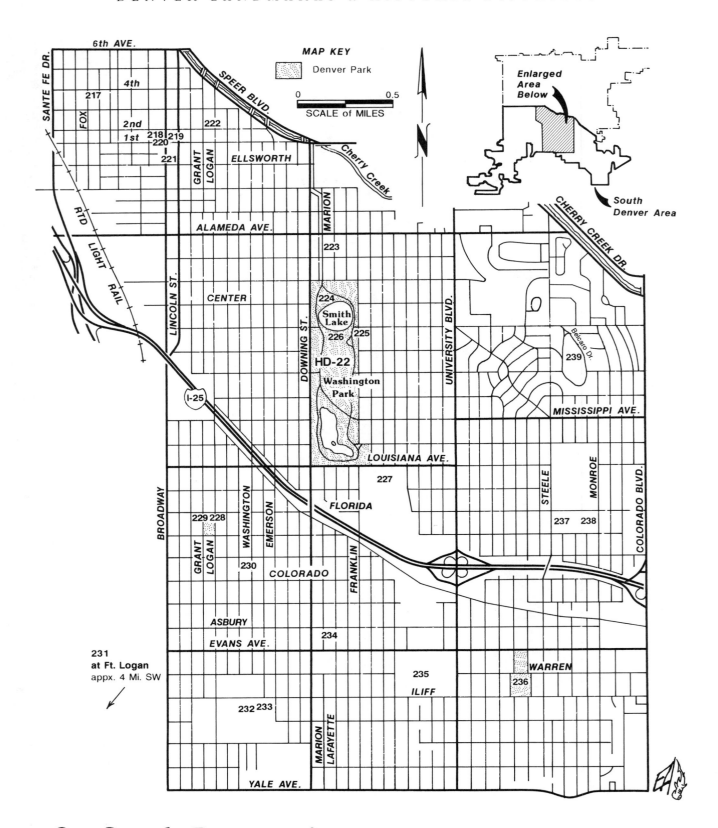

9. South Denver Area

The town of South Denver sprouted along the Broadway tracks as the largest of Denver's streetcar suburbs. Incorporated in 1886, South Denver stretched from Alameda to Yale Avenues and from Colorado Boulevard on the east to Pecos Street on the west. This political and commercial center for the area south of Cherry Creek and West 6th Avenue resisted annexation to the big city to the north until 1893. South Denver's town hall was the landmarked house of Mayor James Fleming at 1510 South Grant Street.

One of south Denver's oldest and finest mansions, the **Thomas M. Field House,** 2340 South Washington Street, is one of two Denver landmarks demolished by fire (the other is Constitution Hall in LoDo). Another grand old mansion, the **Warren Residence** (1892, Frank E. Edbrooke and/or Warren Wheeler), 2169 South Cook Street, built of the same Arizona sandstone Edbrooke used that year for the Brown Palace Hotel, is not a designated Denver landmark. Another undesignated landmark is one of the most prominent buildings in Southwest Denver, Edbrooke's **Old Main,** an edifice with a soaring bell tower on the Teikyo-Loretto Heights College campus on South Federal Boulevard.

In this guide, South Denver is defined as everything within the city limits south of Cherry Creek and West 6th Avenue. This includes the neighborhoods of Barnum, Harvey Park, Overland Park, Platte Park, University Park, Valverde, and Washington Park.

SOUTH DENVER (NORTH OF ALAMEDA AVENUE)

217. Coyle-Chase House

(1891), 532 W. 4th Ave.

This modest two-story brick dwelling has stone trim, a fish-scale-shingled front gable with a sunburst peak, and a wood-columned front porch. Here journalist Mary Coyle Chase wrote her Pulitzer-Prize-winning play *Harvey* (1944), which introduced the world to an imaginary six-foot-tall rabbit. Her home is representative of the Baker neighborhood, a National Register Historic District stretching from West 5th to West Alameda Avenues between Broadway & Fox Streets.

217. Coyle/Chase House. (Photo by Thomas H. Simmons)

This middle-class neighborhood has many small Queen Anne dwellings, as well as some notable larger houses and institutions.

218. Fire Station No. 11

(1936, Charles F. Pillsbury), 40 W. 2nd Ave.

This firehouse is one of the attractions of the Baker National Register Historic District. Pillsbury gave this three-bay, red tapestry brick station Art Deco piers that rise into a parapet. The somewhat stark, modernistic facade retains the original stainless steel lamps, Art Deco signage, and sidewalk bench.

219. Mayan Theater

(1930, Montana Fallis (facade). 1985, restoration by Midyette-Seieroe Architects), 110 Broadway

This rare surviving example of a movie house extensively decorated in pre-Columbian motifs was rescued from the wrecking ball in 1984. The theater's

219. Mayan Theater. (Photo by Tom Noel)

220. First Avenue Hotel, c. 1907. (Courtesy Denver Public Library)

Technicolor terra-cotta ornament and hand-painted and -stenciled walls were rejuvenated, as were the facade's terra-cotta Indian chief and Aztec and Mayan polychrome trim. This exotic facade, largely made by Julius P. Ambrusch of the Denver Terra Cotta Company, fronts an older red brick theater, the homely Queen Theater built around 1915.

220. First Avenue Hotel

(1906, Charles Quayle), 101–115 Broadway

Typical of early twentieth-century commercial buildings, this is neoclassically inspired, with a bracketed cornice and broad eaves hovering over a symmetrical four-story arrangement. The Flemming Brothers, leading south Denver developers, had architect Charles Quayle, the son of architect William Quayle, design this

edifice with generous glass storefronts below hotel units. One of the largest buildings in South Denver, it was restored during the 1980s as a cornerstone of Broadway's revitalization.

221. South Broadway Christian Church

(1891, Edwin J. Miller and Wenzel J. Janisch), 23 Lincoln St., NW corner of E. Ellsworth Ave.

The dominant element of this Richardsonian Romanesque church is a crenelated square bell tower coupled with an engaged smaller round turret. The church's rough-faced rhyolite walls are highlighted by carved stone adorning the gable peaks, buttress caps, and recessed entrance. Decorative wood accentuates the steep peaks of rhythmic rows of gables and dormers.

222. Sherman Elementary School/Denver Art Students League

(1893, Henry Dozier. 1920, bungalow annex. 1987, renovation), 200 Grant St.

This school was named for General William T. Sherman, Yankee hero of the Civil War. The two-and-a-half story building is clad in smooth red-orange sandstone above the rusticated stone basement level. Sandstone is also used for the arch fronting the recessed entry in a protruding bay. After closing in 1982, this building was recycled in 1987 as the home of the Denver Art Students League, with twenty-four thousand square feet of studios and offices.

221. South Broadway Christian Church. (Photo by Tom Noel)

223. Steele Elementary School. (Photo by Tom Noel)

222. Sherman Elementary School/Denver Art Students League. (Photo by Roger Whitacre)

223. Steele Elementary School

(1913, David W. Dryden. 1929, Burnham Hoyt and Merrill H. Hoyt), 320 South Marion St. Pkwy.

Colorful terra-cotta trim and mosaic tile roofs on twin pyramidal towers lend an exotic Art Deco flair to this buff brick and stucco school, which is well sited on the parkway entrance to Washington Park. Dryden's original 1913 school was completely different — a typical neoclassical edifice. Stripped to its structural elements by the Hoyts, the school was reconstructed with Deco-style flat roofs, decorative panels, stringcourses, and faux balconies. The school is named for Robert Wilbur Steele, Sr. (1820-1901), a pioneer judge, politician, and chief justice of the Colorado Supreme Court.

119

WASHINGTON PARK/CITY DITCH

Washington Park (1899, Reinhard Schuetze) is a 162-acre park with Grasmere and Smith Lakes as its centerpieces. The two lakes are connected by a great meadow. This long, narrow rectangular park is enhanced by looping roadways, paths, and the City Ditch, which makes the lakes and greenery possible. Among many park plantings was a now-gone model garden for the average Denver yard. Buildings include the twelve-sided **Shelter House** (1912) on the east side of the Great Meadow, and a picturesque, late nineteenth-century farmhouse and barn tastefully expanded as the park headquarters and maintenance center.

224. Washington Park Bathhouse

(1912. 1996, renovation by Robert Root & Associates), S. Downing St. and E. Center Ave.

This two-story bathhouse recalls Smith Lake's past days as a swimming hole, where a sandy beach and this bathhouse were installed in 1912. Swimming was prohibited in 1957 after the lake became polluted and the polio scare swept the United States. Low-pitched roofs and wide eaves characterize this two-story bathhouse, which has changing rooms on either end and a central gathering area around a fireplace. In 1996, this neglected structure underwent a $600,000 rehabilitation as offices, meeting rooms, a reading room, and headquarters for the Volunteers for Outdoor Colorado.

225. Eugene Field Cottage

(1880?), 715 S. Franklin St., SW corner of E. Exposition Ave. in Washington Park, NR

Denver's first preservation project, spearheaded by Margaret Tobin "Molly" Brown, may have been the 1927 campaign to spare this house from being demolished to make room for a gas station. Molly led the crusade to move the poet's home from 307 West Colfax Avenue to Washington Park and convert it to a branch of the Denver Public Library. Eugene Field was a journalist and poet noted for *A Little Book of Western Verse* and his poem "Wynken, Blyken, and Nod." That children's poem inspired the nearby sculpture fountain (1919, Mabel Landrum Torrey) of three children sailing

225. Eugene Field Cottage. (Photo by Thomas H. Simmons)

off to sleep in a wooden shoe. Field lived in this clapboard cottage while working as a reporter and managing editor of the *Denver Tribune* from 1881–1883 before moving to Chicago. This rare example of the simple 1880s frame cottages once common in Denver now houses the Denver Parks and Recreation Foundation, a nonprofit group known as the Park People, who are devoted to maintaining and improving Denver city parks.

226. Washington Park Boathouse and Pavilion

(1913, J.J.B. Benedict. 1987, restoration by Anthony Pellecchia Associates), south shore of Smith Lake in Washington Park

The boathouse on the south shore of Smith Lake has a two-story lakefront facade with an open pavilion over enclosed boat storage. In winter it served as a warming house for ice skaters. The boathouse is a mix of Prairie-style, Italianate, and Arts and Crafts elements outlined with electric lights to create a dreamy nocturnal reflection.

HD-22 SMITH'S DITCH (CITY DITCH) HISTORIC DISTRICT (see Map 9, page 116)

(1860–1867), in Washington Park, NR

Denver's first major irrigation ditch has the second-oldest water right on the upper South Platte River. This ditch made possible the greening of the semiarid Mile High City, which averages only fourteen inches of

226. Washington Park Boathouse and Pavilion. (Photo by Felix Bauer)

SOUTH DENVER (SOUTH OF ALAMEDA AVENUE)

227. South High School. (Photo by Tom Noel)

227. South High School

(1926, William E. Fisher and Arthur A. Fisher), 1700 E. Louisiana Ave. between S. Franklin and S. Race Sts.

Overlooking Washington Park, this three-story Italian Renaissance Revival school building has red brick walls trimmed in yellowish terra-cotta under a red tile roof. The main entrance has a loggia of five arches with griffins perched above, keeping an eye on students. A large square tower, banded with several dentiled cornices, features a clock face. Inside, the study hall is guarded by an owl, a crowing cock, a parrot, and a penguin symbolizing wisdom, early rising, recitation, and deportment. The Denver School Board set high design standards in the 1920s, granting Denver's leading architects artistic freedom, a policy that proved its worth in South High. The Fishers drew inspiration from St. Ambroggio's Church in Milan and, for the clock tower, Santa Maria in Cosmedin Church in Rome.

228. Sarah Platt Decker Branch Library

(1913, Willis A. Marean and Albert J. Norton. 1993, restoration by David Owen Tryba), 1501 S. Logan St., SW corner of E. Florida Ave.

This fanciful recreation of Anne Hathaway's cottage in Stratford-on-Avon, England, has leaded diamond-

precipitation a year. The Capitol Hydraulic Company, incorporated February 21, 1860, began the twenty-seven-mile-long canal named for John W. Smith, who completed it. Washington Park's Smith Lake is also named in his honor.

The ditch begins as a diversion of the South Platte River in Waterton Canyon southwest of Littleton (the first four miles of the ditch are now inundated by Chatfield Reservoir). It flows for fifteen miles through Englewood, enters Denver through Harvey Park, and flows through Capitol Hill. Dug by hand and by horse-drawn scrapers, the ditch was originally an open, unlined canal, three feet wide on the bottom and seven feet wide at the top. It fed hundreds of lateral canals that ran along the streets of what is now downtown and Capitol Hill. Its water enabled Denverites to plant trees, lawns, and gardens and transformed the city into an oasis. Smith spent $10,000 to build what is still sometimes called Smith's Ditch. The city bought it in 1875 for $60,000 and extended it to City Park, where it fills Ferril Lake. The ditch is now buried, except in Washington Park, where it feeds both lakes. Denver historian Louisa Ward Arps, in her book *Denver in Slices* (1959), calls City Ditch "the oldest working thing in Denver."

228. Sarah Platt Decker Branch Library. (Courtesy Denver Public Library)

pane windows and a gable roof of green tile with ornate multiple chimneys. The walls of this L-shaped, residential-style library are tapestry brick with creamy terracotta trim. Denver artist Dudley Carpenter painted two interior murals, *The Pied Piper of Hamelin* and *The Lady of the Lake and the Sword Excalibur*. Inglenook seating by the fireplaces and a high, open-beam, vaulted ceiling make this a cozy neighborhood haven. It is named for a Denver clubwoman who championed causes ranging from women's suffrage to branch libraries.

229. Fleming House. (Photo by Tom Noel)

229. Fleming House

(1882), 1510 S. Grant St., SE corner of E. Florida Ave.

James A. Fleming, the mayor of South Denver before its annexation to Denver in 1893, used his home as the town hall. This rusticated stone dwelling with

three prominent, round, conical-capped towers is now a senior citizen activity center next door to Decker Branch Library in Platte Park.

230. Grant Middle School

(1953, Gordon D. White), 1751 S. Washington St.

Gordon D. White used an asymmetrical composition, cubic interior spaces, steel girder and concrete construction, smooth exterior surfaces, flat roofs, and horizontal window bands for this example of 1950s school design. On this site stood Grant Elementary School (1890), which was enlarged in 1893 to become South High School until the current South High was constructed in 1926. The old school, with 1907 and 1924 additions, was demolished in 1953 for this school, which is also named for President Ulysses S. Grant.

231. Fort Logan Field Officer's Quarters

(1889, Frank J. Grodavent. 1997, proposed restoration by Edward D. White, Jr.), 3742 W. Princeton Cir.

In 1887, Congress authorized an army fort on the southwestern outskirts of Denver, and Lieutenant General Philip H. Sheridan arrived to select a site along what is still called Sheridan Boulevard. After first mistakenly occupying private land, the army found the right site on the south bank of Bear Creek. Civilian architect Frank J. Grodavent designed the post buildings, including this house and a companion field officer's residence destroyed by fire in the early 1970s. Grodavent's large three-story brick house built in a vernacular Queen Anne style has a foundation and trim of granite.

Fort Logan was named for John A. Logan, a Union Army Civil War general. The post was closed in 1946, and in 1960, Governor Stephen L.R. McNichols acquired part of the site and converted it to the Fort Logan Mental Health Center. The state hospital shares approximately 550 remaining acres with other organizations, including Fort Logan National Cemetery (1949). The Field Officer's Quarters now houses the Friends of Historic Fort Logan, who have begun restoration and plan to open a post museum here in 1997.

231. Fort Logan Field Officer's Quarters. (Photo by Roger Whitacre)

232. Thomas Field House Site

(1893), 2305 S. Washington St. at E. Iliff Ave.

Thomas M. Field, an engineer involved with constructing various Colorado railroads, also served as Denver city treasurer. He built an 11,600-square-foot residence on this eighty-acre site. Following his death, the Field house became, from 1902 to 1971, the main building of the State Home for Dependent and Neglected Children. The Georgian Revival three-story brick and stone landmark was vacant when fire destroyed it in 1987.

233. Nursery Building

(1923, Ernest P. Varian and Lester E. Varian), 888 E. Iliff Ave. in Harvard Gulch Park

Children, not plants, were nourished in this one-story care center. Together with a gym and boiler room, this is a remnant of what used to be the State Home for Dependent and Neglected Children. This structure, distinguished by its curvilinear parapets in the Mission Revival mode, has been converted to a park maintenance building.

234. Asbury Elementary School

(1927, Temple Hoyne Buell), 1320 E. Asbury Ave. between S. Marion and S. Lafayette Sts.

Temple Buell, the son of a prominent Chicago family, was gassed during World War I. That war injury, compounded by tuberculosis, led him to move to Denver. He came here to die, but the sunny, salubrious climate and Buell's own bon vivant nature enabled him to fool — and outlive — his doctors. He died in 1990 at the age of ninety-four and was eulogized as one of Colorado's most successful and prominent twentieth-century architects. Like other early Buell schools, this is an example of Collegiate Gothic, complete with lion gargoyles and shields carved over the doors.

123

235. Evans Memorial Chapel in 1878. (Tom Noel Collection)

235. Evans Memorial Chapel

(1878), University of Denver campus, E. Evans Ave. and S. University Blvd.

In memory of his daughter Josephine Evans Elbert, who died young, former governor John Evans built this $13,000 chapel at the southwest corner of West 13th Avenue and Bannock Street, diagonally across from the Byers-Evans House. This Gothic Revival edifice of Morrison sandstone was later augmented by the larger adjacent Grace Methodist Episcopal Church (1887). Frederick J. Sterner designed Grace in the same Gothic Revival style, using similar brownish sandstone. The University of Denver acquired the site and demolished the larger church in 1959 for a parking lot but kept the Evans Chapel wing. Each stone was numbered, disassembled, and then reassembled in the Harper Humanities Gardens, the centerpiece of the University of Denver campus.

236. Chamberlain Observatory

(1890, Robert S. Roeschlaub), 2930 E. Warren Ave. in Observatory Park, NR

Humphrey B. Chamberlain, a wealthy real estate promoter and amateur astronomer, gave this observatory to the University of Denver. Its skin of random, rusticated red sandstone chunks topped by an iron observa-

tory dome is an elegant combination of forms and styles. Roeschlaub's prototype was an 1887 observatory for Carleton College in Minnesota. In Denver he added lateral gabled wings and a protruding entrance bay and had his name carved into the stone nameplate over the Romanesque arched entry. Still used as an observatory, it is open to the public on certain evenings.

237. Cory Elementary School

(1951, Victor Hornbein), 1550 S. Steele St. between E. Florida and E. Iowa Aves.

Victor Hornbein's horizontal composition, with its asymmetrical yet harmonious layers of projecting flat roofs, is reminiscent of Frank Lloyd Wright's Usonian style. Hornbein, although inspired by Wright, developed his own unique style geared to the high, dry, sunny Colorado climate. Walls of banded glass windows capture abundant natural light and mountain views under prominent projecting eaves that squint into the sun. Brick walls serve as both the exterior and interior finish. This school is named for John Jerome Cory (1890–1945), a Denver teacher who became principal of South High, then assistant superintendent for Denver junior and senior high schools and the Emily Griffith Opportunity School.

238. Merrill Middle School

(1953, Temple Hoyne Buell), 1551 S. Monroe St. between E. Florida and E. Iowa Aves.

Louise A. Merrill was a teacher and principal at Byers Junior High, whose burgeoning student population was divided to fill this modern, flat-roofed school. Merrill Middle School has an orange brick skin trimmed in white limestone. The entrance is sheltered by an overhanging second story that exhibits the school's distinctive ribbon windows.

239. Phipps House

(1932, Charles Adams Platt, William Platt, Geoffrey Platt, and William E. Fisher and Arthur A. Fisher), 3400 Belcaro Dr.

Belcaro (Italian for "beautiful dear one") is what Lawrence C. Phipps called his huge Georgian mansion, which is Denver's grandest residence. On the hilltop of

237. Cory Elementary School. (Photo by Thomas H. Simmons)

238. Merrill Middle School. (Photo by Thomas H. Simmons)

what was once a much larger estate, the fifty-four-room, 33,123-square-foot mansion surmounted by eight massive chimneys was built for $301,063.

Charles A. Platt, a New York architect and one of this country's premier designers of fine country houses, began work on the house before his death in 1933. His architect sons, William and Geoffrey, completed the house with William and Arthur Fisher as supervising Denver architects. The poured concrete building is clad in red brick, with dressed Indiana limestone trim and a slate roof. Beyond the entry, with its columns and broken pediment, are a reception area and stair hall finished in Colorado travertine from Wellsville. The oak paneling of the billiard room was transplanted from a Jacobean house in London. The paneled dining room and other interior fixtures were also brought from England.

The ivy-covered Tudor Revival tennis house on the north side of the mansion was designed by John Gray of Pueblo, the initial project architect who was replaced by the Platts and the Fishers. This glass-and-tile-roofed, 423,000-cubic-foot structure is, like the mansion, clad in brick and Indiana limestone. Exposed steel beams appear in the barrel vault over the court. A loggia entrance is trimmed in artistic wrought iron. The tennis house has a two-bedroom second-floor apartment, dressing rooms, kitchen, soda fountain, and fireplace lounge. A large Allen True mural in the lounge depicts Phipps family members skiing at the Winter Park Ski Area, which they helped develop.

Lawrence C. Phipps, a millionaire vice president and treasurer of Carnegie Steel in Pittsburgh, moved to Denver for his family's health. He served as U.S. senator (1918–1930) and invested successfully in many local ventures. In 1931, the Phipps family's Belcaro Realty and Investment Company began developing the area surrounding the mansion as one of Denver's posher residential enclaves. The estate, now reduced to five acres, was given in 1964 to the University of Denver for use as a house museum and the Lawrence C. Phipps Memorial Conference Center.

CHAPTER 6
East Denver Area

EAST DENVER (SOUTH OF 6TH AVENUE PARKWAY)
LOWRY AIR FORCE BASE
MONTCLAIR
PARK HILL (NORTH OF EAST COLFAX AVENUE)

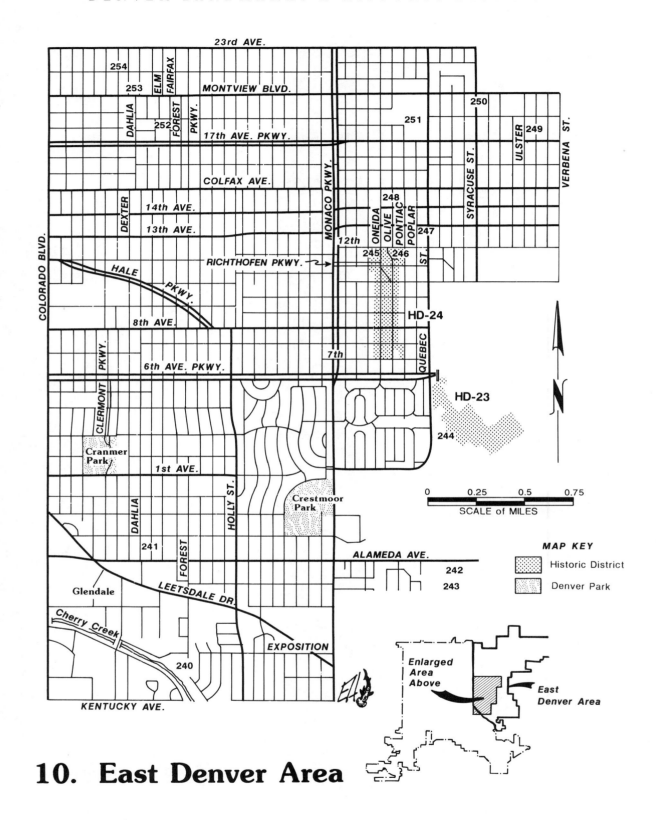

10. East Denver Area

East Denver is a relatively prosperous and largely residential area through which the park and parkway system provides a touring route. East 17th Avenue Parkway, East 6th Avenue Parkway, Montview Boulevard, and Clermont, Forest, Monaco, and Richthofen Parkways are interconnected greenways lined by many fine homes reflecting popular architectural styles of the past one hundred years. Richthofen Parkway leads to Montclair, an 1885 suburban town with much subsequent infill, annexed to Denver in 1902. This heterogeneous historic district resembles a catalog of residential styles from the 1880s to the 1990s. Two historic districts on what was, until 1994, Lowry Air Force Base commemorate the tremendous impact of the military upon Denver's development.

EAST DENVER (SOUTH OF 6TH AVENUE PARKWAY)

240. Four Mile House. (Photo by Marcia J. Tate)

240. Four Mile House

(1859. Later additions. 1976, restoration by Edward D. White, Jr.), 5000 E. Exposition Ave., at S. Forest St., NR

Denver's oldest extant building is this hewn ponderosa pine log cabin, refined over the years with clapboarding, a later frame wing, and a two-story Victorian brick addition. Built as a stage stop along Cherry Creek and the Smoky Hill Trail (now a hike-bike path), it rests on giant cottonwood logs cut with broad axes. With the

help of drawings from the Historic American Buildings Survey, the house has been restored as a living history museum and farm on a seven-acre site. Among the reconstructed outbuildings are a three-hole privy complete with window and roof vent. With the help of many volunteers, the City of Denver owns and operates this retreat to the rural past.

241. Joshel House

(1954, Joseph P. Marlow), 220 S. Dahlia St., NR

Joseph Marlow, an admirer of Bauhaus design, reduced this house to the basics. A wide, recessed carport on the northwest corner incorporates the main entrance, combining porch, garage, and porte cochere. The two-story south elevation is largely glass, opening the house to sunlight and mountain vistas. Marlow set the two-level house with single flat roof plane into a south-facing hillside, protected on the north and west by sculpted evergreens that provide a windbreak, privacy, and insulation — the same treescaping he used for his own International-style house (c. 1949) at the southeast corner of Oneida Street and East 12th Avenue.

242. Fairmount Cemetery Gatehouse. (Courtesy Denver Public Library)

242. Fairmount Cemetery Gatehouse

(1890, Harry T.E. Wendell), 7204 E. Alameda Ave., SE corner of Quebec St.

This Richardsonian Romanesque stone gatehouse was the original grand entry for Colorado's most populous cemetery. Fairmount's founders promised to abandon the "mournful effects of the old-style cemetery" in favor of a romantic rural cemetery park, for which the U.S. prototype was Mount Auburn Cemetery in Cambridge, Massachusetts. Fairmount's developers recruited Reinhard Schuetze, a native of Holstein, Germany, who had studied landscape architecture and engineering at the Royal Academy in Potsdam. Schuetze planted more than four thousand trees in Fairmount, which is still the state's largest and most diverse arboretum. Schuetze, Colorado's first landscape architect, subsequently designed or redesigned many Denver parks. At Fairmount (where he is buried), Schuetze achieved the goal of great cemetery parks — landscaping designed to look as if it had not been designed.

Many well-known Coloradans reside in this necropolis, and a number erected stately mausoleums as their final earthly homes. Frank E. Edbrooke probably designed his own private Neoclassical mausoleum, as did Temple Hoyne Buell, whose polished granite crypt has elaborate wrought-iron doors guarded by gilded maidens. The large communal mausoleum (1930, Frederick E. Mountjoy and Frank W. Frewan), on a hill at the eastern edge of the cemetery, is a huge Greek temple with a granite veneer. Inside, fine stained glass windows, Alabama white marble walls, Tennessee pink marble floors, and soft recorded music create a celestial atmosphere.

243. Fairmount Cemetery Ivy Chapel

(1890, Harry T.E. Wendell. 1995, restoration), 430 S. Quebec St., SE corner of E. Alameda Ave. in Fairmount Cemetery

This delicate French Gothic Revival stone chapel has a multiple-arch grand entry, flying buttresses, and spires in a vertical composition that makes it one of Denver's best Gothic monuments. Grey sandstone serves as both skin and trim.

LOWRY AIR FORCE BASE

HD-23 LOWRY AIR FORCE BASE HISTORIC DISTRICTS (see Map 10, page 128)

(1937. Many additions), Quebec to Havana Streets between E. Alameda and E. 11th Aves.

The base was established on the site of the Agnes Phipps Memorial Sanatorium, a large and lavish tuber-

243. Fairmount Cemetery Ivy Chapel. (Photo by José Dole)

culosis hospital complex opened in 1904 by Lawrence C. Phipps and named for his mother, a victim. The City of Denver purchased the 1,840-acre site in 1937 and donated it to the Army Air Corps, the predecessor of the U.S. Air Force, for an air base and aviation training center. It was named for Denverite Francis B. Lowry, who had been shot down over France during World War I. The commanding officer moved into the hospital superintendent's house (1904, Aaron Gove and Thomas F. Walsh), 520 Rampart Way, the only structure of the sanitarium still standing. Denver architects Gove and Walsh designed the sanitarium in the Mission style, with sleeping porches, open porches, and arcades in stuccoed buildings flaunting curvilinear parapets and red tile roofs.

The base grew tremendously during World War II, when it was a major U.S. training station for bombardiers, artillery personnel, and aerial photographers.

During the Cold War, the base continued to thrive and became the first home of the Air Force Academy before it moved in 1958 to its Colorado Springs campus. More than six hundred structures dotted the site, and some 1.5 million men and women were trained or stationed at Lowry over the years.

On September 30, 1994, the Air Force abandoned Lowry, which was then converted to various uses. Two historic districts were created. The Officers' Row Historic District contains sixteen houses along Rampart Way and East 4th and East 5th Avenues. The Lowry Technical Training Center Historic District consists of Building 349 (the original 3,600-bed brick barracks, which became the Administrative Building); Buildings 379 and 380, Art Deco edifices used for classrooms; and two large aircraft hangars, Buildings 401 and 402. Hangar 401 has been recycled as the Wings Over the Rockies Museum, 7750 East Irvington Place.

244. Lowry/Eisenhower Memorial Chapel No. 1. (Photo by Thomas H. Simmons)

244. Lowry-Eisenhower Memorial Chapel No. 1

(1941), Quince Way/Camp David Way near the SW corner of E. 3rd Ave., NR

The standard military-design chapel is strategically located between the Officers' Row and the Lowry Technical Training Center Historic Districts. Lowry Air Force Building 27 is a rare surviving example of a simple, low-budget, frame military chapel. This humble, little-altered edifice gained fame as a place where President Dwight D. Eisenhower and his wife, Mamie, attended services during his presidential visits to Denver in 1953, 1954, and 1955. It is popularly known as the Eisenhower Memorial Chapel and is easily recognizable by its prominent spire.

MONTCLAIR

HD-24 MONTCLAIR HISTORIC DISTRICT
(see Map 10, page 128)

(1975), Olive and Oneida Sts. between E. 7th and E. 12th Aves.

A German émigré, Baron Walter B. Von Richthofen, founded and promoted Montclair as a suburban town in 1885. The core of the neighborhood is an unusual Denver historic district of scattered large Victorian homes on one-block tracts infilled with many more modest newer residences. The older houses were built as show homes to attract home builders, but the crash of 1893 froze development until after 1900. The neighborhood is a catalog of area styles from the 1880s to the present, with a preponderance of 1950s brick houses incorporating bungalow and ranch-house elements. The three-story brick and stone house (1897; 1987, restoration) at 740 Olive Street was the home of architect Harlan Thomas, who served as a Montclair mayor.

Tuberculosis Houses

(1907–1911, Charles M. Kittredge and Dennis Tirsway, bldrs.), 928, 940, 956 Olive St. and 791 Newport St.

A notable feature of the Montclair district are these so-called TB houses. Other, considerably altered models are at 725, 737, and 920 Newport Street. These single-story homes are a reminder that Denver became one of this country's most health-conscious cities after the 1893 silver crash. Health care became a major industry as tuberculars, asthmatics, and other lung disease patients began a new rush into Colorado. They came for the high, dry, sunny climate, nationally prescribed as a cure for the deadliest disease of that time — tuberculosis. By 1900, Denver was filled with sanitaria, hospitals, and rest homes. Many an old mansion became a boardinghouse for members of the "one-lunged army."

The TB houses were side gabled, with screened porches at either end and open interiors with minimal walls to allow sunlight and fresh air. Subsequent owners have enclosed the sleeping porches. The houses are surprisingly modern in their open floor plans and emphasis on bringing the outdoors inside. Rooms open off a central hall with a fireplace. Ten-foot ceilings, many windows, and large doorways made for bright, open houses, unlike the bungalows being built at the time.

245. Montclair Civic Building (Molkerei)

(c. 1899), 6820 E. 12th Ave. between Newport and Oneida Sts., NR

Modeled after German health spas offering the milk cure, this building started out as a Molkerei (German for "milkhouse") with cattle stabled in the basement. Tuberculosis patients housed upstairs could lounge on the open-air sun porches, drink fresh milk, and breathe the barnyard effluvium. This two-story clapboard structure with a rhyolite foundation and brick columns has a screened porch on three sides. Tuscan columns and the Eastlake trim on the north entry and overhead balcony are among the few pieces of ornament on a utilitarian edifice that found reuse in 1908 as one of Denver's first community centers.

Richthofen Fountain

(1901, Harlan Thomas), E. end of Richthofen Pkwy., SE corner of Oneida St. and Oneida Pl.

To refresh beasts of burden and honor her deceased husband, Baroness Louisa von Richthofen erected this fountain of pinkish, black-flecked Pikes Peak granite. Later, a bronze repository containing her ashes was added to the back wall of the fountain. In addition to the name "Richthofen," the fountain is incised with a line from Samuel Taylor Coleridge's poem "The Rime of the Ancient Mariner": "He Prayeth Well Who Loveth Well Both Bird, and Man, and Beast."

246. Richthofen Castle

(1887, Alexander Cazin? 1910, addition by Maurice Biscoe. 1924, addition by J.J.B. Benedict and Maurice Biscoe), 7020 E. 12th Ave. and Olive Street, NR

Baron Walter von Richthofen erected this rhyolite castle as the show home of Montclair, his suburban real estate scheme. Alexander Cazin, a fellow German, may have designed this mock medieval fortress with its third-story crenelated turrets. On the northwest corner sits the red sandstone bust of Frederick Barbarossa, the medieval ruler who first tried to unify Germany. The original castle, a prickly Prussian affair, was remodeled in 1910 by Edwin Hendrie, who purchased the castle as his home in 1903. Hendrie added a half-timbered west wing, tiled the roof, and remodeled the interior for his daughter, Gertrude, and her husband, William W. Grant. In 1924, the Grants had J.J.B. Benedict design the south wing. Inside the thirty-five-room castle is an entry hall with dark oak paneling and hand-tooled leather walls and a parquet-floored music room seating 150. The gatehouse to the east has been converted to a separate residence, 1177 Pontiac Street. Low-slung modern homes now surround the castle, a private residence that still dominates the Montclair neighborhood.

247. St. Luke's Episcopal Church

(1890, James Murdoch), 1270 Poplar St., SE corner of E. 13th Ave.

Rusticated rhyolite walls pierced by lancet windows, and a square corner tower with a tall, shingled steeple distinguish this church. Despite additions, St. Luke's, with its small buttresses, fine stonework, and large rose window, remains a good example of an English Gothic Revival chapel.

248. Fire Station No. 14

(1937, Charles F. Pillsbury), 1426 Oneida St.

This station occupies the site of the old Montclair town hall, which had also housed the fire station before Montclair's annexation to Denver in 1902. Pillsbury

246. Richthofen Castle. (Courtesy of von Richthofen estate, Tom Noel Collection)

247. St. Luke's Episcopal Church. (Courtesy Denver Public Library)

designed this WPA firehouse to harmonize with the surrounding residential architecture. It resembles the Tudoresque cottages popular in the 1930s in its tapestry brick facade with tile trim, steep-pitched, side-gabled roof, and central projecting entry bay with a prominent doorway under a half-timbered gable.

249. Greeters of America Home

(1900, Peter Maider, bldr.), 1740 and 1760 Ulster St.

The Greeters of America, an organization of hotel employees, established its "national home" for indigent, ill, and retired members in these two houses. The first, 1740 Ulster, had been constructed in 1900 as a private residence. The Greeters built the larger brick residence at 1760 Ulster in the late 1920s. This newer building was once connected to the older house by a now-gone breezeway. The low-slung, unimposing brick complex blends well with the surrounding residential area.

133

PARK HILL (NORTH OF EAST COLFAX AVENUE)

250. Ashley Elementary School

(1930, John M. Gardner and Eugene F. Evans. 1951, addition by S. Arthur Axtens), 1914 Syracuse St.

This school is named for Eli Melville Ashley (1833–1909), a man with bushy eyebrows and a bushy goatee who presided over the Western Chemical Company. He also headed the Denver Chamber of Commerce and served on the Denver School Board, where he helped achieve a consolidated Denver School district. Prominent Denver architect S. Arthur Axtens's 1951 addition of a hallway and more classrooms uses the same zigzag blond brick patterns, ornate iron railings, and vertical window treatment employed by Gardner and Evans.

251. Treat Hall

(1889, Frank H. Jackson), 1800 Pontiac St., NR

Designed in the Richardsonian Romanesque mode, this first building of Colorado Woman's College was named for the college's first president, Jay Porter Treat. It initially housed faculty, students, and classrooms. Rusticated gray stone walls have contrasting red stone banding and round-arched windows. The massive entry arch, steep-pitched roof, and Châteauesque dormers add charm to this imposing monolith. Colorado Woman's College was purchased in 1982 by another private school, the University of Denver, and converted to the University of Denver Park Hill Campus.

252. Park Hill Elementary School

(1901. 1912, addition. 1928, remodel and addition by Frederick E. Mountjoy and Frank W. Frewan. 1969, addition by Phillips-Carter-Reister), 5050 E. 19th Ave. between Elm and Fairfax Aves.

Medallion busts of Beethoven and Shakespeare are part of the florid terra-cotta trim for this school in the Spanish Colonial Revival style. In 1928 Mountjoy and Frewan added a gymnasium on the west and an auditorium on the east. These match the stucco building mass, polychrome terra-cotta detail, floral frieze, and red tile roof of the original 1901 school (architect unknown). In 1968–1969, the architectural firm of Phillips-Carter-Reister designed the kindergarten wing and cafeteria as a horizontal massing that complements the vertical nature of the 1901 three-story central building.

253. Park Hill Branch Library

(1920, Merrill H. Hoyt and Burnham Hoyt. 1994, restoration by David Owen Tryba), 4705 Montview Blvd., NE corner of Dahlia St.

This Italian Renaissance–Revival-style branch library honors Montview Boulevard's grand residential scale. The Andrew Carnegie Foundation helped fund this $27,000 branch library, a stucco one-story building under a red tile roof. Rich details include an entry cartouche featuring the lamp of learning. Acanthus-encrusted balusters divide the diamond-paned front windows. An unfortunate 1964 remodeling was happily undone in a 1994 restoration. Once again, the overwhelming interior impression is of natural light and spaciousness, with dark woodwork and ceiling beams providing contrast.

254. This corner bell tower summons the faithful to St. Thomas Episcopal Church. (Photo by Rutherford C. Witthus)

254. St. Thomas Episcopal Church

(1908, Harry James Manning), 2201 Dexter St.

One of Denver's best examples of the Spanish Colonial Revival mode has a fantastic Churrigueresque entry surround of cast stone. A keystone inscribed with a cross caps the arched doorway beneath a stained glass window crowned by a wreath framing the ark of salvation. A three-arched bell tower, stucco walls, and red tile roof characterize the church, which, with its auxiliary buildings and cloister, frame a lovely enclosed courtyard. Inside on either side of the altar, the reredos features handmade tile shields featuring the twelve apostles.

CHAPTER 7
Denver Mountain Parks

MARTIN RANCH/DANIELS PARK
RED ROCKS PARK
DEDISSE PARK

The Denver Mountain Parks are owned and operated by the City of Denver even though they fall outside the city limits. Other municipalities have undertaken similar projects, but the variety and vastness of Denver's mountain parks are noteworthy. These forty-eight parks encompass roughly 13,500 acres in Clear Creek, Douglas, Grand, and Jefferson Counties. They contain buffalo and elk herds in Genesee Mountain Park, an outdoor amphitheater in Red Rocks Park, and Winter Park Ski Area.

Mayor Robert W. Speer made mountain parks part of his City Beautiful scheme, and voters approved a 1912 city charter change authorizing their acquisition and development. Frederick Law Olmsted, Jr., was engaged to plan a string of parks, which he surveyed on horseback before providing a master plan.

The first mountain park, Genesee, was acquired by the city in 1912 to save Genesee Mountain from being sold to a sawmill company. Subsequent purchases or donations to the city included Lookout Mountain (1917), where the Buffalo Bill Grave and Museum were installed after his death in 1917. Mayor Benjamin Franklin Stapleton and his energetic and resourceful manager of improvements and parks, George E. Cranmer, expanded and improved the park system, building Red Rocks Amphitheater and Winter Park Ski Area by 1941, when the present system was virtually complete. Although the entire Denver Mountain Park system is on the National Register of Historic Places, only a handful of specific sites have been designated as Denver landmarks.

MARTIN RANCH/DANIELS PARK

HD-25 FLORENCE MARTIN RANCH HISTORIC DISTRICT

(c. 1920s), in Daniels Park, west side of Daniels Park Rd., 3.5 miles north of U.S. 85

Florence F. Martin, born in Sydney, Australia, to a governor of New South Wales, became a globe-trotting socialite. She met and became fast friends with Denver department store magnate William C. Daniels and his wife, Cicey. Daniels gave Martin a ranch site in Daniels Park, twenty miles south of Denver in Douglas County.

There Martin assembled a 2,400-acre ranch. Her large house burned, leaving only ruins, but a barn, tiled round silo, bunkhouses, chicken coops, pump houses, and a reservoir survive.

Upon her death in 1957, Martin donated the entire ranch to the City of Denver for use as a mountain park. The Martin Ranch is architecturally notable for its use of native stone foundations with upper walls of tongue-and-groove siding in a ranch complex displaying both rustic and Craftsman-style elements. The 160-acre core of the ranch comprises the historic district.

Adjacent Daniels Ranch parcels were also donated to Denver over the years as part of an effort to put together a greenbelt of mountain parks in the foothills around Denver. Besides making Daniels Park the home of a municipal buffalo herd, the Denver Parks and Recreation Department built a rustic-style picnic shelter of massive field stones with built-in benches around a central fireplace. This public amenity is well sited on a scenic overlook facing the South Platte Valley and the Front Range of the Rockies.

RED ROCKS PARK

255. Red Rocks Amphitheater

(1941, Burnham Hoyt), in Red Rocks Park, near the junction of Colorado Highways 8, 26, and 74, NRD

Selected Colorado's most notable twentieth-century structure for the American Institute of Architects' 1957 centennial exhibit at the National Gallery of Art in Washington, D.C., this acoustically superb outdoor theater is formed by massive sandstone slabs and metamorphic rocks tilted upward by volcanic action. *Architectural Forum*, in May 1945, praised "the admirable restraint with which architect Burnham Hoyt has preserved the original flavor of a majestic setting." Collaborating with nature, Hoyt used the local juniper tree as landscaping and the native red sandstone for drainage canals and outdoor seating. The wonderful simplicity of this design has been marred by a few subsequent additions, such as a stage covering that partially blocks the view of Denver and the high plains. The surrounding 1,640-acre Red Rocks Park offers hiking trails through dramatic foothills scenery.

255. Red Rocks Amphitheater. (Photo by Tom Noel)

256. Pueblo Concession House

(1931, Wilbert R. Rosche), in Red Rocks Park near the amphitheater

The facade of this two-story Southwestern-style structure mixes a Mission Revival parapet and Pueblo Revival vigas, a combination as common as intermarriage between Hispanos and Native Americans. This elegant structure set in a cactus garden contains a visitors' center, cafe, and museum.

DEDISSE PARK

257. Evergreen Lake Warming House

(1934, Civilian Conservation Corps), south shore of Evergreen Lake

A grassy hillside flows onto the roof of this round log shelter dug into the south bank of this picturesque mountain reservoir. Massive logs with corner saddle notching form a low-slung facade angled to fit the contour of the lake's shoreline. The use of peeled logs and the rustic style may have been suggested by the nearby Keys on the Green Clubhouse and Restaurant, a J.J.B. Benedict design for the Denver Mountain Parks golf course bordering the west edge of Evergreen Lake. Reminiscent of sod-roofed log dugouts, this warming house provides a wonderful model for discreet, contextual mountain resort architecture.

This unobtrusive earth-sheltered structure was built as a warming house, skate rental shop, and snack bar for ice skaters who flocked to this Denver Mountain Park. The warming house proved to be too small, and the CCC constructed a mirror-image addition on the east side of the structure, which shares the boardwalk and pier. The warming house, Evergreen Lake, and Keys on the Green Clubhouse and Restaurant are part of Dedisse Park, a National Register Historic District.

139

Appendix A
Denver Landmarks and Historic Districts
by Designation Number

LANDMARKS

1. Emmanuel Sherith Israel Chapel, 1201 10th St. at Lawrence St.
2. Constitution Hall, 1501–1507 Blake St. at 15th St. (demolished)
3. Governor's Mansion, 400 E. 8th Ave., SE corner of Logan St.
4. Immaculate Conception Basilica, 401 E. Colfax Ave., NE corner of Logan St.
5. Byers-Evans House, 1310 Bannock St., NE corner of W. 13th Ave.
6. Trinity United Methodist Church, 1820 Broadway, NE corner of E. 18th Ave.
7. St. John's Episcopal Cathedral, 1313 Clarkson St. between E. 13th and E. 14th Aves.
8. First Baptist Church, 230 E. 14th St., SW corner of Grant St.
9. First Church of Christ Scientist, 1401–1415 Logan St., NW corner of E. 14th Ave.
10. Daniels & Fisher Tower, 1601 Arapahoe St., corner of 16th St. Mall
11. Denver Women's Press Club, 1325 Logan St.
12. Four Mile House, 5000 E. Exposition Ave.
13. Zion Baptist Church, 933 E. 24th Ave., NW corner of Ogden St.
14. St. Elizabeth's Catholic Church, 1062 11th St.
15. South Broadway Christian Church, 23 Lincoln St., NW corner of E. Ellsworth Ave.
16. Evans Memorial Chapel, University of Denver campus, E. Evans Ave. and S. University Blvd.
17. St. Mark's Episcopal Church, 1160 Lincoln St., SE corner of E. 12th Ave.
18. Scott Methodist Church-Sanctuary Lofts, 2201 Ogden St., NW corner of E. 22nd Ave.
19. St. Cajetan's Catholic Church, 900 Lawrence St., corner of 9th St.
20. Molly Brown House, 1340 Pennsylvania St.
21. Brinker Collegiate Institute-The Navarre-Museum of Western Art, 1725–1727 Tremont Pl.
22. Smith Mansion, 1801 York St., NW corner of E. 18th Ave.
23. Pope-Thompson-Wasson House, 1320 Race St.
24. Denver Tramway Company Powerhouse-Forney Transportation Museum, 1416 Platte St.
25. Pearce-McCallister House, 1880 Gaylord St.
26. Tivoli Brewery, 900 block of Larimer St.
27. Buckhorn Exchange Restaurant, 1000 Osage St., NE corner of W. 10th Ave.
28. U.S. Mint, 320 W. Colfax Ave. between Delaware and Cherokee Sts.
29. Tears-McFarlane House, 1290 Williams St., SE corner of E. 13th Ave.
30. Odd Fellows' Hall, 1543–1545 Champa St.
31. Denver City Cable Railway Company Building, 1215 18th St. at Lawrence St.
32. Richthofen Castle, 7020 E. 12th Ave. and Olive St.
33. Croke-Patterson-Campbell Mansion, 428–430 E. 11th Ave., SW corner of Pennsylvania St.
34. Foster-McCauley-Symes House, 738 Pearl St.
35. Sacred Heart Catholic Church, 2760 Larimer St.
36. Thomas Hornsby Ferril House, 2123 Downing St.
37. Asbury Methodist Church, 2215 W. 30th Ave., NW corner of Vallejo St.
38. Heiser House, 3016 Osceola St., NE corner of W. 30th Ave.
39. Queree House, 2914 W. 29th Ave.
40. Mackay House, 3359 Alcott St.
41. Cox House, 3417 Lowell Blvd.
42. Cox Gargoyle House, 3425 Lowell Blvd.

43. Miller House, 2501 High St., NW corner of E. 25th Ave.
44. John Brisben Walker House, 3520 Newton St.
45. Cheesman Park Memorial Pavilion, 1000 High St.
46. Denver Botanic Gardens House, 909 York St., NW corner E. 9th Ave.
47. Boettcher Conservatory, Denver Botanic Gardens, 1005 York St.
48. Eugene Field Cottage, 715 S. Franklin St.
49. Red Rocks Amphitheater, Red Rocks Park
50. Montclair Civic Building, 6820 E. 12th Ave.
51. Fleming House, 1510 S. Grant St., Platte Park
52. Sheedy Mansion, 1115 Grant St., NW corner of E. 11th Ave.
53. Fire Station No. 1, 1326 Tremont Pl.
54. Hallet House, 900 Logan St., NE corner E. 9th Ave.
55. Clarke House, 940 Logan St.
56. Campbell House, 950 Logan St.
57. Clemes-Lipe House, 901 Pennsylvania St., NW corner E. 9th Ave.
58. Taylor House, 945 Pennsylvania St.
59. Hitchings Block, 1620 Market St.
60. Liebhardt-Lindner Building, 1624 Market St.
61. McCrary Building, 1626–1632 Market St.
62. Waters Building, 1642 Market St.
63. Bockfinger-Flint Mercantile, 1644–1650 Market St.
64. Columbia Hotel, 1320–1732 17th St., corner of Market St.
65. U.S. Post Office and Federal Building, 1823 Stout St., between 18th and 19th Sts.
66. St. Elizabeth's Retreat Chapel, 2825 W. 32nd Ave.
67. St. Andrews Episcopal Church, 2015 Glenarm Pl.
68. Half-Moon House, 3205 W. 21st Ave.
69. Voorhees House, 1471 Stuart St.
70. Smith House, 1435 Stuart St.
71. Raymond House-Castle Marne, 1572 Race St.
72. Bliss House, 1389 Stuart St.
73. Bosworth House, 1400 Josephine St., NE corner of E. 14th Ave.
74. Malo Mansion, 500 E. 8th Ave., SE corner of Pennsylvania St.
75. John Porter House, 777 Pearl St., SW corner of E. 8th Ave.
76. Adams-Fitzell House, 1359 Race St.
77. Corona School-Dora Moore School, 846 Corona St. between E. 8th and E. 9th Aves.
78. Coyle-Chase House, 532 W. 4th Ave.
79. Dunning-Benedict House, 1200 Pennsylvania St., NE corner of E. 12th Ave.
80. Keating House, 1207 Pennsylvania St., NW corner of E. 12th Ave.
81. Treat Hall, 1800 Pontiac St.
82. St. Luke's Episcopal Church, 1270 Poplar St., SE corner of E. 13th Ave.
83. Neef House, 2143 Grove St.
84. Creswell House, 1244 Grant St.
85. Daly House, 1034 Logan St.
86. McNeil House, 930 Logan St.
87. Fairmount Cemetery Gatehouse, 7204 E. Alameda Ave.
88. Fairmount Cemetery Ivy Chapel, 430 S. Quebec St.
89. Spangler House, 1444 Stuart St.
90. Baker-Plested Cottage, 1208 Logan St.
91. The Cornwall, 921 E. 13th Ave., NW corner of Ogden St.
92. Sykes-Nicholson-Moore House, 1410 High St.
93. Watson House, 1437 High St.
94. Kerr House, 1900 E. 7th Ave., SE corner of High St.
95. Grant-Humphreys Mansion, 770 Pennsylvania St.
96. Damascio House, 3611–3615 Osage St.
97. St. Thomas Episcopal Church, 2201 Dexter St., NW corner of E. 22nd Ave.
98. Phipps House, 3400 Belcaro Dr.
99. Zang Mansion, 709 Clarkson St., NW corner of E. 7th Ave.
100. All Saints Episcopal Church-Chapel of Our Merciful Savior, 2222 W. 32nd Ave., SE corner of Wyandot St.
101. Our Lady of Mount Carmel Catholic Church, 3549 Navajo St., SW corner of W. 36th Ave.
102. St. Patrick's Catholic Church, 3325 Pecos St., NW corner of W. 33rd Ave.
103. Equitable Building, 730 17th St., corner of Stout St.
104. Gates House, 1375 Josephine St., SW corner of E. 13th Ave.
105. Ideal Building (Colorado Federal Building), 821 17th St., corner of Champa St.
106. Rosenzweig House, 1129 E. 17th Ave. and Park Ave. between Downing and Marion Sts.
107. Walters-Brierly House, 2259 Gilpin St., SW corner of E. 23rd Ave.
108. Stearns House, 1030 Logan St.
109. Wells Fargo Depot, 1338 15th St., corner of Market St.
110. Edbrooke House, 931 E. 17th Ave.
111. McNulty House, 1390 Stuart St., SW corner of W. 14th Ave.
112. Woodbury House, 2841 Perry St.
113. Lobach House, 2851 Perry St., SW corner of W. 29th Ave.
114. Thomas Field House (demolished), 2305 S. Washington St.
115. Mitchell-Schomp House, 680 Clarkson St., SE corner of E. 7th Ave.
116. Zang Townhouse, 1532 Emerson St.

117. Guerrieri-Decunto House, 1650 Pennsylvania St.
118. Moses House, 4001 W. 30th Ave., NW corner of Perry St.
119. Gebhard-Smith-Brantigan House, 2253 Downing St., SW corner of E. 23rd Ave.
120. Lee House, 2653 W. 32nd Ave.
121. Kistler-Rodriguez House, 700 E. 9th Ave., SE corner of Washington St.
122. Foster House, 2533 W. 32nd Ave.
123. Clements Row House, 2201–2217 Glenarm Pl.
124. Mattie Silks House, 2009 Market St.
125. Baerresen-Freeman House, 1718 Gaylord St.
126. Fleming-Hanington House, 1133 Pennsylvania St.
127. Butters House, 1129 Pennsylvania St.
128. Flower-Vaile House, 1610 Emerson St.
129. Wheeler Block, 2114–2152 W. 29th Ave.
130. Cerrone's Grocery, 3617 Osage St.
131. Lowry-Eisenhower Memorial Chapel No. 1, Lowry Air Force Base, Quince Way-Camp David Way near the SW corner of E. 3rd. Ave.
132. Wolcott School, 1400–1414 Marion St., NE corner of E. 14th Ave.
133. Denver City Railway Company, 1635 17th St., corner of Wynkoop St.
134. Chappell House, 1555 Race St.
135. McCourt House, 1471 High St.
136. Masonic Temple, 1614 Welton St., corner of 16th St. Mall
137. Denver Athletic Club, 1325 Glenarm Pl. between 13th and 14th Sts.
138. Barney Ford Building, 1512–1514 Blake St.
139. Curry-Chukovich-Gerash House, 1439 Court Pl.
140. Kettle Building, 1426 Larimer St.
141. Apollo Hall-Congdon Building, 1421–1425 Larimer St.
142. Barnum Building, 1412 Larimer St.
143. Sussex Building, 1430 Larimer St.
144. Granite Hotel, 1456–1460 Larimer St.
145. Crawford Building, 1439–1441 Larimer St.
146. Gallup-Stanbury Building, 1445–1451 Larimer St.
147. Lincoln Hall Building, 1413–1419 Larimer St.
148. McKibben Building, 1409–1411 Larimer St.
149. Gahan's Saloon-Lanktree Hotel, 1401–1407 Larimer St.
150. Edward W. Wynkoop Building, 1738 Wynkoop St.
151. Denver Gas and Electric Company (Insurance Exchange Building), 910 15th St., corner of Champa St.
152. Oxford Hotel, 1612 17th St., corner of Wazee St.
153. Bosler-Yankee House, 3209 W. Fairview Pl.
154. Mayan Theater, 110 Broadway
155. Emerson School-Ralph Waldo Emerson Center, 1420 Ogden St., NE corner of E. 14th Ave.
156. Sarah Platt Decker Branch Library, 1501 S. Logan St., SW corner of E. Florida Ave.
157. Anfenger House, 2900 Champa St., corner of 29th St.
158. Philip Milstein (1907–1993), Denver's only human landmark
159. Wood-Morris-Bonfils House, 707 Washington St., NW corner of E. 7th Ave.
160. Hotel Hope Building, 1404 Larimer St.
161. Barth Hotel, 1514 17th St., corner of Blake St.
162. Windsor Stables Building, 1732–1770 Blake St., corner of 18th St.
163. Fire Station No. 15, 1080 Clayton St., SE corner of E. 11th Ave.
164. Hose Company No. 1, 1963 Chestnut St., corner of 20th St.
165. Sweet House, 1075 Humboldt St.
166. First Avenue Hotel, 101–115 Broadway
167. Denver Press Club, 1330 Glenarm Pl.
168. Temple Emanuel Center, 1595 Pearl St., SW corner of E. 16th Ave.
169. Brind-Axtens House, 1000 Logan St., NE corner of E. 10th Ave.
170. Hannigan-Canino Terrace, 3500 Navajo St. and 1421–1439 W. 35th Ave.
171. Neusteter Building, 720–730 16th St., corner of Stout St.
172. Wyatt School, 3620 Franklin St. between E. 36th and E. 37th Aves.
173. Milheim House, 1515 Race St.
174. Central Bank Site, 1100–1108 15th St., corner of Arapahoe St.
175. Paramount Theater, 1621 Glenarm Pl.
176. Harman Town Hall-Greenleaf Masonic Temple, 400 St. Paul St., NE corner E. 4th Ave.
177. Scottish Rite Masonic Temple, 1370 Grant St., SE corner of E. 14th Ave.
178. Brown Palace Hotel, 321 17th St., NW corner of Broadway
179. Boston Building, 828 17th St., corner of Champa St.
180. Park Hill Branch Library, 4705 Montview Blvd., NE corner of Dahlia St.
181. Byers Branch Library, 675 Santa Fe Dr., SW corner of W. 7th Ave.
182. Smiley Branch Library, 4501 W. 46th Ave. at Utica St. in Berkeley Lake Park
183. Woodbury Branch Library, 3265 Federal Blvd.
184. Hill Mansion, 150 E. 10th Ave., SW corner of Sherman St.
185. U.S. National Bank-Guaranty Bank, 815 17th St., corner of Stout St.
186. Ferguson-Gano House, 722 E. 7th Ave.
187. Annunciation Catholic Church, 3601 Humboldt St., NW corner of E. 36th Ave.

188. Henry M. Porter House, 975 Grant St.
189. Greeters of America Home, 1740 and 1760 Ulster St.
190. Moffat Station, 2101 15th St., corner of Bassett St.
191. Fort Logan Field Officer's Quarters, 3742 W. Princeton Cir.
192. East High School, 1545 Detroit St., corner of E. Colfax Ave.
193. Cass House, 733 E. 8th Ave., NW corner of Clarkson St.
194. Robinson House, 1225 Pennsylvania St.
195. Stevens Elementary School, 1140 Columbine St. between E. 11th and E. 12th Aves.
196. Denver Municipal Auditorium, 920 14th St. between Curtis and Champa Sts.
197. South High School, 1700 E. Louisiana Ave. and Franklin St.
198. Twentieth Street Bathhouse, 1101 20th St., corner of Curtis St.
199. Brown-Garrey-Congdon House, 1300 E. 7th Ave., SE corner of Marion St.
200. Smedley Elementary School, 4250 Shoshone St. between W. 42nd and W. 43rd Aves.
201. Jane Silverstein Ries House, 737 Franklin St.
202. West High School, 951 Elati St. between W. 9th and W. 11th Ave.
203. Ashley Elementary School, 1914 Syracuse St. between E. 19th and E. 20th Aves.
204. Ebert Elementary School, 410 Park Ave. at Tremont Pl.
205. Lydon House, 2418 Stout St.
206. Douglass Undertaking Building, 2745 Welton St.
207. Cody House, 2932 Lafayette St.
208. McBird House, 2225 Downing St.
209. Whitehead-Peabody House, 1128 Grant St.
210. Burlington Hotel, 2201 Larimer St., corner of 22nd St.
211. Grant Middle School, 1751 S. Washington St.
212. Skinner Middle School, 3435 W. 40th Ave. between Irving & King St.
213. Romeo Block, 2944–2958 Zuni St., SE corner of W. 30th Ave.
214. Denver Dry Goods, 700 16th St., corner of California St.
215. Bluebird Theater, 3315–3317 E. Colfax Ave. between Adams and Cook Sts.
216. Denver Tramway Building, 1100 14th St., corner of Arapahoe St.
217. House With the Round Window, 3240 W. Hayward Pl.
218. Morey Middle School, 840 E. 14th Ave. between Clarkson and Emerson Sts.
219. Denver Public Schools Administration Building-Denver Art Museum Administration Building, 414 14th St., corner of Glenarm Pl.
220. Chamberlain Observatory, 2930 E. Warren Ave.
221. Graham-Bible House, 2080 York St.

222. Washington Park Bathhouse, S. Downing St. and E. Center Ave.
223. Nursery Building, 888 E. Iliff Ave.
224. Golda Meir House, 1146 9th St.
225. First National Bank of Denver-Holtze Executive Place Hotel, 818 17th St., corner of Stout St.
226. Park Hill Elementary School, 5050 E. 19th Ave. between Elm and Fairfax Aves.
227. Ogden Theatre, 935 E. Colfax Ave. at Ogden St.
228. Joshel House, 220 S. Dahlia St.
229. Cory Elementary School, 1550 S. Steele St. between E. Florida and E. Iowa Aves.
230. Merrill Middle School, 1551 S. Monroe St. between E. Florida and E. Iowa Aves.
231. Washington Park Boathouse and Pavilion, Washington Park
232. Pueblo Concession House, Red Rocks Park
233. Evergreen Lake Warming House, Dedisse Park, south shore
234. Savage Candy Company, 2158–2162 Lawrence St., SE corner of 22nd St.
235. Fire Station No. 3, 2500 Washington St.
236. Holmes House, 2330 Downing St.
237. Asbury Elementary School, 1320 E. Asbury Ave. between S. Marion and S. Lafayette Sts.
238. Hayden, Dickinson, and Feldhauser Building-Colorado Building, 1615-1623 California St.
239. Austin Apartments, 2400–2418 E. Colfax Ave., SE corner of Josephine St.
240. El Jebel Temple-Rocky Mountain Consistory, 1770 Sherman St., SE corner of E. 18th Ave.
241. Steele Elementary School, 320 S. Marion St. Pkwy.
242. Fager Residence, 2947 Umatilla St.
243. Tallmadge & Boyer Terrace, 2925–2947 Wyandot St.
244. Fire Station No. 7, 3600 Tejon St.
245. Our Lady of Guadalupe Catholic Church, 3559 Kalamath St., SW corner of W. 36th Ave.
246. German House-Denver Turnverein, 1570 Clarkson St.
247. Horace Mann Middle School, 4130 Navajo St. between W. 41st and W. 42nd Aves.
248. Sherman Elementary School-Denver Art Students League, 200 Grant St.
249. Cowie House, 3147 Umatilla St.
250. Fox-Schlatter House, 3225 Quivas St.
251. Cole-DeRose Apartment House, 1940–1946 W. 33rd Ave., SE corner of Tejon St.
252. Horan House, 2839 Wyandot St.
253. Elitch Gardens Theater, W. 38th Ave and Tennyson St.
254. Benson-Orsborn House, 1305 Elizabeth St., NW corner of E. 13th Ave.
255. Sayre's Alhambra, 801 Logan St., NW corner of E. 8th Ave.

256. Fire Station No. 11, 40 W. 2nd Ave.
257. Fire Station No. 14, 1426 Oneida St.
258. Fire Station No. 18-Denver Police Gang Unit, 2205 Colorado Blvd., NW corner of E. 22nd Ave.

HISTORIC LANDMARK DISTRICTS IN ORDER OF DESIGNATION

D-01 Larimer Square Historic District
D-02 Humboldt Street Historic District
D-03 Ninth Street Park Historic District
D-04 Clements Addition Historic District
D-05 Montclair Historic District
D-06 Civic Center Historic District
D-07 Smith's Ditch (City Ditch) Historic District
D-08 Morgan Addition Historic District
D-09 Potter Highlands Historic District
D-10 West 28th Avenue (Stonemen's Row) Historic District

D-11 Old Highland Historic Business District
D-12 Snell Addition Historic District
D-13 Potter Highlands Historic District (expanded boundaries)
D-14 Lafayette Street Historic District
D-15 Lower Downtown Historic District
D-16 Speer Boulevard Historic District
D-17 City Park Pavilion Historic District
D-18 Country Club Historic District
D-19 Quality Hill Historic District
D-20 Witter-Cofield Historic District
D-21 East Seventh Avenue Historic District
D-22 Wyman Addition Historic District
D-23 East Park Place Historic District
D-24 Florence Martin Ranch Historic District
D-25 Curtis Park "B" Historic District
D-26 Curtis Park "A" Historic District
D-27 Lowry Officers' Row Historic District
D-28 Lowry Technical Training Center Historic District

Appendix B
Denver Landmark Preservation Commissioners

Archuletta, Lena (1984–1987)

Arndt, Helen Millett (1967–1983)

Atchison, Philip (1967–1969)

Barry, Joseph B. (1974–1985)

Catherwood, Jean (1986–1992)

Falkenberg, Ruth (1979–1991)

Ferril, Thomas Hornsby (1972–1978)

Fisher, Alan (1967–1978)

Flores, Philip A. (1991–)

Foster, Paul (1983–1988)

Fuller, Mrs. Pierpont (Frances Walker) (1967–1979)

Hart, Gerald T. (1967–1974)

Hoeft, Kathy (1990–1992)

Hornbein, Marjorie (1986–1992)

Hornby, Barbara Sudler (1992–)

Leonard, Stephen J. (1994–)

Mazzula, Fred M. (1967–1981)

Milstein, Philip (1967–1984, 1987–1990)

Morgan, James C. (1978–1992)

Morris, Langdon E., Jr. (1972–1983)

Noel, Thomas J. (1983–1994)

Norgren, Barbara S. (1979–1991, 1993–)

Nunally, Sharon L. (1992–)

Pouw, Stanley (1991–1992)

Rogers, John B. (1996–)

Root, Robert (1992)

Rosenman, Seth (1992–95)

Schneider, Roz Yamashita (1990–)

Stearns, Robert L. (1967–1972)

Sudler, James A. (1967–1972)

Swett, B. Storey (1992–)

White, Edward D., Jr. (1969–1990, 1992–)

Appendix C
Lost Undesignated Landmarks

Aladdin Theater (1926, Frederick W. Ireland, Jr.), E. Colfax Ave. at Race St. Demolished 1984.

Albany Hotel (1885.1930s, remodel and expansion by Burnham Hoyt), 17th and Stout Sts. Demolished 1977.

Apollo Hall-City Hall (1859, Libeus Barney), 1425 Larimer St. Demolished 1870s.

Arapahoe County Courthouse (1883, Frederick C. Eberley), 16th St. and Court Pl. Demolished 1933.

Arapahoe School (1872), 18th and Arapahoe Sts. Demolished 1955.

James Archer House-Denver Medical School (1870s), 13th and Welton Sts. Demolished 1925.

Argo Smelter (1878, Robert S. Roeschlaub), I-25 and I-70. Demolished 1910.

Ashland School (1874. 1882, William Quayle. 1894, addition), W. 29th Ave. between Zuni St. and Firth Court. Demolished 1975.

Bancroft Block (1880, Robert S. Roeschlaub), 16th and Stout Sts. Demolished 1902.

Barth Block (1882, Robert S. Roeschlaub), 1210 16th St. Demolished 1946.

Horace Bennett-Chappell House, 1300 Logan St. Demolished 1970.

W. D. Bethell House (1893, Theodore D. Boal), 1154 E. Colfax Ave. Demolished 19??

Charles Boettcher House (1880s, John J. Huddart), 1201 Grant St. Demolished 1953.

Charles Boettcher II House (1922, J.J.B. Benedict?), 777 Washington St. Demolished 1963.

Boettcher School (1940, Burnham Hoyt), 1900 Downing St. Demolished c. 1992.

Brinton Terrace (1882, Ernest P. Varian and Frederick J. Sterner), 23–37 E. 18th Ave. and 1803–1807 Lincoln St. Demolished 1956.

Broadway School (1875, Robert S. Roeschlaub), 1300 Broadway. Demolished 1923.

Henry C. Brown-H.A.W. Tabor Mansion (1870s), E. 17th Ave. and Broadway. Demolished 1903.

John Sidney Brown House (1890s), 909 Grant St. Demolished 1968.

Byers-Porter House (1883), 1510 Sherman St. Demolished 19??

Cactus Club (1925, Burnham Hoyt), 441 14th St., corner of Glenarm Pl. Demolished 1969.

California Building (1892, Frank E. Edbrooke), 17th and California Sts. Demolished 1961.

John F. Campion House (c. 1900, Aaron M. Gove and Thomas F. Walsh), NE corner of E. 8th Ave. and Logan St. Demolished 1964.

Central Presbyterian Church (1875, Robert S. Roeschlaub), 18th and Champa Sts. Demolished 19??

Chamber of Commerce Building (1884, Frank E. Edbrooke), 14th and Lawrence Sts. Demolished 1967.

Cheesman Block (1881), 17th and Larimer Sts. Demolished 1971.

Chever Block (1879, Robert S. Roeschlaub), 1701 Larimer St. Demolished c. 1971.

John B. Church Residence (1890, Robert S. Roeschlaub), 900 Pennsylvania St. Demolished 1960s?

William Church "Castle" Residence (1890, William Lang and Marshall R. Pugh), 1000 Corona St. Demolished 1965.

Clark, Gruber & Co. Bank and Mint (1860), 16th and Market Sts. Demolished 1907.

Club Building (1892, Frank E. Edbrooke), 1725–1739 Arapahoe St. Demolished 1955.

Colorado National Bank (1882, William H.J. Nichols and Leo Canmann), 1701 Larimer St. Demolished 1939.

Continental Oil Building (1927, William N. Bowman), 1755 Glenarm Pl. and 18th St. Demolished 1976.

Cooper Building (1895, Frank E. Edbrooke), 17th and Curtis Sts. Demolished 1970.

Curtis & Clarke Building (1874), 1644–1650 Larimer St. Demolished c. 1964.

Delgany School (1885, Robert S. Roeschlaub), 21st and Delgany Sts. Demolished 1917.

Denham Theater, 635 18th St. at California St. Demolished 1974.

Denver City Hall (1883), 14th and Larimer Sts. Demolished 1937.

The Denver Club (1889, Ernest P. Varian and Frederick J. Sterner), 17th St. and Glenarm Pl. Demolished 1952.

Denver High School (1889, Robert S. Roeschlaub), from 19th to 20th Sts. between Stout and California Sts. Demolished 1929.

Ebert School (1880, Robert S. Roeschlaub), 22nd and Logan Sts. Demolished 1924.

Eleventh Street School (1861. 1873, addition), 11th and Lawrence Sts. Demolished c. 1884.

Ernest & Cranmer Building (1890, Frank E. Edbrooke), 17th and Curtis Sts. Demolished 1963.

Essex Building (1887, Frank E. Edbrooke), 1617 Lawrence St. Demolished c. 1970.

John Evans House (1860s), 14th and Arapahoe Sts. Demolished c. 1910.

John Evans II House (1911, William E. Fisher and Arthur A. Fisher), 2001 E. Alameda Ave., NE corner of Race St. Demolished c. 1968.

John A. Ferguson Mansion, E. 7th Ave., corner of Washington St. Demolished.

First Baptist Church (1883, Frank E. Edbrooke), 1747 Stout St. Demolished 19??

Donald K. Fletcher Mansion (1892), 1575 Grant St. Demolished 1961.

Gettysburg Cyclorama Building (1886), 1726 Champa St. Demolished 1906.

Gilpin School (1881, Robert S. Roeschlaub), 29th St. between Stout and California Sts. Demolished 1951.

Golden Eagle Dry Goods (1880, Frank E. Edbrooke), 1600 Lawrence St. Demolished c. 1970.

Peter Gottlesben Residence (1888, Robert S. Roeschlaub), 1901 Sherman St. Demolished 19??

Grant Smelter Stack (1892), 4100 Arkins Court. Demolished 1950.

Guldman-Bonfils Mansion (1912, Aaron M. Gove and Thomas F. Walsh), 1500 E. 10th Ave., SE corner of Humboldt St. Demolished 1960s.

Haish Manual Training School (1888, Robert S. Roeschlaub), 14th and Arapahoe Sts. Demolished 1970s.

Nathaniel P. Hill Residence (1881, Robert S. Roeschlaub), 14th and Welton Sts. Demolished 1934.

Holzman House (1890, Ernest P. Varian and Frederick J. Sterner), 1772 Grant St. Demolished 19??

Lafayette Hughes Mansion (1920s, William E. Fisher and Arthur A. Fisher), 2755 E. Exposition Ave. Demolished 19??

Hyperbolic Paraboloid (1958, I. M. Pei), 16th St. and Court Pl. Demolished 1996?

Interstate Trust Building (1891, Frank E. Edbrooke), 1132 16th St. and Lawrence St. Demolished 1970.

Iron Building (1891, John W. Roberts), 17th and Arapahoe Sts. Demolished 1969.

Charles M. Kittredge Mansion (1893, John J. Huddart), E. 8th Ave. and Oneida St. Demolished 1956.

Charles B. Kountze Home (1875, William H.J. Nichols), 14th and Welton Sts. Demolished.

Charles B. Kountze Mansion (1882, A. W. Fuller), 1601 Grant St., NW corner of E. 16th Ave. Demolished 1959.

Lafayette (Maria Mitchell) School (1898–1901, Robert S. Roeschlaub), Lafayette St. and 1335 E. 32nd Ave. Burned 1970.

Longfellow School (1882, Robert S. Roeschlaub), 13th and Welton Sts. Demolished 1956.

Majestic Building (1894, Frank E. Edbrooke), 16th St. and Broadway. Demolished 1977.

Markham Hotel (1882, Frank E. Edbrooke?), 1654 Lawrence St., corner of 17th St. Demolished 1969.

John McMurtrie–John Good Mansion (1892, Frank E. Edbrooke), 1007 Pennsylvania St. Demolished 1965.

McPhee Block (1890, Frank E. Edbrooke. 1920, remodeled as the C. A. Johnson Building), 17th St. and Glenarm Pl. Demolished 1975.

Metropole Hotel and Broadway Theater-Cosmopolitan Hotel (1890, Frank E. Edbrooke), 18th St. and Broadway. Demolished 1984.

Mining Exchange Building (1891, Kirchner and Kirchner), 15th and Arapahoe Sts. Demolished 1963.

Moffat House, 14th and Curtis Sts. Demolished 1920s.

Moffat Mansion (c. 1900, Harry James Manning), NE corner of E. 8th Ave. and Grant St. Demolished 1972.

Morey-Guggenheim House (1890s, Aaron M. Gove), 1555 Sherman St., SW corner of E. 16th Ave. Demolished 1953.

John K. Mullen House (1898), 896 Pennsylvania St. Demolished 19??

New Isis Theater (1912, Robert S. Roeschlaub), 1716–1726 Curtis St. Demolished 1954.

Old Post Office, Customs House, and Federal Building (1892), Arapahoe and 16th Sts. Demolished 1965.

Orpheum Theater (1903. 1930, demolished and rebuilt as the New Orpheum Theater), 1537 Welton St. Demolished 1967.

Patterson Block (1924), 17th and Welton Sts. Demolished 1975.

Thomas M. Patterson Residence (1883, Robert S. Roeschlaub), 17th and Welton Sts. Demolished c. 1923.

People's National Savings Bank (1890, Frank E. Edbrooke), 16th and Lawrence Sts. Demolished.

Quincy Block (1890s, Frank E. Edbrooke), 1012 17th Street, corner of Arapahoe St. Demolished 1960s?

Republic Building (1928, George Meredith Musick, Sr.), 16th St. and Tremont Pl. Demolished 1981.

Robert S. Roeschlaub Residence (1880, Robert S. Roeschlaub), W. Colfax Ave. and Delaware St. Demolished 19??

Platt Rogers Mansion (1884, Ernest P. Varian), E. Colfax Ave., corner of Washington St. Demolished 1996.

Security-Midland Bank (1927, William E. Fisher and Arthur A. Fisher), 17th and California Sts. Demolished c. 1993.

Shorthorn Building (1889, Frank E. Edbrooke), 23rd and Larimer Sts. Demolished 1990s.

Sloans Lake Depot (1890, Robert S. Roeschlaub), Sheridan Blvd. and W. 25th Ave. Demolished 19??

Sopris Duplex (1886, Robert S. Roeschlaub), 1337 Stout St. Demolished 19??

St. Leo's Church (1898?), 10th St. and W. Colfax Ave. Demolished 1965.

Strand Theater-State Theater (1914. 1925, modernization as the State Theater), 1630 Curtis St. Demolished 1953.

Tabor Block (1879, Willoughby J. Edbrooke and Frank E. Edbrooke), 16th and Larimer Sts. Demolished 1972.

Tabor Grand Opera House (1880, Willoughby J. Edbrooke and Frank E. Edbrooke), 16th and Curtis Sts. Demolished 1964.

Tabor Mansion, 1260 Sherman St. Demolished 1968.

Charles S. Thomas House (1882. 1892, expansion and remodeling by Frederick J. Sterner), 1609 Sherman St. Demolished 1960.

Times Building (1881, Robert S. Roeschlaub), 1547–1572 Arapahoe St. Demolished 19??

Tuxedo Place (1880, Robert S. Roeschlaub), E. Colfax Ave., NE corner of Downing St. Demolished 19??

Twenty-fourth Street School (1879, Robert S. Roeschlaub), 2345 Walnut St. at 24th St. Burned 1934.

Uncle Dick Wootton's Hall (1859, Richens L. Wootton), 11th and Walnut Sts. Demolished 18??

Union Block (1882, Robert S. Roeschlaub), 16th and Arapahoe Sts. Demolished 1963.

Unity Temple (1887, Frank E. Edbrooke), 19th St. and Broadway. Demolished 19??

Welcome Arch (1906, Mary Woodsen), 17th and Wynkoop Sts. Demolished 1931.

West Court Hotel (1911, Robert Willison and Montana Fallis), 1415 Glenarm Pl. Demolished 1982.

Whittier School (1883, Robert S. Roeschlaub), Marion St. between E. 24th and E. 25th Aves. Demolished 1974.

Windsor Hotel (1880), 18th and Larimer Sts. Demolished c. 1960.

Henry Wolcott Townhouse-The Paddock-Cactus Club (c. 1890, Harry Ten Eyck Wendell), 1751 Glenarm Pl. Demolished 1925.

Wolfe Hall (1867), 17th and Champa Sts. Demolished 1888.

Roger W. Woodbury Mansion (1889, Leonard Cutshaw), 2501 Woodbury Court, Demolished 1958.

B. F. Woodward Residence (1890s, Frank E. Edbrooke), 1530 Sherman St. Demolished 19??

Wyman Elementary School (1890, Robert S. Roeschlaub), E. 17th Ave. and Williams St. Demolished 1975.

Zang Brewing Company Complex (1859. Many additions), 6th to 9th Sts. between Platte and Water Sts. Mostly demolished.

Bibliography

GENERAL WORKS

Abrams, Jeanne E. *Historic Jewish Denver.* Denver: Rocky Mountain Jewish Historical Society, 1982. 26 p., maps, illus.

Arps, Louisa Ward. *Denver in Slices.* Denver: Sage Books, 1959 (1983 reprint). 274 p., maps, illus., endnotes, index.

Brettell, Richard E. *Historic Denver: The Architects and the Architecture, 1858–1893.* Denver: Historic Denver, Inc., 1973. 240 p., illus., notes, bib., index.

City Club of Denver. *Art in Denver.* Denver: Denver Public Library, 1928. 59 p., illus., index.

Colorado Historical Society, Office of Archaeology and Preservation. *State Register of Historic Properties.* Denver: Colorado Historical Society, 1995. This publication is frequently updated. This office also has extensive files on designated and potential landmarks.

Dallas, Sandra. *Cherry Creek Gothic: Victorian Architecture in Denver.* Norman: University of Oklahoma Press, 1970. 292 p., illus., bib., index.

Davis, Sally, and Betty Baldwin. *Denver Dwellings and Descendants.* Denver: Sage Books, 1963. 250 p., illus., bib., index.

Denver Landmark Preservation Commission. Files of individual and district designations. Denver Planning Office.

Denver Landmark Preservation Commission. *Historic Buildings Inventory.* Rev. ed. Denver: Denver Planning Office, 1981. Maps.

Denver Landmark Preservation Commission. *Design Guidelines for Landmark Structures & Districts.* Denver: Denver Planning Office, 1995. 54 p., illus.

Etter, Don D. *Denver Going Modern: A Photographic Essay on the Imprint of the International Style on Denver Residential Architecture.* Denver: Graphic Impressions, 1977. 132 p., illus., index.

Etter, Don D. *Denver's Park and Parkway System National Register Nomination.* Denver: Colorado Historical Society, 1986.

Forest, Kenton, Gene McKeever, and Raymond McAllister. *History of the Public Schools of Denver: A Brief History and Complete Building Survey.* Denver: Tramway Press, 1989. 64 p., illus., bib.

Goodstein, Phil. *Denver Streets: Names, Numbers, Locations, Logic.* Denver: New Social Publications, 1994. 144 p., maps, illus., bib., index.

Haber, Francine, Kenneth R. Fuller, and David R. Wetzel. *Robert S. Roeschlaub: Architect of the Emerging West, 1843–1923.* Denver: Colorado Historical Society, 1988. 168 p., illus., endnotes, index.

Kohl, Edith Eudora. *Denver's Historic Mansions.* Denver: Sage Books, 1957. 268 p., illus.

Leonard, Stephen J., and Thomas J. Noel. *Denver: Mining Camp to Metropolis.* Niwot: University Press of Colorado, 1990 (1994 reprint). 544 p., maps, illus., endnotes, appendices, bib., index.

McAlester, Virginia, and Lee McAlester. *A Field Guide to American Houses.* New York: Knopf, 1984. 525 p., illus., bib., index.

Morris, Langdon E., Jr. *Denver Landmarks.* Denver: Charles W. Cleworth, 1979. 324 p., illus., index.

Murphy, Jack A. *Geology Tour of Denver's Buildings and Monuments.* Denver: Denver Museum of Natural History and Historic Denver, Inc., 1995. 96 p., illus., bib., index.

Musick, G. Meredith, Sr. *Wayfarer in Architecture.* Denver: privately printed, 1976.

Noel, Thomas J. *Colorado Catholicism and the Archdiocese of Denver, 1857–1989.* Niwot: University Press of Colorado, 1989. 468 p., maps, illus., bib., index.

Noel, Thomas J., and Barbara S. Norgren. *Denver: The City Beautiful and Its Architects.* Denver: Historic Denver, Inc., 1987 (1993 reprint). 248 p., 400 illus., bib., illustrated glossary of architectural terms, biographical dictionary of Denver architects, index.

Smiley, Jerome C. *History of Denver.* Denver: Denver Times-Sun Publishing, 1901 (1978 reprint, Western Publishing). 1,115 p., maps, illus., index.

Wilk, Diane. *A Guide to Denver's Architectural Styles and Terms.* Denver: Denver Museum of Natural History and Historic Denver, Inc., 1995. 96 p., illus.

CENTRAL DENVER

Bakke, Diane, and Jackie Davis. *Places Around the Bases: A Historic Tour of the Coors Field Neighborhood.* Englewood, Colorado: Westcliffe, 1995. 177 p., map, illus., index.

Ballast, David Kent. *Denver's Civic Center: A Walking Tour.* Denver: City Publishing, 1977. 30 p., maps, illus.

Brenneman, Bill. *Miracle on Cherry Creek: An Informal History of the Birth and Rebirth of a Neighborhood.* Denver: Central Bank & Trust, 1973. 130 p., illus., bib.

Etter, Don D. *Auraria: Where Denver Began.* Boulder: Colorado Associated University Press, 1972. 99 p., maps, illus.

Gibson, Barbara. *The Lower Downtown Historic District.* Denver: Denver Museum of Natural History and Historic Denver, Inc., 1995. 96 p., illus., index.

Noel, Thomas J. *Denver's Larimer Street: Main Street, Skid Row, and Urban Renaissance.* Denver: Historic Denver, Inc., 1982. 196 p., maps, illus., index.

Noel, Thomas J. *The Denver Athletic Club, 1884–1984.* Denver: The Denver Athletic Club, 1983. 106 p., illus., bib., index.

Noel, Thomas J. *Growing Through History With Colorado: The Colorado National Banks, 1862–1987.* Denver: University of Colorado at Denver, Colorado Studies Center, 1987. 160 p., illus., bib., index.

CAPITOL HILL AREA

Goodstein, Phil. *Denver's Capitol Hill.* Denver: Life Publications, 1988. 182 p., maps, illus., index.

Grinstead, Leigh A., Steve Grinstead Fletcher, and Gheda Gayou. *Molly Brown's Capitol Hill Walking Tour.* Denver: Historic Denver, Inc., 1995. 63 p., map, illus., bib.

Wilk, Diane. *The Wyman Historic District.* Denver: Denver Museum of Natural History and Historic Denver, Inc., 1995. 96 p., illus.

NORTHEAST DENVER

Etter, Carolyn and Don. *The Denver Zoo.* Niwot: Roberts Rinehart Publishers, 1996. 237 p., illus., sources, index.

Peters, Bette D. *Denver's City Park.* Rev. ed. Boulder, Colorado: Johnson Publishing, 1986. 67 p., maps, illus., notes, index.

West, William A. *Curtis Park: A Denver Neighborhood.* Boulder: Colorado Associated University Press, 1980. Photos by Don Etter. 88 p., maps.

NORTHWEST DENVER

Sagstetter, Beth, ed. *Side by Side: A History of Denver's Witter-Cofield Historic District.* Denver: C & M Press, 1995. 229 p., maps, illus., bib., index.

Wiberg, Ruth Eloise. *Rediscovering Northwest Denver: Its History, Its People, Its Landmarks.* Boulder, Colorado: Pruett Publishing, 1976 (1995 reprint, University Press of Colorado). 212 p., illus., notes, bib., index.

Zelinger, Michael Jay. *West Side Story Relived.* Denver: West Side Reunion Committee, 1987. 228 p., illus.

SOUTH DENVER

Breck, Allen D. *From the Rockies to the World: The University of Denver, 1864–1989.* Denver: University of Denver, 1989. 228 p., illus., index.

Etter, Don D. *University Park: Four Walking Tours.* Denver: Graphic Impressions, 1974. 55 pp., illus.

Goodstein, Phil. *South Denver Saga.* Denver: New Social Publications, 1991. 250 p., illus., bib., index.

Van Wyke, Millie. *The Town of South Denver: Its People, Neighborhoods, and Events Since 1858.* Boulder, Colorado: Pruett Publishing, 1991. 150 p., maps, illus., bib., index.

EAST DENVER

Halaas, David F. *Fairmount and Historic Colorado.* Denver: Fairmount Cemetery Association, 1976. 104 p., illus.

Levy, Michael H., and Patrick M. Scanlan. *Pursuit of Excellence: A History of Lowry Air Force Base, 1937–1987.* Denver: Lowry Air Force Base History Office, 1988. 71 p., illus., chronology, index.

Noel, Thomas J. *Richthofen's Montclair: A Pioneer Denver Suburb: A Brief History, Illustrated Walking Tour, and Research Guide to Denver Houses and Neighborhood History.* Boulder, Colorado: Pruett Publishing, 1976. 116 p., maps, illus., bib., index.

Index

F

G

H

I

T

About the Author

Thomas J. Noel received a B.A. in history and an M.A. in library science from the University of Denver and an M.A. and Ph.D. in history from the University of Colorado at Boulder. He teaches history at the University of Colorado at Denver and is a columnist for *The Denver Post.* Tom conducts walking tours of Denver neighborhoods, specializing in cemeteries, churches, libraries, saloons, and other landmarks. He served as a Denver Landmark Commissioner and chair during the 1970s and 1980s and is now a National Register Reviewer for Colorado. He and his wife, Vi, live in the historic Montclair neighborhood of East Denver.

HIS OTHER BOOKS INCLUDE:

Richthofen's Montlcair: A Pioneer Denver Suburb (1976)
Denver: Rocky Mountain Gold (1980)
Denver's Larimer Street: Main Street, Skid Row & Urban Renaissance (1981)
The City and the Saloon (1982)
The Denver Athletic Club (1983)
The Colorado National Banks (1987)
Denver: The City Beautiful & Its Architecture, with Barbara S. Norgren (1987)
Colorado Catholicism, 1857–1989 (1989)
Denver: Mining Camp to Metropolis, with Stephen J. Leonard (1990)
The University Club of Denver, with Peg Ekstrand (1991)
Historical Atlas of Colorado, with P. Mahoney and R. Stevens (1994)
Colorado: The Highest State, with Duane Smith (1995)